MODELLING FOR POPULATION AND SUSTAINABLE DEVELOPMENT

ECCO – Enhancement of Population Carrying Capacity Options – is a computer modelling approach developed at the Centre for Human Ecology, University of Edinburgh, to help guide policy making towards more sustainable development. ECCO comprises both the modelling approach to issues of population, resources, environment and development and the various computer models that have grown out of it. These models have been constructed from national pilot studies in which the ECCO approach has been applied to specific national issues.

This book, which reports on the proceedings of an international workshop held at Soest in the Netherlands, presents a technical evaluation of ECCO, an analysis of the policy relevance of ECCO and assesses other approaches – with emphasis on ecology, economics, energy, agriculture and population – and examines the possibilities for their integration within ECCO.

The contributors come from developing and developed countries, from international and national organisations, and from a variety of research fields. This diversity of experience and expertise has produced a rigorous assessment of the various modelling approaches and a book that will be essential reading for professionals responsible for policy analysis in the fields of population, resources, environment and development.

MODELLING FOR POPULATION AND SUSTAINABLE DEVELOPMENT

Edited by
A. J. Gilbert and L. C. Braat

Published by Routledge and
The International Social Science Council
with the co-operation of
UNESCO
and
The Institute for Environmental Studies,
Free University, Amsterdam

ROUTLEDGE

London and New York

First published in 1991
by Routledge
11 New Fetter Lane, London EC4P 4EE

Simultaneously published in the USA and Canada
by Routledge
a division of Routledge, Chapman and Hall Inc.
29 West 35th Street, New York, NY 10001

Filmset from author's disks by
J&L Composition Ltd, Filey, North Yorkshire
Printed and bound in Great Britain by
Biddles Ltd, Guildford and King's Lynn

British Library Cataloguing in Publication Data
Modelling for population and sustainable development.
1. Economic planning. Econometric models
I. Gilbert, A. J. II. Braat, Leon C. III. International Social Science Council
338.90011

Library of Congress Cataloging in Publication Data
also available

ISBN 0-415-06187-3

The seminar on which this work is based was organised by the Institute for Environmental Studies, Free University, Amsterdam, on behalf of the Unesco Division of Population and Human Settlements.

Funding was provided by Unesco and the Dutch Ministry of Foreign Affairs, Directoraat Generaal voor Internationale Samenwerking (DGIS).

CONTENTS

FIGURES AND TABLES

FIGURES

TABLES

PREFACE

The workshop on modelling for population and sustainable development was organised by the Institute for Environmental Studies, Free University of Amsterdam, and funded conjointly by the Dutch Ministry of Foreign Affairs and Unesco's Division of Population and Human Settlements. Unesco has continued to participate in the elaboration and application of the model in fulfilment of its mandate in the social sciences, namely, to fund or undertake theoretical research, and to identify and make available methodological tools to assist Member States in dealing with the long-term planning of population growth and socio-cultural development.

ECCO (Enhancement of population Carrying Capacity Options) has significant theoretical and practical applications. It links in a dynamic manner population issues and development concerns, considering population growth in relation to the available resource base. It draws attention especially to 'carrying capacity', that is, the capacity of a given territory to sustain its population – a population with a given quality of life, cultural particularity and foreseeable impact on the environment. Four key concepts – population, resource, environment and development – are thus linked, and projected over a relatively long-term time scale, that is, within the context of sustainability.

At the heart of the model is the method of resource accounting, initially developed as a simulation model for Unesco's Population and Human Settlements Division in order to assess the potential for enhancing the sustainable population carrying capacity of nation states. The concept rests on the observation that, if an economy is analysed retrospectively in physical terms, ultimately all output is found to rest on present and past energy use. Since labour, in terms of quantity if not quality, is generally in surplus in economies enjoying technological progress, one can quantify economic activities in terms of present and past energy use to establish the future level of material welfare in an economy and further, the sustainability of that level in the context of its present status and known resources.

During the conceptual phase of the development of the methodology – conducted by Unesco's Division of Population in order to investigate the 'relationship between population, environment and technological progress' – Unesco collaborated with UNFAO, and benefited from financial support from UNFPA, the United Nations Trust Fund, and UNDP. At the second stage, and with the co-operation of the University of Strathclyde Resource Use Institute and the University of Edinburgh Centre for Human Ecology, training in ECCO was provided to participants from developing countries to help them initiate pilot projects using the methodology. Ten years after the theoretical development of the methodology and its application at national level in various countries, there was felt a need to assess the simulation model critically and to confront it with other similar modelling approaches. This was the objective of the workshop on modelling for population and sustainable development organised in the Netherlands in November 1987.

The proceedings now being published attest to the high quality of the work presented and it constitutes another significant milestone in the promotion and development of the ECCO methodology. It demonstrated its potential in integrating various issues, the most important being environmental issues which were not considered originally. This possibility of constant improvement makes it a dynamic tool worthy of investment.

At the workshop, countries – as diverse as Kenya, Thailand, China, Zimbabwe and Mauritius – which had experimented with ECCO pilot projects were given the opportunity to share their experience with those wishing or about to initiate similar projects. For funding agencies, this was a demonstration that ECCO, far from being a piece of purely academic research, had become an applied tool for development. As more countries become interested in the model and its application, it is hoped that plans for further refinement and training in ECCO will continue to receive support from Unesco and other agencies interested in population dynamics and their relationship with resource, environment and sustainable development. Unesco, in fact, in its Medium-Term Plan for 1991–95 has made provision for activities related to planning for sustainable development in line with the enhancement of population carrying capacity options. Such provision includes the involvement of more countries in the use of the model and regional training of specialists in its methodology.

Other than Unesco, organisations concerned with long-term planning of resources and the environment also participated in the workshop, and the presence there of representatives from FAO, ILO and IISA augurs well for ECCO's future development. The United Nations Environment Programme, IUCN, the World Bank and regional development banks have also expressed interest in the model.

The potential of the methodology as a significant tool for sustainable development also merits the attention of policy and media leaders. It is becoming more evident today that only those models that seek to ensure the welfare of the present generation without jeopardising the future of our children and their environment should be given support. In this sense, ECCO deserves support from national as well as interregional organisations interested in restoring the balance between population growth and total development policy.

1

INTRODUCTION: ISSUES AND PERSPECTIVES

A. J. Gilbert

1.1. INTRODUCTION

Sustainable development is receiving increasing attention in developing and developed countries, and in national and international organisations. It derives from concern over the interrelationships between (human) populations, natural resources, environment and economic development. The World Commission on Environment and Development detailed the issues and the urgency of moving towards sustainable development in its report *Our Common Future* (WCED, 1987). However, the means of achieving or identifying alternative paths towards sustainable development remain elusive.

This document presents the proceedings of the Seminar/Workshop – 'Modelling for Population and Sustainable Development' – which was held at Soest, the Netherlands, in November 1987. The central element of the meeting was ECCO (Enhancement of population Carrying Capacity Options), a computer modelling approach developed at the Centre for Human Ecology, University of Edinburgh, to guide policy making towards more sustainable development. ECCO comprises both the modelling approach to issues of population, resources, environment and development (also known as PRED), and the various computer models which have been developed using this approach.

ECCO is a policy assessment instrument cast in energy terms, as a prelude, or for use in parallel, to an 'economic' approach. It may be characterised as follows:

1 it distinguishes physical outputs of an economy (and externally purchased physical capital) from all other outputs;

2 it quantifies physical resource use (minerals, water, energy, etc.) in terms of one numeraire – energy;
3 it quantifies food output in terms of protein and relates intensification in terms of kg protein/ha as a function of inputs/ha expressed;
4 it seeks to match the primary requirements of the economy (e.g. water) in physical terms and affording supply through rate of capital investment; and
5 it recognises exogenously imposed ecological and physical thresholds derived from separate studies.

Other approaches to modelling for population and sustainable development have, of course, been developed in many places, and a range of these were presented. Participants came from developing and developed countries, from international and national organisations, and from a variety of research fields. This diversity in backgrounds encouraged a rigorous assessment of these modelling approaches.

1.2. OBJECTIVES OF THE SEMINAR/WORKSHOP

The seminar/workshop had three main objectives:

1 to conduct a technical evaluation of ECCO;
2 to evaluate the policy relevance of ECCO; and
3 to assess other modelling approaches and the opportunities which may exist for their integration within ECCO.

The meeting's programme and this document were constructed with these objectives in mind.

Part I of this document describes the ECCO approach – its background, objectives and technical aspects including preliminary validation. This provided the basis for technical evaluation. Criteria included flexibility, adequacy, transferability, skill requirements, data (requirements, availability and quality) and validation of the approach and its models.

Part II presents summaries of pilot studies conducted in Kenya, Mauritius and Thailand. The models constructed in each pilot study were also subjected to technical evaluation. However, the ultimate purpose of such models is to guide policy development, and so evaluation of the policy relevance of ECCO began with these pilot studies. Criteria for this include transparency and credibility of the models and their output.

Part III discusses the future development of ECCO via new national pilot studies and the greater detailing of select sectors. There are also plans to develop a regional version of ECCO (see Chapter 3), but further information on this was not yet available. These presentations permitted an exchange of ideas between those developing new ECCO programmes, those with experience in developing ECCO models, possible funding organisations, and other experts.

Part IV presents a range of other modelling approaches to population and sustainable development, derived from the following fields: ecology, economics, energy, agriculture and demography. The third objective seeks to assess the potential, desirability and logistics of integrating or in some way incorporating aspects of these other approaches within the ECCO framework. As a part of this objective, those aspects of ECCO which need improvement, and those aspects from other approaches which could contribute to this improvement are identified.

Part V presents the conclusions of the seminar/workshop. The participants' evaluations of ECCO and assessments of other modelling approaches are summarised. Part V also makes recommendations on future directions for ECCO, as well as providing a checklist or guidelines for those setting up future ECCO activities.

1.3. ISSUES OF POPULATION AND SUSTAINABLE DEVELOPMENT

Before being able to discuss model relevance, two central concepts require discussion and definition: human carrying capacity and sustainable development.

Carrying capacity has its roots in population ecology, where it represents the maximum number of individuals in a population that can be sustained by a given environment. Human carrying capacity may be defined (Unesco and FAO, 1985) as 'the number of people sharing a given area or territory who can, for the foreseeable future, sustain the existing standard of living [through the utilisation of] energy, land, water, skill and organisation'. Quantification of carrying capacity in general is difficult;

the given environment is not a constant. Quantification of human carrying capacity is even more difficult because of the interplay between economic and social factors in the human environment and the subjective elements within 'standard of living'.

A population in a bounded system can become unsustainable if it exceeds the environment's carrying capacity (the earth may be viewed as a bounded system, leading to questions and concerns regarding human carrying capacity). In an open system, imports may be used to supplement the goods and services of the immediate environment, and so increase the carrying capacity. Nations are examples of open systems – a country may import that which its environment does not supply, and so provide for its domestic population. This enlargement of carrying capacity then becomes tied to economic development – imports must somehow be balanced by exports (at least in the current political and economic climate).

Economic development in developed and developing countries follows very different paths, partly in response to different import–export environments. Developed countries tend to have relatively stable populations, but growing rates of per capita consumption. Economic development aims to support this growth in the quality of life. Such countries use their domestic resources of skills and technology to convert raw materials, often imported, to finished products. They are usually more than self-sufficient in the production of both food and manufactured goods, and the surplus is exported.

Developing countries, by definition, have not yet reached a stage of economic development characterised by the levels of industrialisation and national income yielding sufficient domestic savings to finance investment for further growth. Consequently, they tend to import capital (loans), as well as skills and technology to fuel development. They have high population growth rates, are often not self-sufficient in food production, and so must also import food. These imports are to be repaid from the earnings of development projects which are necessarily oriented towards export and not domestic markets.

The consequences of economic development are also different. In developed countries, the adverse impacts of economic activity on environmental quality threaten to constrain future growth in the quality of life. In developing countries, economic development and the emphasis on export earnings threaten to deplete the natural resource base on which current and future economic activity is dependent. However, it is becoming evident in both types of country that not only do economic activities have an adverse impact on the environment, but that poor environmental quality can, in turn, have an adverse impact on economic activity.

'Sustainable development' is relatively easy to conceptualise. It involves finding a balance between resource/environmental use, and the satisfaction of human needs. Goodland and Ledec (1985) define sustainable development as 'a pattern of social and structural transformations which optimises the economic and other societal benefits available in the present without jeopardising the likely potential for similar benefits in the future'. A number of similar definitions exist, some of which are presented elsewhere in this document. The value of such definitions is that they provide a basis for communication. Unfortunately, they do not provide any guidance on how sustainable development can be achieved or on how to identify paths towards it.

It is obvious that the paths towards sustainable development in developing countries will differ markedly from those in developed countries. Each country has its own set of population, natural resource, environment and economic development issues which require analysis before a range of possible paths can be identified.

The key to sustainable development lies in harmonising economic production functions, environmental production functions and the physical laws of thermodynamics. The approach must be multi-disciplinary, integrating the social sciences, particularly economics, and the natural sciences, particularly ecology and physics.

1.4. PERSPECTIVES FOR POPULATION AND SUSTAINABLE DEVELOPMENT

Human populations tend to identify themselves with relatively small spatial areas, often associated with local or provincial boundaries. Control over human activities tends to be exercised at correspondingly small spatial levels, largely for historical reasons. However, recent developments in communications and trade have encouraged the development of a national perspective.

Economic development today is dominated by this national perspective. Consequently, many analytical approaches, both traditional macroeconomic and others such as ECCO, are conducted at this spatial level. However, there is an inherent inconsistency in this approach. The factors which influence decisions usually reflect a regional perspective (a region may be loosely defined as some spatial level intermediate between national and local). Examples of such factors are the quantity, quality and distribution of natural resources, transport networks, energy availability and supply, labour and unemployment, impact of economic activity on environmental quality and of poor environmental quality on economic activity.

Of course, other factors reflecting different spatial levels are also involved. With respect to resource and environmental issues, Braat et al. (1987) identified three groups of issues which span many regions, and require multiregional, national or even multinational management. These may be summarised as follows:

1 the shared resource issues, where a resource is used by more than one region – e.g. large river systems such as the Rhine in Europe, transboundary pollution, overfishing in the Mediterranean and the North Sea;
2 the shared market issues, where local resources are endangered by economic pressure originating in a limited common or world market – e.g. the European Common Agricultural Policy encourages land mismanagement through the overapplication of fertilisers and pesticides;
3 the common problem issues, where similar resource, resource-using or resource-impact problems exist in a number of regions – e.g. fresh water supply, forest die-off, desertification and drylands management.

ECCO was designed to focus on the national level. However, plans to construct a regional version of ECCO indicate that the importance of smaller spatial levels is recognised. The important point is that analysis for population and sustainable development must be flexible with regard to spatial level, so that the interests of all (relevant) spatial levels can be reflected.

This discussion has concentrated on the spatial perspective. Three additional perspectives relevant to issues of population and sustainable development have been identified: intergenerational trade-off, multiple use of resources, and risk management. These are discussed briefly below.

The use of the word 'sustainable' implies a long-term perspective. Sustainable development implies protection of the interests of future generations. Intergenerational trade-off refers to the choice between use, by the present generation, of natural resources for economic development, and their conservation for and subsequent use by future generations.

One of the main challenges for sustainable development is the resolution of multiple-use conflicts. Multiple use refers to the deliberate, multiple and simultaneous use of natural resources for different economic objectives. The most common example, relevant to both developing and developed countries, is the use of fresh water for both drinking purposes and for sewage or other waste disposal. Multiple use is most important in areas where resources and space are in scarce supply. The central issue is the optimal combination of the different uses. It is evident that the time scale is again a crucial element.

Risk and uncertainty have received much attention over the last ten years. The following types of risk can be identified:

1 uncertainty due to stochastic features of the natural environment;
2 uncertainty due to changes in human preferences and behaviour; and
3 uncertainty related to our limited understanding and therefore control over economic activity and ecological processes.

There will be a need for knowledge regarding the extent of these uncertainties and their consequences when sustainable development becomes a serious objective of government and management policy. Risk management for sustainable development means the design of policies and the making of decisions which render these risks as explicit as possible, and reduce them to more acceptable levels.

1.5. CONCLUDING REMARKS

Economic development has been stimulated by human needs, and is traditionally an important objective of policy makers.

More recently, attention has focused on sustainable development in addition to more typical economic issues such as income, labour and technology.

A number of perspectives to population and sustainable development have been outlined. However, their effective incorporation into policies and management programmes has not always been achieved, usually due to ambiguities and the absence of techniques facilitating this incorporation. ECCO is one of a number of approaches which attempt to clarify these ambiguities and to provide a technique for use in policy formulation.

At this stage, the only common element in these approaches is the multidisciplinary nature of analysis. It has become obvious that no one discipline holds all the answers, at least as yet. Meetings, such as that reported in this document, encourage better, more effective communication between disciplines, individuals and organisations with very different interests.

REFERENCES

Braat, L. C., F. M. Brouwer, A. J. Gilbert, E. Hulzebos and W. A. Hafkamp. 'Integrated modeling of renewable natural resources: the economic–ecologic interface.' FAST Occasional Paper No. 172, Commission of the European Community, March 1987.

Goodland and Ledec. 'Neoclassical economics and principles of sustainable development.' Paper presented at the Third International Environmental Accounting Workshop, sponsored by the World Bank and UNEP, Paris, 1985.

Unesco and FAO. *Carrying capacity assessment with a pilot study of Kenya: a resource accounting methodology for exploring national options for sustainable development*. Unesco and FAO, Paris and Rome, 1985.

World Commission on Environment and Development. *Our Common Future*. Oxford University Press, Oxford, 1987.

Part I

ECCO

2

INTRODUCTORY COMMENTS: THE CHALLENGE FOR THE FUTURE

U.E. Loening

We start with three basic words: sustainability, development and carrying capacity. These are three concepts with profound implications.

Carrying capacity is basically a biological concept: an old-established idea, used by biologists and ecologists for many different species. It becomes a rather different concept when applied to the human species because of our capacity to enhance the carrying capacity of the land for our species. One of the purposes of this workshop is to assess the role of these three concepts in assisting the global community to survive the next period, the most dramatic period of change that has ever occurred in the history of the planet. Never before has there been such a dominance by a single species whose consumption is so avid that the renewable natural resources of the earth are threatened. I think we can document that man's effect on the biosphere and on long-term sustainability has been negative – we have lived off the principal and exceeded the carrying capacity of the globe.

Our challenge for the future is therefore what to do next and how to do it. It is a challenge that involves the interplay between caring for the growing human family and conserving the diversity, resources and sustainable productivity of the biosphere. Many people have already cried 'Wolf!' in the face of this problem which stretches back a very long way indeed. Plato was quite aware of what was happening to the soil, water and productivity of Attica through deforestation. However, the changes that are now occurring have never before been on such a planetary scale. John Stuart Mill, 130 years ago, foresaw the situation, defined a stationary but not static economy, and hoped that people 'will be content to be stationary, long before necessity compels them to it'.

I believe we are now close to being compelled. So our first question is: What is the carrying capacity of the earth as a whole for humans? That is, not a disaggregated version for each country, but a wholly aggregated one for the planet. While no one country need be self-sufficient, obviously the earth as a whole must be. The question is complex: firstly, since carrying capacity can be, and has been, enhanced, the limits depend on the criteria applied; secondly, one must assume that the objective is to provide for human needs, sustainably and within the carrying capacity. But what are these needs?

The 'material standard of living' is a measurable quantity and one that is discussed at this conference. It is relatively simple to define and to fulfil, but it is by no means the only criterion or measure of human needs. It is not the same as the 'quality of life'. More fundamental needs that lead to more basic criteria have been listed, reviewed and are being worked on by Manfred Max-Neef[1]: permanence or subsistence, protection, affection, understanding, participation, leisure, creation, identity or meaning, and freedom. One can systemise these. For instance, freedom is a necessity for participation.

To provide for such fundamental needs which are universally applicable and which cut across cultures will bring us into difficult questions and dilemmas. The first of these concerns the first of those three words: what is development? Development is so often seen as a (rather primitive) way of providing material resources by a process of industrialisation.

We need to see it in the wider context of what the aims really are. If development of the human spirit and fulfilling to some extent those fundamental needs is the aim, then it is probable that the carrying capacity of the earth has already been exceeded. A paper recently presented in Edinburgh by Arthur Westing of SIPRI[2] suggested that 2000 million may be the upper long-term carrying capacity of the earth. Clearly one can argue about the numbers, but it is apparent that we have exceeded the carrying capacity and this means, of course, that we are not sustainable in our present lifestyle.

Unsustainability is readily seen if one looks around the globe at past and present civilisations. Indeed all industrial societies in the European tradition – and here I include ancient societies such as those of Sumeria, Egypt, Greece and Rome – have squandered and degraded their lands and in the end have reduced their carrying capacity. The increases they achieved were temporary, and only appeared as increases because they came from conquest – both conquest of each other and conquest of their natural resource base. As I mentioned, Plato was very aware of that problem. None of these civilisations have been sustainable in principle or in practice.

China has perhaps been the nearest to sustainability with agriculture continuing on the same land for forty centuries. However, this was at the cost of deforestation and soil erosion in the mountains. That massive debt is now beginning to be repaid in China with a vast reforestation programme. Maybe our turn has now come to repay those debts that have accrued from development but that are now actually preventing progress towards a more sustainable and happier planet. It is worth reflecting that Greece, southern Italy, Spain and Portugal are now the poorer members of the European Community; they were once its richest birth places.

For the last few centuries and especially the last few decades, the rest of the globe has been serving European industrial development. The import of raw materials into Europe and North America and now Japan has in effect been in exchange for the export of a cultural approach that led to unsustainable development. Thus, these two words are a challenge for the First World even to understand and similarly a challenge for the richer parts of industrialising, developing nations to take into account. It is the first time in our historical tradition that we require to heed, control and remain within an enhanced carrying capacity if we are to survive at all. That is a revolutionary change in the course of history.

Sustainability means that the evolution and development of the future should be based on continuing and renewable processes and not on the exploitation and exhaustion of the principal or the capital of the living resource base. Social institutions, created by cultural evolution from earlier ages in which there were always other ways out and other places to go, will have to change to serve the new purposes. This is clearly stated in the report of United Nations Commission on the

Environment and Development, the Brundtland Report: 'The time has come to break out of past patterns. Attempts to maintain social and ecological stability through old approaches to development and environmental protection will increase instability'.

I wonder how many of those who read these sentences truly appreciate their significance and the enormity of the change that is needed? Such approaches as ECCO, which incorporate aspects of resource accounting and carrying capacity, will help us both to understand the problem and to provide some methods for its solution.

New approaches require the development of two basic methodologies: firstly, techniques and methods guiding use, recycling and replacement of our natural resources, the productivity of the earth's surface; secondly, techniques for evaluating and quantifying the effects of what we are actually doing. Carrying capacity assessment – a realistic method of measuring the attainable, testing the development programmes and thus defining for each region its capacity to develop in an appropriate way – is involved in the latter. By summation one hopes thus to define for the whole world a sustainable development programme.

As to the first, the techniques of natural resource use, among the innovations needed is the ability to appreciate the issues as a whole and not to work in sectoral compartmentalised ways. The productivity and sustainability of the biosphere are now, inevitably and for the first time in history, under mankind's profound influence and the planet therefore faces a man-made future. All the aspects of that future, the desired and the unwanted effects, are interconnected and must be considered together as a whole. I will not dwell on that now, except to emphasise that this is an essential scientific approach for survival – survival let us say of the most fitting in the environment rather than in the crude Victorian, Darwinian sense of the fittest. From such a broad holistic science one can see that we may actually deduce a new ethic that demands fairness and co-operation, both with each other and with nature, in place of the competitive conquest that has been so successful in the past. It results also in a process of optimisation in place of maximisation.

Methods for evaluating and quantifying possible achievements of the new options and technological approaches is the second requirement. Here we have to say that economic analyses of all sorts in their present form are not adequate for those tasks, and never have been. They largely neglect the major component behind all economic activity – the natural resource base.

The productivity of the biosphere is not a part of economic appraisal; the time scales are different, as are the values. Economics deals with humans and their activities and tends to neglect nature. Science deals with nature and tends to neglect humans and their culture. Economics has allowed and continues to allow an irrational and destructive system of development to appear rational and thus to encourage one to exploit instead of to husband resources. The apparent success of economics, nevertheless, still makes us believe in the prospects and promises of rescue by technical innovation. This was very apparent in the Institute of Systems Analysis in Moscow which I visited recently and where the four major economic systems of Japan, the EEC, the USA and the USSR were being appraised, compared and projected into the future. I am not a pessimist and nor are they, but they concluded that all of these economic superpowers will decline in their economic futures – curves falling steeply. They indicated that the only solution would be a dramatic technical innovation. This must be a mistaken belief if applied internationally.

Instead of conventional economics we have to apply another system. The alternative suggested here is called resource accounting, which may become a fundamental way to measure humankind's activities. From a resource-accounting base we rapidly develop methods to assess carrying capacities. These are not methods for predicting the future; rather, they are methods to assess the physical consequences over the medium-term of different policy options; they help to demonstrate to decision makers what is possible for the future. But resource-accounting methods also bring us face to face with areas that need better understanding and knowledge such as the choice of different technologies for the use of natural resources. The carrying capacity approaches can lead to the development of appropriate technologies for the future.[3]

Through this workshop we are to evaluate the present state of our carrying capacity models. I shall raise only one aspect that needs careful appraisal here. This is the question of aggregation of the scale of the data. I have talked in rather global terms; we do not have a model for the globe although some attempts towards one are being made. The question is at what spatial level do we make a carrying capacity model? To make one for national boundaries is, to my mind, absolutely vital because we have national boundaries. However, national boundaries do not respect ecological boundaries which are ultimately fundamental, and if we are going to go to a fundamental carrying capacity then the micro must add up to the macro. Consequently, to correlate aggregated with disaggregated models, the choice of size and boundaries must be considered carefully. In practice national sovereignty in our present world has to be respected and therefore nations probably provide the most appropriate level for evaluation.

Malcom Slesser and colleagues are involved in developing a model that is subnational, that of the Central Region of Scotland.

Finally, I have a couple of comments for discussion or challenge. We need to appreciate that globally there is no longer a case to be made for a trade-off between development and environmental conservation. The biosphere has suffered dramatically. The resource base throughout has been reduced. Ecological rehabilitation must now be an essential component of any new development programme in all countries. The international agencies, including especially the World Bank as a catalytic agency for maybe fifty or sixty times as much financial development funds as it provides, are crucial in this. I am glad to see that they are beginning to incorporate environmental issues into their planning – the World Bank's Environmental Office has increased tenfold when the World Bank staff as a whole has been reduced by 30 per cent. But that is not enough. A policy is now needed to reverse past trends of destruction. It is no longer acceptable to have a trade-off because that still takes us in a negative direction, and will not lead to sustainable development. The resource base now needs to be improved instead of diminished.

These conclusions show that changes to more appropriate technologies have profound implications for the future. Carrying capacity models based on suitably integrated, biospheric and human data should allow a way forward.

I have some vision of a long-term future. The long term is that the world finally learns to have the human family live within its carrying capacity. And that may well be much less than 2,000 million. The question is how to get from here to there? We have a very large hump to overcome which is where the whole approach of modelling perhaps has its greatest impact and its greatest value – that the innovations and new social institutions needed to get over that large hump of living beyond our present carrying capacity is a major function of the modelling studies.

NOTES

1 See, for example, his speech for the Alternative Nobel Prize, the Right Livelihood Foundation: *People and Planet*, Green Books, 1987; or his paper on the TOES conference, 1984.
2 3rd. Int. Conf. Environmental Futures: Maintenance of the Biosphere, Sept. 1987.
3 One of those that I am much concerned with as a biologist and which I think we should be able to assess and develop, is closed cycle or biological agriculture. I make the case that our existing agriculture is one of short circuiting or bypassing natural processes rather than understanding and using them. It is likely that far from reducing food supply and reducing the carrying capacity of the world as a whole, biological agriculture is the only way in which a sensible level can be maintained into the longer term. Obviously the existing agrochemical agriculture has been extremely successful in certain senses and indeed the Common Agricultural Policy is suffering from that success. But it is not a long term one. It is probably unique to Europe anyway and it is one example of where a carrying capacity assessment can let us evaluate the more appropriate biological methods for the future.

3

THE ECCO APPROACH TO PLANNING SUSTAINABLE DEVELOPMENT

J. King

3.1. INTRODUCTION

ECCO is not simply an independent application of modelling to population and development problems. It evolved from some ten years of debate within the United Nations system about the nature of the interactions between population, resources, environment and development – PRED as this has come to be called – and the means of quantifying those interactions. The ECCO approach was developed by Unesco with the financial support of the United Nations Population Fund (UNFPA) and the United Nations Development Programme (UNDP). In 1984 it was pilot tested in Kenya with the collaboration of the United Nations Food and Agriculture Organisation (FAO) and the Nairobi-based economic consultants Mwenge Associates, under the sponsorship of a United Nations trust fund established specifically to encourage co-operation within the United Nations system on research into PRED relationships. By the end of 1987, ECCO had been applied in two more countries, Mauritius and the United Kingdom, although still on an experimental basis. Three further studies had been initiated in Thailand, Zimbabwe and China.

In the pages which follow an attempt will be made to explain the changes in thinking which have occurred over the last few decades about population and economic growth. It will also describe the contribution we believe ECCO has to make in assisting governments to identify paths to sustainable development.

3.2. THE POPULATION–RESOURCE–ENVIRONMENT ISSUE

Post-war faith in economic growth as the sole way to prosperity started to fade as the complications of rapid population increase and environmental degradation entered the scene. It became evident that in many countries economic development would have to proceed very quickly indeed if it were to respond to the needs generated by that increase in human numbers, quite apart from the question of improving living standards. At the same time the prospects of development appeared to be compromised by pressure on the environment both from industrial and agricultural activity in the modern sector, and from subsistence populations compelled for their survival to exploit the land beyond its sustainable yield.

The 1984 Population Conference held in Bucharest was significant in the sense that it recognised that population had to be seen as part of development rather than as an independent issue. This recognition was taken further at the International Population Conference in Mexico ten years later when both population and environment were placed squarely in the development context, as is reflected in Recommendation 1 of the report (UN, 1984):

> Considering that social and economic development is a central factor in the solution of population and interrelated problems and that population factors are very important in development plans and strategies and have a major impact on the attainment of development objectives, national development policies, plans and programmes as well as international development strategies should be formulated on the basis of an integrated approach that takes into account the interrelationships between population, resources, environment and development.

This recommendation was adopted despite the turn-about in policy of the United States from the previous conference, and was introduced mainly on the insistence of the developing-country group. It followed a similar line of thought to that expressed at a number of regional meetings held in the months leading up to the Mexico conference.

Although the population–resource–environment link was now

firmly rooted in international development thinking, the question of how to quantify this relationship in such a way that it was meaningful to national planners did not appear to receive much attention for the reasons, perhaps, suggested below. It was, however, implicitly accepted that an understanding of how demographic, environmental and resource factors interacted was essential if sustainable forms of development were to be achieved.

The notion of sustainable development has now come to receive high priority on the list of international issues and it occupies an important place in the report of the World Commission on Environment and Development, *Our Common Future* (1987). Here sustainable development is defined as 'development that meets the needs of the present without compromising the ability of future generations to meet their own needs'. It is recognised that since rapid population growth adds to pressure on resources and slows improvements in living standards, 'sustainable development can only be pursued if population size and growth are in harmony with the changing productive potential of the ecosystem'. The report even ventures to suggest that for most developing countries the imbalance between population growth and resource development will worsen unless deliberate measures are taken.

The World Commission goes further than most other international statements in recognising that some quite radical changes will be required if the concept of sustainable development, including the linkages between population, resources and the environment, is to be taken seriously into account in national planning. Not only will production have to be linked with conservation measures and social and economic goals defined in terms of sustainability; fundamental institutional changes will also need to be made within governments in order to overcome long habits of decision-making based on compartmentalised concerns and for the most part excluding agencies concerned with population or natural resource issues from direct participation in economic planning. While, however, significant attention is given to institutional change, the problem of necessary innovation in development planning methodology is barely touched upon. The question therefore still remains: on what basis can governments identify the trade-offs between, say, population growth and standard of living or between intensification of agriculture and soil conservation? How can they determine development strategies through which actions taken in different components of the economy are mutually reinforcing, guiding the economy towards sustainable development? The Commission's report states that such development is required not only to meet the basic needs of all but to increase opportunities for fulfilling people's aspirations for a better life.

The report does not, however, indicate how all this might be done.

3.3. ECONOMICS AND DEVELOPMENT PLANNING

There has been an instinctive tendency to rely on economics and economic modelling to solve the problem of bringing population and environmental issues into development planning; but so far traditional techniques appear to have failed to meet this challenge.[1] Conventional economic models were constructed to reflect the workings of the market economy where growth is determined by market expectations and the values attributed to goods and services. They are concerned with the internal logic of the economy rather than with external physical influences which may ultimately affect the direction of growth over the long term. As long as resource and environmental constraints do not have to be considered, or are not perceived as having to be considered, it is perfectly reasonable to proceed, say, by setting a target for economic growth and then deciding on the fiscal and other economic policies needed to achieve that target. The trouble begins when attempts are made to forecast over the long term, for it involves estimating the values underlying prices over a long period ahead and with increasing uncertainty.

A United Nations task force on long-term objectives (1981) touched on this problem when it referred to the uncertainties involved in estimating the long-term price and supply of oil which would justify investments in alternatives. What the task force really implied was that the physical as well as the economic determinants of oil availability needed to be understood before prices could be estimated with any degree of accuracy. Economic planning techniques can serve their function admirably over the short term, but they cannot guarantee that the objectives that they pursue are compatible with physically realisable development prospects over a long period. There may be environmental implications which are concealed because environmental factors are 'externalised'. There may be physical restrictions affecting the supply of resources as these become harder to access. If economic forecasts are taken too far ahead, they may be leading the national system towards a state which is ultimately unsustainable. One suspects that ignorance of this possibility provides grist to the mill of the likes of Julian Simon (1983).

This does not imply that governments are doing nothing to take account of the demographic and resource trends underlying the development of their economies. In a number of countries national planning has managed to adjust to a certain extent. Some efforts are being made to improve individual aspects of resource management, particularly in the case of water, and attention is being given in certain quarters to the question of internalising the environmental and social costs of production. Long-term population forecasts are beginning to be used to calculate school enrolment, housing or health needs, although generally on a sectoral basis only. A start has been made to quantify factors outside the formal economy, such as fuel-wood gathering as it contributes to energy consumption.

When a long-term planning horizon is adopted it turns attention onto anticipated problems which may not be justifiable or which appear superfluous in the context of short-term planning, but which at the same time cannot be postponed to a time when action may be too late or prohibitively expensive. Increases in population, deterioration of soils or land lost through desertification are examples of such changes which are barely perceptible over five or even ten years, but over longer periods become increasingly evident. By this time they may well be compromising a nation's prospects of attaining sustainable development.

Certain long-term targets may be found in national plans, when common sense dictates that action is necessary. This includes the setting of population growth targets which, generally speaking, are determined on the basis of the likely response to family planning measures. In other areas, including the following, targets for action are most likely to be lacking:

- the allocation of heavy initial investments which may be required, for example, to build up the infrastructure necessary for ensuring the transition to a new energy regime

(perhaps based on renewable energy systems), or to maintain environmental quality – an activity which is easily discounted by economic accounting methods;
- the husbanding of natural resources to ensure the sustainable productive capacity of renewable resources and to plan for the rate of exploitation of non-renewables in a manner which will allow for the availability of substitutes and give time for social adjustment;
- the formulation of material goals which accord with long-term prospects of physical development;
- the planning of research and development to meet problems identified in advance and taking account of relevant lead times;
- the creation of a basic understanding of the overall national situation, as it affects both present and future generations, so that people may realise the importance of, and give support to population and other policies designed to secure a satisfactory life both for themselves and for their children and descendants.

Now that the notion of sustainable development is gaining ground the understandable reaction of both the international community and of individual governments has been to seek as much improvement as possible on all fronts: economic growth through the intensification of agriculture and industry, the stepping-up of family planning programmes, and greater attention to the control of environmental degradation and to the conservation of natural species. An instructive example can be taken from a sessional paper issued by the Government of Kenya (1986) which proposes a development strategy destined to form the basis of the 1989–93 plan. The paper recognises that anticipated rapid population growth constitutes a serious problem, stating that at the end of the century the nation will have a population of some 35 million people, 75 per cent more than in 1984. The threat of increasing strain on the environment – land, water and forests – is similarly recognised. In response to this situation, an economic growth target of 5.6 per cent annual increase is to be set to generate the means of satisfying basic needs and to create employment. This is to be accompanied by stricter attention to resource management and conservation.

The question which immediately arises, quite apart from that of the feasibility of maintaining a 5.6 per cent growth rate, is whether these different goals are mutually consistent. Can agriculture be intensified to the point of maintaining a population one-and-three-quarters as large as that of today (and without danger to the productivity of the soil)? If so, how are the necessary inputs to be obtained, through local industry or through imports? If it is to be through imports, will these be acquired through currency earned from manufacturing or through cash crops? And if through cash crops will this mean that land has to be taken from food production, limiting yet further arable land or that which might be used for fuel-wood plantations or for other purposes? Such questions can only be answered if the dynamics are understood of the national system as a whole and of the feedbacks which operate between the different components of the system. The sessional paper has the merit, though, of pointing out that a trade-off exists between rates of population increase and standards of living expressed in GNP per capita.

Table 3.1 indicates that if today's total fertility rate were to remain constant at 7.9 per cent (projection A), average incomes between 1984 and 2000 would increase by 2.7 per cent, assuming

Table 3.1 Kenya: Population and income per capita in 2000

	1984	*2000*	
		Projection A	*Projection B*
1. Population (million)	19.5	38.5	34.8
2. Fertility rate	7.9	7.9	5.6
3. Implied average growth rate (%/year)	–	4.4	3.7
4. Dependency ratio	1.22	1.24	1.04
5. GDP per capita in 1984 prices with GDP growth			
(1) 4.5%/year	220	226	250
(2) 5.6%/year	220	267	295
6. 16-year increase (%) in income/capita			
(1)		2.7	13.6
(2)		21.4	34.1

Source: Government of Kenya Sessional Paper No. 1 of 1986, citing Development Plan 1984–88.

that there was an average annual growth rate in GNP of 4.5 per cent. Incomes would increase by as much as 21.4 per cent if a GNP growth rate of 5.6 per cent could be maintained. If instead a fertility rate of 5.6 per cent could be achieved (projection B), then incomes would grow by 13.6 and 34.1 per cent respectively. The sessional paper concludes, naturally, that for the next fifteen years economic growth is the only way to make a significant impact on average incomes and on employment, given anticipated population increase. After that time, it states, family planning measures undertaken today can have a marked effect. It is not within the scope of that report to ascertain whether those methods will prove to be sufficient or not. An annual economic growth rate of 5.6 per cent does, however, appear to be an extremely ambitious target.

Table 3.2 The effect of population growth on selected variables

	Current fertility	*2-child families*
1. Population 2025	9.8×10^6	3.5×10^6
2. Social Service expenditure to 2025 to maintain current standard	14×10^6*	50×10^6*
3. Water deficit by 2010	370×10^6 m^3	220×10^6 m^3
4. Arable land per capita 2025	0.037 ha	0.11 ha
5. Food imported to feed population to current standard	increase	reduction
6. Males in labour force	1,250,000	900,000
7. GNP/capita (1975 units)	500	1000

Source: Jordan report to USAID by Futures Group, Washington DC Population Growth.
* Values in Jordan dinars, 1 JD (1984) = $US 2.72.

Attempts have been made to assess the somewhat longer-term impacts of population growth on different components of a nation's economy. In a report on Jordan's development prospects, made by the Futures Group on behalf of USAID, the effect of alternative population growth variants were calculated in relation to a number of other variables (Table 3.2).

A series of discontinuous snapshots are obtained in this way of what the future may hold. Again, however, there is no feedback of output to input data. The question has not been addressed as to whether the economy, considered as a total system, can generate rates of growth without damage to the environment and can provide for the needs of the population indefinitely; that is, on a sustainable basis.

3.4. SUSTAINABLE DEVELOPMENT AND THE ASSESSMENT OF CARRYING CAPACITY

The concept of carrying capacity provides a useful framework for investigating the nature of sustainable development. If a national economy is developing in a direction which will ultimately lead the country to overshoot its carrying capacity, then that country cannot be said to be on a sustainable course of development. Sustainable development implies that the various components of the system are interacting in such a way that all inputs necessary to secure the needs or aspirations of the population can always be met at a rate corresponding to the rate of population increase. If population growth exceeds that rate, the country will sooner or later exceed its carrying capacity. An early sign of this may well be reflected in an over-exploitation of resources, leading to deforestation or to desertification as people are compelled to disregard natural cycles of regeneration in their search for survival. A nation may also be set on the way to exceeding its carrying capacity if it is relying excessively on fossil fuels without allocating the capital necessary to create an alternative energy system for future years: capital which will have to be foregone in some part of the economy.

Carrying capacity assessment can provide a basis for identifying targets for sustainable development; for as long as a country's development proceeds within the confines of national carrying capacity, that development will be sustainable. Carrying capacity constitutes, as it were, a frame representing the physical potential for development: the space which is available for expansion in terms of both population and economic growth. The size of that frame may of course be changed, whether outwards or inwards. Not only do cultural, economic or social factors come into play; societies have the possibility of expanding their carrying capacity through the deliberate selection and pursuit of development options which allow for the enhancement of necessary physical resource flows (through technology and through conservation for example) while ensuring that economic growth is not surpassed by population growth and the material demands of society.

3.5. MODELLING NATIONAL CARRYING CAPACITY[2]

The assessment of carrying capacity requires a systems approach since the national system needs to be seen as a whole with the feedbacks perceived between the different components and competing demands ascertained. It is inevitable, therefore, that recourse be sought to modelling.

Starting from *Limits to Growth* (Meadows et al., 1972), there have, of course, been several attempts to assess global carrying capacity. One of the more recent, made by Arthur Westing (1981), calculates two alternative levels of standard of living and the corresponding levels of population which might be carried. The first assumes the level of an average of the world's twenty-seven most affluent nations, and the second, the average of forty-three nations of medium wealth. The sizes of population which result are only about 2 billion for the affluent variant and 3 billion for the medium variant. Both alternatives, being well below today's figure, assume that strong emphasis would need to be placed on population control and that aspirations would need to change for the world as a whole, at least for a time. However, the method of calculation (which did not involve any modelling techniques) consisted of ascertaining the per capita utilisation of five different resource areas considered separately – total land area, cultivated land area, forest land area, cereals and wood. No attempt was made to integrate the different sectors and assess the effects of alternative uses. Nor was the question of substitution of materials considered. One suspects that had such considerations been taken into account a rather different outcome might have resulted.

A number of models have been applied to the estimation of carrying capacity at national level. Four of these are described briefly and a review of their principal features is given later in Table 3.3.

3.5.1. Land resources for populations of the future

This FAO study (FAO, 1986) was conducted with the collaboration of the International Institute for Applied Systems Analysis. The methodology adopted was to divide a national territory into identifiable agro-ecological zones classified by soil, climate, degree of slope, tendency to degradation, etc. A large amount of data was collected and computerised to provide filters for assessing the food-producing potential of the different zones according to three hypothetical levels of input: low, intermediate and high. According to the outcome of this study sixty-four countries, mostly in Africa, would not be able to feed their populations from their own territories under the low input assumptions, thirty-six with intermediate inputs and nineteen with high inputs.

The conclusions reached through the model are the result of exogenous decisions which ignore the question of how the different levels of input are to be acquired. The conclusions do take account of population growth (using the United Nations Medium variant) and allow for land requirements for housing and domestic infrastructure. However, the model does not reflect the dynamic behaviour of the economy and was not designed as a tool for long-term planning.

3.5.2. Carrying Capacity Incorporated

This American group published an assessment of the US carrying capacity in 1982. While it lacked the detailed agro-ecological data of the FAO study, it did try to take account of the costs of achieving the necessary inputs. It further quantified food output per hectare in terms of inputs per hectare expressed as the energy requirement of these inputs. The study unfortunately had a very small data base. Nevertheless the report stressed the large energy requirements of agriculture and the problem of soil depletion. It examined the national energy position into the future and came to the conclusion that the account was running into a deficit situation. It then allocated to agriculture in 2020 the same fraction of the country's energy as in 1982 and concluded that the US would by that time be able to produce enough food for rather less than the total population. As in the case of the FAO study, the model is static. Details of the model have not been released, making it impossible to judge how useful it might be for the purpose of development planning.

3.5.3. Odum's eco-energetic models

In Odum's (1983) models, natural energy flows and non-renewable energy are seen as interacting in the process of stimulating development. Odum argues that the computation of the maximum rate of work (energy) that can be generated within a country represents its ultimate maximum performance, and thus the numbers that can be carried at a given standard of living. Odum has advanced his own terminology which is highly complex, and it is not always easy to penetrate the logic behind his numerical processes; why, for example, is what he terms 'developed carrying capacity' simply eight times that of renewable carrying capacity? Odum's approach is concerned very largely with the purely energy aspects of the economy. Once again, the models are static and no suggestions are offered as to how to proceed from a current to a desired situation.

3.5.4. Review

Table 3.3 summarises features of these various models.

The models serve different purposes, none of which is as a tool for development planning and for assessing the impact of population change on development. As Table 3.3 indicates, a model designed to fulfil that function clearly needs to be dynamic and able to reflect feedbacks between different sectors of the national system; and it needs to include specifically both the food and the energy sectors (the rationale for using energy as a numeraire will be touched upon later). The object of such a model will be to explore, in the context of planning, how long-term strategies may be devised to enhance national carrying capacity, taking account of the modification of physical factors through social, cultural and political factors.

Table 3.3 Some features of existing approaches to measuring national carrying capacity

Model	*D*	*S*	*G*	*Fo*	*Ec*	*Fe*	*En*
FAO/IIASA		*		*			
Carrying Capacity Inc.				*	*		*
Odum eco-energetic		*					**
Desired planning model	*			*		*	**

D = dynamic
S = static
Fo = specific food sector
Ec = econometric
Fe = feedback
En = treats energy separately
** also uses energy as a numeraire.
Source: Slesser, 1984.

3.6. ECCO AND RESOURCE ACCOUNTING

Having surveyed existing efforts to quantify national carrying capacity it was decided to develop a model drawing on the strengths of these and having the express purpose of assisting governments to identify strategies for long-term development, with particular attention to the implications of population growth.

ECCO is a dynamic simulation model which quantifies feedback among the different sectors of the national system in physical resource terms. The reason for doing this is to avoid the thorny problem of having to predict monetary values over a long period ahead – the bane of long-term economic forecasting. That this is an area where there can be no rigour of measurement is reflected in Figure 3.1 which shows how widely forecasts of oil prices differ. Prices do, of course, respond to scarcity but only when scarcity becomes evident. Until then, the perceived

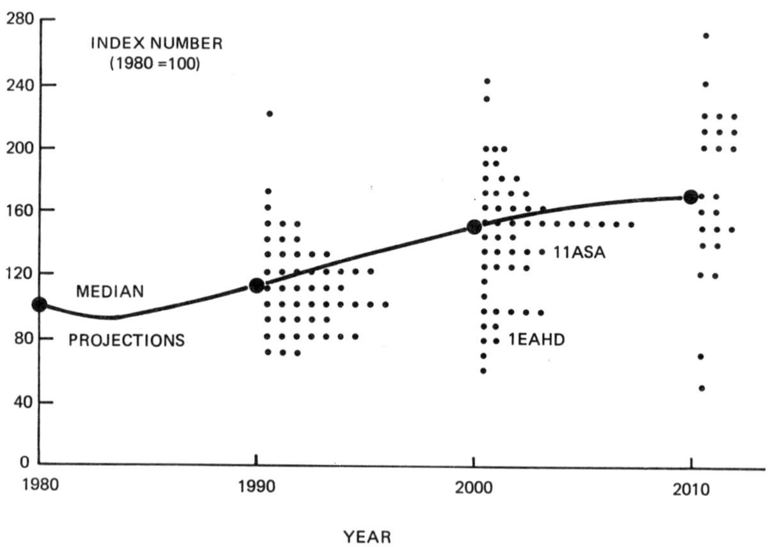

Figure 3.1 Predictions of the international price of crude oil (1980 = 100).
Source: Schrattenholzer and Manne (1984).

value of a commodity may not change and may even command no monetary price at all, as in the case of environmental factors which are usually treated as externalities.

In planning, fiscal devices are used to direct investment towards the economic outcome sought, and even quite small changes in the fiscal climate of a country can have a marked effect over the short term. However, if the direction pursued is incompatible with physically realisable development prospects, it may well result in a distortion of the system. There may be resource implications which are not evident, perhaps because resources such as air, water or soil are treated as a 'free good', or because of incorrect assumptions about the potential for improvement through technological change. There may also be failure to quantify adequately the investment needed to maintain the flow of resources.

In ECCO, resources are quantified through the energy required to release them and to produce any good or service in the economy. Inputs and outputs associated with all activities are thus expressed in energy terms, using the already well-established technique of energy analysis. In this way the problem of the changing, time-dependent values attached to money is overcome, since physical relationships are predictable.

The rationale of using energy as a common numeraire is explained in depth in Professor Slesser's paper in this book which also describes the structure and operation of the model. A few further observations are, however, in order here.

3.6.1. Development and growth potential

The more resources – land, water, forests, minerals or sources of energy – a country has in relation to its population, the greater its ultimate scope for development. If it is to be sustainable, that development will include laying down the infrastructure required for meeting the needs of the population in perpetuity and, in order to do this, ensuring that the environment does not deteriorate beyond the point of no return.

Until relatively recently it was tacitly assumed that as much room for manoeuvre remained as needed. Then, as pressure on the resource base increased with rising populations and higher material demands, constraints appeared on the horizon and the notions of conservation and of efficiency of resource use began to take firm root. There is no doubt about the validity of efficiency measures; considerable gains may be achieved through energy saving, for example. At the same time such gains can only be made once. There must be parallel efforts to see that the capital, structures and processes necessary are put in place for maintaining the life support system indefinitely. The purpose of carrying capacity assessment through ECCO is to see how this may be done through the exploration of policies and evaluation of trade-offs, in such a way as to leave open sufficiently broad options for change.

3.6.2. Physical and social carrying capacity

Physical carrying capacity is determined not only by population but also by material demands per capita. In an article by Gifford et al. (1975), for example, it was noted that a 1946 estimate of the carrying capacity of Australia was given at 25 million whereas an estimate in 1956 put it at 480 million. The lower figure assumed the living standards current at the time and the higher figure a subsistence existence for everyone. Beyond the question of material standard of living there can also be social factors which effectively decrease physical carrying capacity. It may be that importance is attached to wilderness areas and the prospect of heavy population densities disliked. Society may be unwilling to accept not only nuclear energy but also the prospect of large areas being covered by the solar devices necessary to produce energy in an alternative manner. Carrying capacity could also be affected in the other direction by the willingness of people to exchange the encumberances of industrial society for a different, more physically sparse life style.

Such considerations can be incorporated in ECCO and the implications of alternative social choices examined. Few countries have explicit social goals. However, by exploring the courses of action open and determining the trade-offs involved, a country can begin to identify the kind of future it wishes to pursue, and to balance aspirations with means and in the context of what is materially possible.

3.6.3. ECCO and socio-cultural variables

Models are often held in suspicion as being unable to cope with social and cultural factors, the ‘stuff’ of life.

It is probably true that such factors cannot be directly quantified in a satisfactory manner. But they may be taken into consideration in an indirect, but nevertheless precise way. Physical carrying capacity will in theory be the population which can be supported given the way resources are used. The reason is that outputs, given a constant resource mix in identical circumstances, are mediated through socio-cultural variables. In Kenya, for example, it was found that farmers in the modern sector produced more per unit input than subsistence farmers, the cause lying in management. The output differential could easily be incorporated into ECCO. Other types of output differential explained by land tenure systems, industrial organisation, education and training, etc., can be treated in a similar manner.

3.6.4. ECCO and environmental factors

Environmental factors have not yet been sufficiently accounted for in ECCO. This is not so much because of technical problems, but because of lack of agreement on the degree of degradation considered acceptable. Where norms have been established they can be incorporated in an ECCO model without undue difficulty. This may involve respecting certain thresholds in relation to permitted effluent levels or perhaps the exploitation of forest land. With regard to the former this will mean, grosso modo, calculating the effort required to ensure that the rate of dissipation of pollutants is kept within the territory's means of absorbing or dispersing it.

3.6.5. Data base of ECCO

It is frequently commented that ECCO must be hard to implement due to the lack of an adequate data base. This is more apparent than real. It is, however, important that physical data be collected. A typical example is that in most economic statistical tables water and electricity are combined within a single category, and expressed in financial terms. This renders the information useless for the purpose of an ECCO model. But the physical data on water flows, etc., and electricity supply in physical units must have been measured in the first place in order to arrive at the financial statistics. In addition, one does require in the team applying ECCO at least one person competent in the field of energy analysis.

3.7. THE ROLE OF RESOURCE ACCOUNTING

As a conclusion to this paper, resource accounting (which may alternatively be termed physical planning) as applied in models like ECCO represents an adjunct to economic planning rather than an alternative. To be useful, however, the application of ECCO must precede economic planning.

The functional role of resource accounting is to explore how a country's carrying capacity may be enhanced and to identify an interlocking set of long-term policies which can set that country on the way to sustainable development through means which are physically possible, economically feasible and politically acceptable. Having been identified, these policies constitute a framework for the operation of economic planning which will then devise strategies to direct economic choice in accordance with long-term reality.

Certain innovations will need to be introduced. Investment programmes will tend, for example, to run beyond current planning horizons so that some mechanism will be necessary to ensure proper articulation between one planning period and the next. The relationships, also, among economic sectors will now be defined with much greater precision and means will need to be found to ensure horizontal co-ordination between different ministries.

ECCO has not yet been applied in the broad sense described above. It has, however, been experimentally tested in a few countries and the results are presented in other papers written for this meeting.

NOTES

1 See, however, Chapter 11 of this document.

2 This section draws on an analysis made by M. Slesser, in a report presented to UNESCO in 1984, unpublished.

REFERENCES

Edwards, W. and D. Philips. 'Metal Prices as a Function of Ore Grade'. In: *Resource Policy*, 1, 1976.

FAO. *Potential Population Supporting Capacities of Lands in the Developing World*. FAO, Rome, 1986.

Gifford, R. M., et al. 'Biophysical Constraints in Australian Food Production: Implications for Population Policy'. In: *Search*, Vol. 6, No. 6, June 1975.

Government of Kenya. 'Economic Management for Renewed Growth.' Sessional Paper No. 1, Government Printer, Nairobi, Kenya, 1986.

Meadows, D., et al. *Limits of Growth*. Universe Books, 1972.

Odum, H. and E. Odum. 'Energy Analysis Overview of Nations'. Working Paper WP—83 82. IIASA, Laxenburg, Austria.

Schrattenholzer, L., and A. S. Manne. 'International Energy Workshop poll response', *The Energy Journal*, Vol. 5, 1984, pp. 45–64.

Simon, J. *The Ultimate Resource*. Princeton University Press, 1981.

UN *International Development: Critical Policy Issues. A Study of the Task Force on Long Term Development Objectives*. UN, New York, 1981.

UN *Report of the International Conference on Population*. UN, New York, 1984.

Westing, A. H. 'A World in Balance.' In: *Environmental Conservation*, Vol. 8, No. 3, 1981.

World Commission on Environment and Development. *Our Common Future*. Oxford University Press, 1987.

4

PLANNING FOR SUSTAINABLE DEVELOPMENT

M. Slesser

4.1. A RESOURCE ACCOUNTING APPROACH TO MEASURING SUSTAINABILITY

4.1.1. Carrying capacity

The need for development to be sustainable has been increasingly implied in recent times, especially in United Nations circles. This theme was the first recommendation of the World Population Conference in Mexico (1985). More recently it has even been argued for by a politician of an aid-donating developed country (Patten, 1987). However, the quantification of sustainable development has remained ellusive, the concept of sustainability being mostly identified with environmental issues (Redclift, 1987). In 1980, King, then at Unesco, realised that it had much broader ramifications, and touched on the interconnections between population, resources, environment and development (PRED; see King, 1987). She felt it had to be articulated through the quantification of the physical determinants of development rather than the economic. Following this lead, Slesser with the support of the United Nations and UNDP (Slesser, 1984) developed a resource accounting approach under the rubric of 'Carrying Capacity'.[1]

To the ecologist, carrying capacity of a particular terrain is seen in terms of thresholds or limits. This, however, is the attainable level of development of a natural system driven purely from solar flux. In man-made systems, stored energy sources like coal and oil, and systems calling for capital structures like hydro-electric dams vastly increase the potential for development. Thus the Unesco study perceived it as the number of people who, sharing a given territory, can be supported at any moment in time on a sustainable basis, taking into account its known resources, as well as factors of a socio-cultural nature.

By 1987 carrying capacity studies on various economies (e.g. Baguant, 1987; Sintunawa, 1986; Unesco, 1984) had shown that energy analysis offered a means of making a precise statement of what is implied in the word 'sustainability' of an economy. The argument is as follows (Slesser and Hounam, 1979).

Economic growth depends on the growth of capital stock (= embodied energy) to enable labour to provide enhanced output (= dissipation of energy). If this is to be sustainable, then the rate of energy flow must be maintainable (up to a point it can be compensated by technical progress). Since part of the energy flow must, through capital and operating energy, be recycled to drive the energy transformation system by which resources in the ground become economically useful, fuel, the energy requirements for this must also be taken into account. As energy resources become less accessible, the energy that must be dissipated in the process of acquiring fuel rises, that is the energy requirement for energy (ERE; see IFIAS, 1974) rises. In money terms it becomes more expensive to extract. In a classic study, Peckham and Klitz (1978) have evaluated ERE for North Sea oil fields as a function of cumulative depletion.

Sustainability may thus be defined as a state where the rate of growth of energy flow into the economy is sufficient to liberate and harness the resources needed to maintain indefinitely or enhance the material standard of living of the people living within that economy in such a manner as to maintain the quality of those potentially degradable resources, like soils, forests and acquifers. While few calculations have yet been carried out on individual economies, the same principle has been applied at the global level (Slesser, 1985), where it has been shown that the rate of useful energy available to the world economy can grow at about 2 per cent annually. Thus the economy of the planet Earth would appear to be sustainable, but at a limited growth rate, in which population growth must detract from economic growth. This study was made using energy as a numeraire, that is to say, the flows within the world economy were measured in terms of the energy required to make them occur, not in terms of money.

As to ultimate world population, if one takes into account the available land resources and considers the growing of crops on them in the context of the energy required for intensification, it is estimated that ultimately it might be possible to feed 90 billion people, but only at subsistence level, and it is questionable how long that would be sustainable (Unesco, 1984).

4.1.2. The money numeraire

A besetting problem of the resource accounting approach, which uses energy as a numeraire, is that those accustomed to making decisions based on financial evaluations have difficulty in interpreting figures expressed in energy terms, such as so many gigajoules of capital. It is therefore worth explaining where resource accounting and the energy numeraire can usefully replace conventional economics and the money numeraire, and how the two units relate to each other.

Money is the way in which people express their values and preferences and in which economists express relative prices. Certainly no other system has been invented which expresses choice so succinctly. While the use of the valuation concept has proved enormously useful in permitting economics to explain how people make and change their choices, and interpreting past economic events, its role in forecasting has proved less successful, except for the very short term, where current values can be assumed to persist (Ascher, 1978). Schrattenholzer, who has made himself the focus of a world survey of energy forecasting at the International Institute for Applied Systems Analysis, recently highlighted the issue with the words 'Long-term energy projections become obsolete quite rapidly'! And as he further remarked of the assumptions made in econometric modelling, 'there is a strong herd instinct in macro-economic forecasting' (Schrattenholzer and Manne, 1984).

One consequence has been a growing distrust of econometric models in development planning, and a trend away from their use. Unhappily this merely results in the replacement of a hitherto explicit statement of one's assumptions, whatever its merits, by hunch, prejudice or, worse still, normative goals without any demonstration of feasibility.

The estimation of sustainability is pointless unless one can also compute how it will change as time passes. Helpful though the valuation concept is for understanding economic decisions and making short-term forecasts, it would appear to have nothing whatsoever to offer the study of sustainability. How may one measure sustainability in terms of value? This may explain the lack of interest within the economics profession on this topic, and the fact that the question of sustainability is largely considered an environmental problem. It is in fact an all-embracing question, and the task is to be able to measure it and predict how various policies may affect it in the future.

It is worth noting, in passing, that this inability to forecast is not a failure of economics, but of the numeraire used – money. But, one might suggest, it may be partly due to an implicit assumption of economics, namely that the economy is entirely wrought by man; that it may be designed and change may be implemented at will.

An equally plausible hypothesis is that the economy is the natural outcome of human greed, demand, inventiveness, population pressure, topography, climate, cultural values and competition from neighbours. That is, the economy is a system of which the tendency for growth or decay is endogenous, and economic measures simply tamper with the mechanism, and create temporary changes (Marchetti, 1985, and on other occasions).

Money can be controlled, however. Money is a concept, not a reality. As such it has neither mass, nor form. It has neither intensive nor extensive properties. It is a convention. It is a very clever invention, the effectiveness of which is based on trust. This trust is continually abused by governments and banks. Many bankers have come to think of money as a commodity. Governments debase the value of money constantly to suit their political convenience. But the greatest problem of all is that the mass of people grow up to think of money as a reality; are conditioned by money. Nevertheless on a day-to-day basis it plays a vital role for common folk going about their business. But it fails as a numeraire for looking at the future. How can one make calculations using a numeraire the value of which is constantly and unpredictably changing? Economics must be the only science that uses a numeraire of unknown and changing value in its computations.

The role of resource accounting, then, is to identify the physically possible, within which the economically feasible must, by the laws of nature, operate. While money is the vehicle

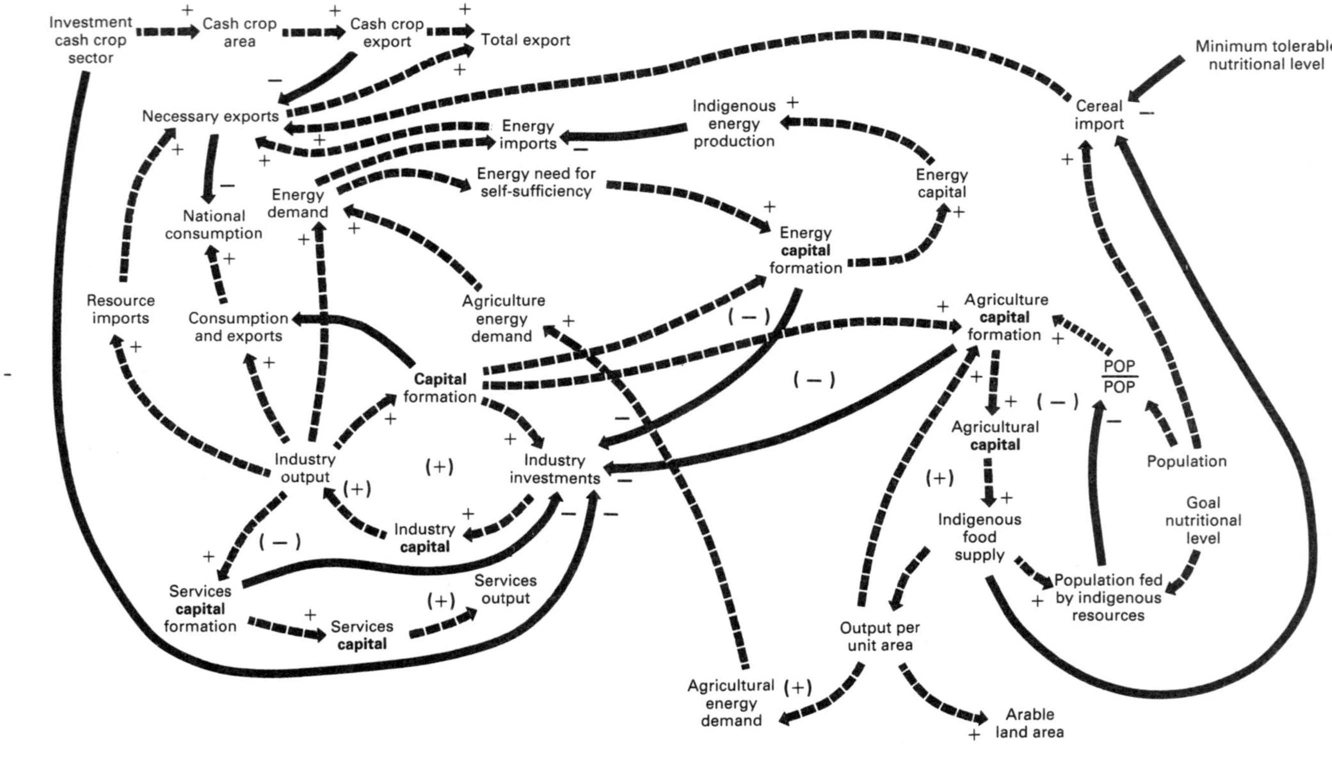

Figure 4.1 Influence diagram of industrial growth cycle.

through which decisions are turned into action, resource accounting and the energy numeraire may be the means by which the possible may be measured.

4.1.3. Resource accounting

In the resource accounting approach the 'cost' of carrying out some economic process or act is measured in terms of the physical effort entailed. Output is quantitively linked to input as a causal relationship. As will be shown below, that effort may be most conveniently measured in terms of the energy required to create all the inputs that go to produce an output, plus the energy to drive the process. This is not to imply that energy is held to be scarce, but that it is unique among physical resources in that it may only be used once.

The question that must immediately arise in the economist's mind is how such a single measure of activity can be used for economic planning. The answer, as it is hoped to demonstrate, is that by using energy as a numeraire, one may compute the feasible set of outcomes of a given set of policies. Reality must lie within that feasible set, for if an action is not physically possible, then it can never be economically possible.

Consider the distinction between a model of economic growth expressed in money terms as opposed to energy. Figure 4.1 depicts, as an influence diagram, a simple industrial growth cycle. In money terms, money flows round the system. It is not consumed. The system has positive feedback, so leading to exponential growth. If the same model is expressed in resource accounting terms – that is, energy – though the arrows and the feedback mechanism of the influence diagram remain unchanged, it is no longer possible to visualise a circular flow, for at each stage the energy used is dissipated. Only the embodied energy[2] in the output moves on.

In order to put resource accounting to work, we now need to consider the underlying concepts and accepted conventions. Before doing so, however, it is necessary to make the connection between physical resources and energy.

4.1.4. Energy and resources

Physical resources, with the possible exception of helium and mercury, are so abundant in the earth's crust that mankind cannot conceivably run out of them. Furthermore though they be used, unlike energy, they are never used up. Many researchers have shown that provided there is energy, know-how and capital, one can always access physical resources, though the energy requirement of so doing may rise to very high levels (Cook, 1977; Chapman and Roberts, 1983; Weinberg and Goeller, 1977). Table 4.1 (for copper) is a typical example of the nature of the situation. As for labour, it is being progressively substituted by energy as a source of work. Labour, in all but the most primitive economies, is a decision-making element in production rather than a source of effort.

Table 4.1 The energy requirements of copper by ore grade

	USA 1970	*Year 2000*	*Basic rocks*
Ore grade, % copper	0.7	0.2	0.001
Recovery of copper, %	82	80	80
Tonnes waste rock/t copper	355	940	6300
t tailings/t copper	145	620	12500
Total waste t/t copper	500	1560	18800
Energy dissipated/t copper, GJ:			
Mining	25	93	1875
Beneficiation	33	127	2543
Smelting and refining	30	30	30
Total GJ/t copper	88	250	4448
Coal equivalent per t copper	3.5	10.1	178

Source: Kellog, 1976.

The price that must be paid for this economic advance is not inconsiderable, for as an economy develops, it becomes ever more dependent on a flow of fuel to maintain the effort required to drive the economy. If a given standard of living is to be maintained, then it is a sine qua non that a flow of energy be sustained. Nor can we take too much refuge in technical progress. Chapman and Roberts (1983) have shown that for many metals technical progress can no longer compensate for declining ore grades. Fleming (1974) showed that on thermodynamic grounds certain technologies have already reached the limits of their feasible technical advance. Thermodynamics can be used as a guide to threshold limitations.

4.1.5. Derivation of resource accounting

The derivation of resource accounting may be considered through the medium of the production function. Traditionally that has expressed output in terms of capital and labour. The rise in OPEC oil prices in 1973 induced a re-appraisal in which energy was sometimes included as a separate factor. In a different approach Slesser (1978) showed that if one networked back all the inputs to a production process, every input could be traced to the twin actions of prior energy and labour use. Stated in another way, time (= labour) and energy (= resources) were the only inputs to production irretrievably dissipated.

Thus, for example, capital is represented by capital goods, themselves the result of manufacture, for which were needed prior capital goods, physical inputs and labour. Similar reasoning applies to all other inputs, including the life-support system for labour itself. It may be shown that of physical resources none are irretrievably dissipated except energy.

Thus the resource accounting (RA) form of a production function states:

$$P = \phi\ (L,L',E,E')$$

where L and E are operational labour and energy and L' and E' prior labour and prior energy.

It should be noted that, unlike economic production functions which use money as a numeraire, the labour terms are not couched in the same numeraire as the energy terms, and so cannot be added or multiplied. In fact, each term stands apart, each determining a rate process, so that it is possible for each to be a limiting factor – a constraint.

An analogous example is the combustion of coal, a rate process, which at low temperatures is entirely dictated by the chemical reaction of oxygen with carbon, but at high temperatures is controlled by the mass transfer of oxygen to the coal surface. Only within a very circumscribed range of conditions is the rate of combustion affected by both. In the case of an economy analysed by resource accounting it would only be where the fossil and fossil energy use per unit of result was of the same magnitude as the human energy effort, measured in energy terms; that is, where the national per capita human work effort was of the same order as the fossil plus solar energy use.

This is of the order of 100 kg of coal energy per capita per year. There are few economies at such a low level, and if solar-energy capture through plants is not taken into account, there are none. In other words, beyond an energy use of about 100 kg coal equivalent per capita, labour, as a source of work, is not the means of enhancing output. The dissipation of energy in the production process is a measure of the non-renewable resource consumption of each and every economic activity (for solar energy, see Slesser, 1980).

4.1.6. Labour

The foregoing does not imply that labour is irrelevant. It remains important in two senses. Firstly, labour equals people, and people make decisions. Labour is used less and less to provide physical work. The workers on the assembly line using power tools are essentially making decisions. A developing economy needs an increasing proportion of educated and trained labour. Secondly, labour is the consumer. An economy is developed in order to furnish this labour with a better life style.

4.1.7. Energy analysis

Resource accounting cannot be put into practice without the aid of the newly-developed discipline of energy analysis (Chapman and Roberts, 1983). Each time energy is used, either wastefully or usefully, that energy is irrevocably dissipated. It is common jargon to talk of the 'embodied' energy in a good or service. The procedure for evaluating economic activity in energy terms is well established (e.g. IFIAS, 1974; Slesser, 1978).

4.1.8. Energy transformation system

But how is the energy provided in the first place? It arises through the ability of the industrial system to extract and refine energy resources, whether fossil, fissile or renewable, and so deliver the fuel where needed. In order to accommodate this fact, Gilliland (1978) has redrawn the conventional economic model of the economy (Figure 4.2): part of the system output (= embodied energy) is devoted to gaining access to energy resources. This prior energy expenditure yields current fuel

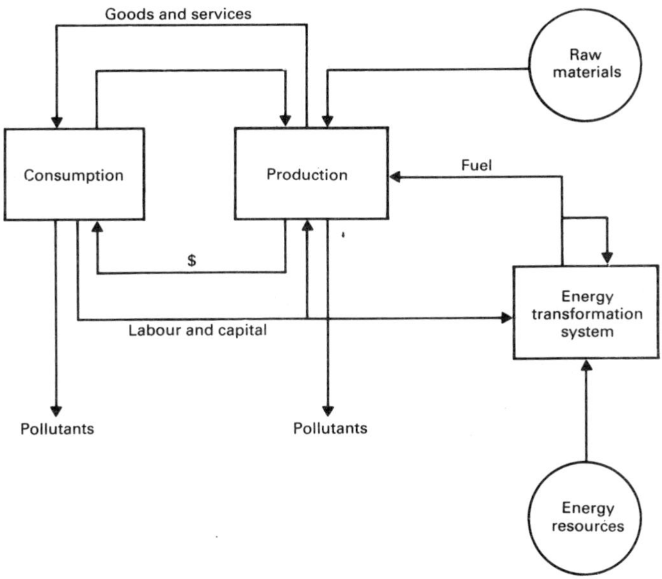

Figure 4.2 Model of an economy, after Gilliland.

supplies. The lower the ratio of primary energy extracted to fuel delivered, the greater the potential rate of economic expansion per unit investment. In energy analysis it is called the energy requirement for energy (ERE), values of which for many resources have been quoted in the literature, e.g. Peckham and Klitz (1978); Chapman, Leach and Slesser (1974); Colorado Energy Research Institute (1976).

4.1.9. Energy allocation mechanism

Energy analysis has been shown to be a perfectly workable way of making economic appraisals of energy systems (Slesser, 1987). In so doing, one of the crucial uncertainties in financial analysis, namely future discount rates, becomes redundant. If one accepts the definition of economics as the science of the allocation of scarce resources, then energy analysis may be seen to be a rather rigorous means of considering the optimal depletion of the one non-substitutable resource in the world (energy), that is, by depleting first those resources which require the least ERE. However, the value system reflects more than just this aspect of scarcity. It reflects market conditions, in turn affected by a host of geopolitical factors.

4.1.10. Resource accounting and development planning

Since no economic activity can be intensified or expanded without the dissipation of energy, one may model an economic system in energy terms. The objection often made to doing this is that energy cannot be used as an allocation mechanism since people, it is argued, do not make their choices on the basis of energy requirement per unit of output. It seems, however, that we may do so unawares. Roberts (1982) in a telling paper on energy and value showed how close were the relationships between embodied energy and value for many goods. However the merits of this argument are not crucial to the use of resource accounting as a means of quantifying the interactions of an economy.

The economic approach to development planning is to move iteratively through the cycle:

WANTS -----→ TECHNOLOGY ------→ RESOURCES -----→ FEASIBLE WANTS

until convergence is obtained. The reliability of the result rests very much on the assumptions made as to resource costs and how people, collectively, may in future value aspects of life and goods.

Considerable use is made of the concept of income and price elasticity of demand. Yet such relationships are too fickle to carry one many years forward in time, as we see by the failure of energy forecasting in recent years.

4.1.11. Using resource accounting

By its nature, resource accounting must analyse development in the reverse way to economic planning. Resources must be liberated in order to liberate further resources. That is:

RESOURCES--→TECHNOLOGY FEASIBLE OUTPUT--→CAPITAL--→RESOURCES

One can impose normative goals, but if these are too many or too demanding, the system may not develop, and in modelling one deliberately restricts them to the basic requirements of survival aims, such as goal nutritional level per inhabitant, domestic energy provision, or minimal water supply, seeking to establish the potential of the system to do better.

The fact that resource accounting is a systems approach does not create an inevitable future; far from it. On the contrary, it enables one to assess the outcome of any policy option that is capable of being quantified. Examples would be birth rate, type of agriculture, fiscal policy, degree of sustainability or self-sufficiency sought in food or energy, export/import policy and so forth. It can be used to explore, as in the real world, many criteria, often political, that enter into the decision-making process. However, being a systems approach it can only give information about the long-term consequences of these decisions for it cannot handle the variations wrought by short-term market forces which may only be expressed in value terms. In fact it identifies the feasible, not necessarily the probable. This aspect of resource accounting renders it very suitable for making carrying capacity studies of a country, whereby one can assess whether investment matches supply needs, and output matches investment needs within a sustainable context. If development is to occur at the best possible rate, yet remain sustainable or move towards sustainability, then all sectors of the economy must grow in harmony, while the implied energy supply must be sustainable. For example, investments in water and energy supply must match industrial, agricultural, domestic and service needs. There are many ways to feed a country's population, of which the extremes are self-sufficiency (e.g. USA) or large food imports (e.g. Hong Kong). Imports imply exports. Both have embodied energy. Energy needs may be met indigenously or by imports. But just as many of the developing countries have come to realise that a high degree of food self-sufficiency must now replace the former priority for industrial development, the rise in OPEC oil prices has introduced a similar concern for energy. For example, self-sufficiency in energy is a cornerstone of EEC energy policy.

Through an assessment of the physical potential, one would seek to identify those policies consistent with sustainable development. In the long term that implies maintainance of food and energy provision, perhaps with a measure of food and energy self-sufficiency (the degree chosen is a political option to be tested). Clearly population growth is a key parameter in the entire equation.

4.1.12. ECCO and sustainability

An economy, sustainable or otherwise, is the product of one or more driving forces. The application of resource accounting to the problem of modelling an economy with a view to testing for sustainability calls for identifying those driving forces, and formulating a structure which reflects their role in the economy. Figure 4.3 depicts this in a basic structure which is called ECCO – Enhancement of Carrying Capacity Options, and more recently, Economic Co-ordination model. It is a dynamic simulation model using energy as a numeraire.

ECCO is a feedback model – that is, any change (effect) within it takes place because change (cause) occurs elsewhere in the

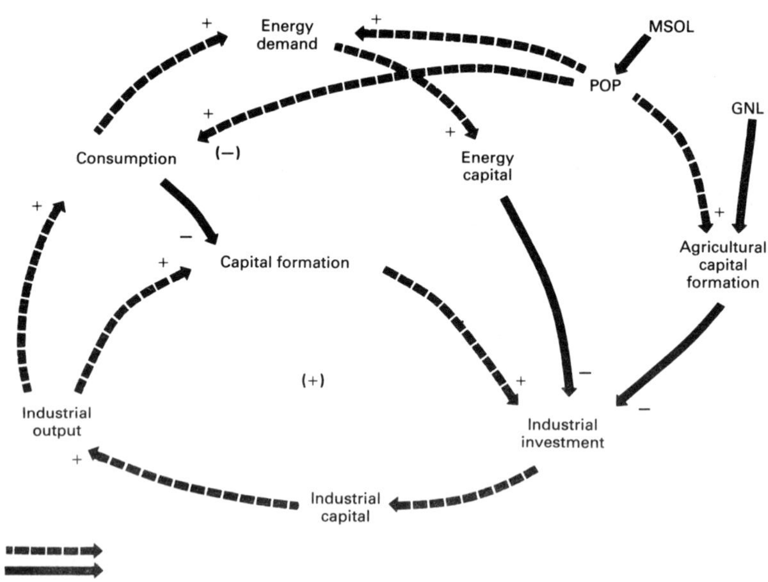

Figure 4.3 Influence diagram for ECCO (principal elements).

model. It is crucial to the effective operation of the model that it be made as simple as possible, yet contain the primary feed-back mechanisms. ECCO runs endogenously once the policy decisions have been inserted. For example in its initial form two normative values were imposed upon it: a goal nutritional level for all inhabitants and a minimal per capita availability of domestic energy.

ECCO has been described in detail elsewhere (e.g. FAO/UNESCO, 1984; Slesser, 1987; and King, 1987) and its use in development planning discussed by King and Slesser (1988).

4.1.13. Sustainability

In ECCO, sustainability is defined as:

SUST = EOUT/EIN, where

EOUT is the energy produced within the country, including captured solar energy, and other renewable energies, and

EIN is the energy used to drive the economic system of the country, both being in the terms of identical energy quality.

Typically EIN will comprise fossil and fissile energies extracted in the country, plus solar[3] and renewable energies whether utilised as crops or biomass.

EOUT must take account of imports and exports, the GER[4] of imports being added, those of exports subtracted. For information on energy qualities of different fuels, Patterson's study (1984) is useful.

4.2. VALIDATION OF ECCO

4.2.1. Introduction

ECCO was first applied in a pilot study of Kenya supported by Unesco and FAO. It was later used in Mauritius, and in training courses for several other countries. To most planners an approach to long-term planning which describes an economy in non-money terms is at best an absurdity, at worst misleading. It was therefore necessary to demonstrate the validity of the resource accounting approach by comparing an ECCO output with historical data. Ideally one would have done this for a developing economy, since it was with such economies in mind that ECCO was developed. However, a reliable long-term data base simply does not exist. Thus the validation study was made on a developed economy, the United Kingdom. The resulting model is called BRITECCO.

4.2.2. Numeraire

In the case of BRITECCO a decision was taken to make it more transparant to users unaccustomed to the energy numeraire. Hence, except for allocation mechanisms, which remain in energy terms, most numbers are expressed in constant (1980) pounds. It must be remembered that though the numbers are in money units, in fact they are simply surrogates for the energy units, and that unlike money, they do not go round and round the economy.

4.2.3. Investment goods

In the UK study, the opportunity was taken to develop the resource accounting concept further than was possible in studies in less-developed countries due to the lack of data there. In manufacturing a distinction was made between capital stock that could be used to create physical capital, but which could not of itself form physical capital. These were termed investment goods and operational goods respectively. For the system to grow, capital stock is required. The sole sources of formation of this capital stock are investment goods, foreign earnings and international borrowings spent on capital stock. Figure 4.4 depicts the structure of this part of ECCO. The numbers in the figure refer to the situation in the United Kingdom in 1974, expressed in billion 1980 pounds. A major difference between the United Kingdom and developing economies is the extent of capital inflow and outflow.

4.2.4. Data

The data for the manufacturing sector was obtained exclusively from the United Kingdom Central Statistical Office's Blue Book,

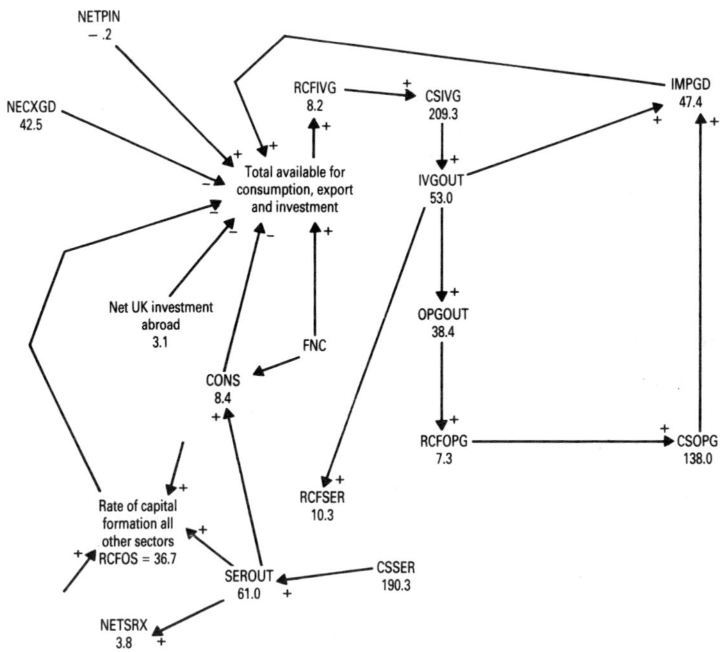

Figure 4.4 Influence diagram of the manufacturing sector of BRITECCO (numbers are in billion 1980 £ in the year 1974).

an annual publication. The details of the United Kingdom version of ECCO are available in report form (Slesser, 1987). Apart from the separation of manufacturing into these two categories, BRITECCO differed little from the Kenya and Mauritius models, being somewhat more disaggregated in certain sectors.

CSOPG	– Capital stock Operational goods	1980 £
HCSOPG	– Historical CS Operational goods	1980 £
OPGOUT	– Output operational goods	1980 £ /y
HOPGOT	– Historical output OPG	1980 £ /y
CSIVG	– Capital stock investment goods	1980 £
HCSIVG	– Historical CS investment goods	1980 £
EDWAT	– Energy for water supply system	GJ/y

FRXP	–	Fraction exported for balance of payments	
HFRXP	–	Historical FRXP	
IVGOUT	–	Investment goods output	1980 £ /y
HIVGOT	–	Historical output IVG	1980 £ /y
IMPGD	–	Rate of import of manufactured goods	1980 £ /y
MSOL	–	material standard of Living	1980 £ /cap.y
NECXGD	–	Necessary exports (to meet balance of payments)	1980 £
NUKINV	–	Net UK investment abroad	1980 £
OWCP	–	Cumulative oil output	t
OWOUT	–	Rate of oil output	t/y
RCFOW1	–	Rate of investment in oil extraction	1980 £ /y
RUKIO	–	Rate of UK investment abroad	1980 £
TCSAG	–	Total capital stock agriculture	1980 £

4.2.5. Comparison of Reference Profile for the United Kingdom with historical data

Reference Profile is the name given to the BRITECCO output when the model was initialised in 1974. In order to appreciate the level of match achieved it is necessary to know what exogenous time-variant data were fed to the model. These essentially represent policy actions during the ten-year period, 1974 to 1984:

- agricultural areas;
- desired output from hill (i.e. less favoured) areas;
- goal nutritional level in cereal and animal protein;
- level of UK food self-sufficiency desired (= 90%);
- rate of UK investment abroad;
- rate of foreign investment in the UK;
- level of UK aid to developing countries;
- level of research funding;
- tourism both into and out of the UK;
- capital invested by British Coal;
- desired rate of penetration of nuclear energy.

The outputs and historical data are shown in Table 4.2. Historical data have the prefix 'H' on the acronym. Table 4.3. summarises the discrepancies in the data in the year 1984. Not all output

Table 4.2 BRITECCO Reference Profile to 1997, starting 1974

BRITRPDOC – Investment goods sector: actual (H) and E

TIME E+03	*CSIVG E+09*	*HCSIVG E+09*	*IVGOUT E+09*	*HIVGOT E+09*	*RCFIVG E+09*	*HRCFIG E+00*
1.9740	175.50	175.50	56.160	57.000	7.329	8.2000
1.9750	177.17	184.60	57.800	55.750	7.533	7.6500
1.9760	179.45	193.70	57.706	54.500	8.778	7.1000
1.9770	182.92	197.70	57.522	57.050	9.857	7.4500
1.9780	187.15	201.70	57.491	59.600	10.606	7.8000
1.9790	191.92	205.50	57.652	56.300	11.162	7.3500
1.9800	196.95	209.30	57.829	53.000	11.379	6.9000
1.9810	201.90	209.95	57.935	52.550	11.338	6.1000
1.9820	206.59	210.60	57.795	52.100	11.150	5.3000
1.9830	210.87	211.30	57.582	52.100	10.795	5.6500
1.9840	214.60	212.00	57.306	52.100	10.299	6.0000
1.9850	217.72		56.807		9.883	
1.9860	220.49		56.142		9.831	
1.9870	223.24		55.520		9.984	
1.9880	226.02		54.966		10.050	
1.9890	228.70		54.123		9.905	
1.9900	231.04		53.149		9.491	
1.9910	232.74		52.296		8.699	
1.9920	233.39		51.343		7.408	
1.9930	232.60		50.071		5.833	
1.9940	230.23		48.435		4.150	
1.9950	226.24		46.526		2.389	
1.9960	220.62		44.372		0.570	
1.9970	213.36		41.938		–0.273	

BRITRPDIC – operational goods and dwellings: actual

TIME E+03	*CSOPG E+09*	*HCSOPG E+09*	*OPGOUT E+09*	*HOPGOT E+09*	*CSDOM E+09*	*HCSDOM E+09*
1.9740	137.00	137.90	38.360	39.400	287.50	287.50
1.9750	139.39	140.50	39.789	39.500	294.32	296.00
1.9760	141.77	143.10	39.889	39.600	301.02	304.50
1.9770	144.05	146.00	39.636	41.150	307.80	212.70
1.9780	146.22	148.90	39.303	42.700	314.69	320.90
1.9790	148.34	152.10	38.989	41.000	321.71	328.85
1.9800	150.40	155.30	38.640	39.300	328.84	336.80
1.9810	152.40	156.10	38.266	39.200	336.10	343.30
1.9820	154.34	156.90	37.781	39.100	343.49	349.80
1.9830	156.18	158.65	37.318	40.950	351.03	357.50
1.9840	157.93	160.40	36.903	42.800	358.70	365.20
1.9850	159.58		36.432		366.50	
1.9860	161.09		35.890		374.43	

Table 4.2 (cont.)

TIME E+03	*CSOPG E+09*	*HCSOPG E+09*	*OPGOUT E+09*	*HOPGOT E+09*	*CSDOM E+09*	*HCSDOM E+09*
1.9870	162.46		35.355		382.51	
1.9880	163.72		34.837		390.72	
1.9890	164.85		34.135		399.08	
1.9900	165.82		33.377		407.64	
1.9910	166.64		32.762		416.39	
1.9920	167.32		32.206		425.26	
1.9930	167.84		31.613		434.24	
1.9940	168.16		30.954		443.35	
1.9950	168.25		30.274		452.63	
1.9960	168.08		29.579		462.13	
1.9970	167.63		28.830		471.86	

BRITRPDOC – Total thermal and electrical use, CS AGR

TIME E+03	*TED E+09*	*HTED E+09*	*EED E+09*	*HEED E+09*	*TCSAG E+09*
1.9740	7.3699	6.8000	218.68	218.00	21.000
1.9750	7.5592	6.7200	226.17	216.80	22.338
1.9760	7.5011	6.6400	227.68	218.60	23.070
1.9770	7.3930	6.5600	227.97	226.40	23.590
1.9780	7.2817	6.4800	228.16	225.00	23.969
1.9790	7.1804	6.4000	228.56	219.00	24.246
1.9800	7.0751	6.3200	228.85	217.20	24.450
1.9810	6.9700	6.2400	229.25	216.80	24.599
1.9820	6.8554	6.1600	229.64	219.20	24.709
1.9830	6.7431	6.0800	230.10	220.00	24.790
1.9840	6.6368	6.0000	230.71	220.00	24.850
1.9850	6.5192		231.00		24.894
1.9860	6.3908		230.98		24.927
1.9870	6.3126		231.10		24.952
1.9880	6.2478		231.84		24.970
1.9890	6.1573		232.00		24.983
1.9900	6.0588		231.98		24.993
1.9910	5.9848		232.69		25.001
1.9920	5.9186		233.62		25.006
1.9930	5.8419		234.22		25.010
1.9940	5.7506		234.36		25.013
1.9950	5.6763		233.92		25.016
1.9960	5.5971		233.36		25.017
1.9970	5.5070		232.49		25.019

Table 4.2 (cont.)

TIME E+03	*NECXGD E+09*	*FRXP E−03*	*HFRXP E−03*	*IMPGD E+09*	*NUKINV E+09*	*MSOL E+03*
1.9740	45.200	478.21	421.25	41.589	3.200	1.0700
1.9750	45.040	461.53	432.19	42.118	6.644	1.0495
1.9760	44.404	454.98	445.63	42.733	8.587	1.0648
1.9770	43.733	450.12	465.31	43.501	9.031	1.0888
1.9780	43.224	446.56	485.00	44.366	7.975	1.1146
1.9790	42.704	441.88	504.69	45.298	6.075	1.1398
1.9800	42.051	435.90	524.38	46.259	4.175	1.1661
1.9810	41.496	431.35	530.00	47.203	2.275	1.1932
1.9820	41.327	432.40	530.00	48.102	0.375	1.2239
1.9830	41.357	435.80	530.00	48.932	–0.186	1.2539
1.9840	41.379	439.23	530.00	49.673	–0.972	1.2822
1.9850	40.892	438.57		50.316	–0.983	1.3123
1.9860	40.373	438.68		50.892	–0.219	1.3447
1.9870	40.132	441.62		51.447	–0.019	1.3767
1.9880	39.970	445.09		51.995	1.181	1.4080
1.9890	39.680	449.59		52.510	2.381	1.4468
1.9900	39.607	457.75		52.959	3.581	1.4884
1.9910	40.216	472.81		53.300	4.825	1.5239
1.9920	40.621	486.19		53.475	6.169	1.5565
1.9930	40.658	497.75		53.428	7.612	1.5906
1.9940	40.327	507.96		53.134	9.156	1.6276
1.9950	39.629	516.00		52.583	10.756	1.6650
1.9960	38.609	522.09		51.770	12.356	1.7024
1.9970	37.263	526.55		50.693	13.956	1.7420

TIME E+03	*CSOW E+09*	*OWOUT E+06*	*HOWOUT E+06*	*OWCP E+09*	*RCFOW1 E+09*
1.9740	0.000	0.00	0.00	0.0000	1.3600
1.9750	1.320	9.76	6.05	0.0043	2.4800
1.9760	2.620	19.36	12.10	0.0182	3.6000
1.9770	4.143	30.56	33.00	0.0423	3.3500
1.9780	6.078	44.70	53.90	0.0788	3.1000
1.9790	8.315	60.90	67.20	0.1305	3.1183
1.9800	10.631	77.44	80.50	0.1986	3.0786
1.9810	12.879	93.19	91.85	0.2831	3.0389
1.9820	14.990	107.63	103.20	0.3827	2.9948
1.9830	16.941	120.58	114.55	0.4961	2.9515
1.9840	18.727	132.02	125.90	0.6218	2.9108
1.9850	20.353	142.00			2.8760
1.9860	21.828	150.63			2.8358
1.9870	23.163	156.69			2.8174
1.9880	24.368	159.32			2.8046
1.9890	25.459	160.98			2.7799
1.9900	26.448	159.13			2.7510

Table 4.2 (cont.)

TIME E+03	*CSOW E+09*	*OWOUT E+06*	*HOWOUT E+06*	*OWCP E+09*	*RCFOW1 E+09*
1.9910	27.345	149.49			2.7329
1.9920	28.157	141.70			2.7179
1.9930	28.890	135.19			2.6977
1.9940	29.553	129.59			2.6704
1.9950	30.151	124.68			2.6652
1.9960	30.687	120.30			2.6569
1.9970	31.170	116.35			2.6425

TIME E+03	*ERESC E−03*	*EREA E−03*	*OWOUT E+06*	*COPR E+09*	*CAPCM E+06*	*EDWAT E+06*
1.9740	12.500	12.500	0.00	2.9172	110.50	46.620
1.9750	12.504	12.504	9.76	2.7931	105.80	47.931
1.9760	12.518	12.518	19.36	2.7292	103.38	48.382
1.9770	12.542	12.542	30.56	2.7081	102.58	48.537
1.9780	12.579	12.579	44.70	2.7109	102.68	48.590
1.9790	12.630	12.625	60.90	2.7438	103.93	48.608
1.9800	12.699	12.650	77.44	2.8148	106.62	48.615
1.9810	12.783	12.675	93.19	2.9011	109.89	48.617
1.9820	12.883	12.700	107.63	2.9766	112.75	48.618
1.9830	12.996	12.725	120.58	3.0061	113.87	48.618
1.9840	13.122	12.750	132.02	2.9483	111.68	48.618
1.9850	13.258	12.825	142.00	2.8478	107.87	48.618
1.9860	13.404	12.900	150.63	2.7554	104.37	48.618
1.9870	13.674	12.975	156.69	2.6704	101.15	48.618
1.9880	14.148	13.050	159.32	2.5923	98.19	48.618
1.9890	14.628	13.125	160.98	2.5204	95.47	48.618
1.9900	15.373	13.200	159.13	2.4544	92.97	48.618
1.9910	16.921	13.275	149.49	2.3936	90.67	48.618
1.9920	18.380	13.350	141.70	2.3377	88.55	48.618
1.9930	19.768	13.425	135.19	2.2863	86.60	48.618
1.9940	21.095	13.500	129.59	2.2390	84.81	48.618
1.9950	22.368	13.650	124.68	2.1955	83.16	48.618
1.9960	23.596	13.800	120.30	2.1556	81.65	48.618
1.9970	24.781	13.950	116.35	2.1188	80.26	48.618

data has a 1974 value which is identical with the real 1974 value. This is because only level equations are initialised with exogenous data. Derivative data, such as energy use in a particular sector, are derived from auxiliary output, generated within the model.

Table 4.3 Values of outputs in 1984 compared with actual

Output name	*ECCO output*	*Unit*	*Historical value*	*% error by 1984*
CS Services	260.2 e9	1980£	282.6 e9	−8.0
Services Output	71.55 e9	1980£	75.1 e9	−5.3
CS Investment goods	214.6 e9	1980£	212.0 e9	+1.2
Investment goods Out	57.3 e9	1980£	52.1 e9	+9.1
CS Operational goods	157.9 e9	1980£	160.4 e9	+1.6
Operational goods Out	36.9 e9	1980£	42.8 e9	−16.9
CS Dwellings	360.16 e9	1980£	365.2 e9	−1.3
CS UK agriculture	24.85 e9	1980£	25.0 e9	−0.06
Goods imported	49.6 e9	1980£	56.0 e9	−13.0
Fraction industrial output exported	0.439	–	0.530	−20.1
Electricity demand	230.7 e9	kWh	220.0	+4.6
Thermal energy demand*	6.6 e9	GJ/y	6.6 e9	*

* United Kingdom energy statistics are expressed in 'heat supplied' units, whereas ECCO considers the primary energy required to furnish the 'heat supplied'. Here the United Kingdom statistics have been modified to conform with the conventions of the model by multiplying by the GER of the 'heat supplied', which is about 1.1.

It is perfectly possible to massage the parameters within any model to obtain a better result than in Table 4.3, but such may only be obtainable with hindsight. For example FNC, the fraction of manufacturing output not consumed, can be slightly modified. The quality of the output may be judged in that the technical coefficients, in particular those of the output to capital ratio for investments and operational goods, are endogenous to the model, while the rates of capital formation in all important sectors are also endogenous. Chapter 11 discusses the evolution of these technical coefficients.

4.2.6. Model sensitivity

The first test of BRITECCO was its interaction sensitivity – the degree to which the feedback loops affected elements of the economy remote from where the changes were made. However, because in the United Kingdom population has been virtually stable for the past decade, certain features of the economy do not react much. For example, there being no change in food demand, changes in the agricultural sector impact on subsidies and improved yields per unit input but do not affect demand.

Test 1: 10 per cent reduction in domestic energy use: TEDDOM

This reduction is achieved by an increase in rate of capital formation RCFDOM in dwellings. A figure of £1000 additional investment per £40,000-worth of house has been used. The outcome for 1984 is:

TEDDOM	minus 10%
CSDOM	plus 2%
CSIVG	minus 0.8%
NETPXP	plus 5.7%
NECXGD	minus 0.9%
FIPAI	negligible
MSOL	plus 0.2%

The outcome shows that fuel exports can thereby rise by 16.0 E6 GJ/y or 3.6 million tonnes oil equivalent per year.

Test 2: An increase of one billion pounds a year in private investment abroad

The effect is to reduce by almost one billion pounds a year investment in United Kingdom industry. The following values relate to 1984, had such a policy or initiative existed. The last two columns reflect the opposite events, namely one billion pounds a year less investment abroad, with concomitant added investment in United Kingdom industry.

Additional investment abroad					*Less investment abroad*	
CSIVG	224.25	e9 £	(223.38)	up	222.51	down
NECXGD	44.53	e9	(45.23)	down	45.94	up
NUKINV	8.028	e9	(−1.97)	up	−11.97	down
MSOL	1258	£	(1248)	up	1248	down
NETPXP	2.68	e9 GJ/y	(2.63)	up	2.58	down

Test 3: Abandon further investment in nuclear energy after 1974

PETUSE	2.7984	e9	GJ/y	(2.5276)	up
NETPXP	2.3641	e9		(2.6349)	down
TEDEL	2.2761	e9	kWh/y	(2.0561)	up
RCFEL	4.7564	e9	£/y	(4.4428)	up
IVGOUT	61.62	e9		(61.28)	down
NUCMW	3.71		GW	(6.76)	down
CTMW	60.67		GW	(54.10)	up

The surprising outcome at first sight is the increase in the rate of investment in electrical power generation (RCFEL) since cost per installed MW is higher for nuclear than conventional thermal stations. However a decline in conventional construction due to over-capacity has had to be suddenly overtaken, and when the model is run to 1997, the outcome is a net reduction of RCFEL.

Sensitivity testing

A study of BRITECCO reveals that the most sensitive parameter is FNC – the fraction of industrial output not consumed, that is, invested. It is sensitive in the sense that a value in excess of 0.67 the rate of capital formation to investment goods enhances CSIVG and drives up production, but lowers immediate MSOL. A value below 0.67 incurs a falling output.

Though the model is sensitive to FNC, it is not unstable. The introduction of a random number generator for FNC with values oscillating between 0.88 and 0.07 introduced no sign of instability.

Reference Profile run to 1997

In Table 4.2, the output of key variables is shown when the model is run forward to 1997 (historical values to 1984 are also shown). The manufacturing sector continues to grow, though as 1997 approaches there are indications of a weakening rate of investment in investment goods. The material standard of living, MSOL, continues to rise, 63 per cent higher than in 1984, twenty-three years earlier.

One could run BRITECCO further forward, but this could

be misleading without specific policy options in mind. Policy options should be inserted by a user with a clear objective in mind and ready to interact with the result. While the author could explore his own predilections, he does not do so in order to be able remain neutral in later consultation with political parties, interest groups, and industry.

Re-initialisation of the model in 1984

A tougher test of the model is to compare 1997 output for models initialised at different times with actual capital stock data but using OCRs computed by the Reference Profile commencing 1974. This adjusts endogenously the OCRs and certain other coefficients.

A version, called BRIT84ST (ST=start), was initialised in 1984 with known capital-stock data but within OCRs calculated endogenously from 1974 input data then run forward to 1997, and outcome compared with the Reference Profile run to the same date. Table 4.4. compares some of outputs for the year 1997.

The match is not at all bad; the worst being CSIVG, the

Table 4.4 1997 outcome of Reference Profile comparison between 1974 and 1984 model initialisation dates

	Values in 1997 1974 *initialisation*	1984 *initialisation*		*Difference* %
OWOUT	116.35	112.9	e9 tonnes	3
NETPXP	5.27·	5.53	e9 GJ	5
TED	5.51	5.15	e9 GJ	6
EED	232.50	215.9	e9 kWh	7
CTMW	46.93	39.7*	GW	16
RCFEL	1.1	0.95	e9 £	14
SEROUT	103.23	104.6	e9	1
MSOL	1742	1846	£	6
NECXGD	37.26	34.0	e9 £	8
CSIVG	213.3	252.9	e9 £	19
IVGOUT	41.9	43.4	e9 £	3
CSOPG	167.6	165	e9 £	2
OPGOUT	28.3	29.5	e9 £	4

* CTMW was initialised at the actual 1984 value, which is actually much higher than required CTMW, due to faulty forecasting by the CEGB, resulting in over-construction in the 1970s.

most important factor in an industrialised export-dominated economy. It is interesting to note that CSIVG peaks in 1993 in the case of initiation in 1984, and in 1992 in the case of initiation in 1974. However MSOL does not go through a peak – at least up to 1997.

Statistical testing: inequality coefficient

A statistical test of predictive accuracy put forward by J. C. K Ash and D. J. Smyth in their book *Forecasting the United Kingdom Economy* is Theil's inequality coefficient (Henri Theil in *Who Forecasts Best?*, International Economic Papers, No. 5 (1955) and in *Techniques of Economic Forecasting*, OECD, Paris, 1965). A perfect forecast gives a coefficient of zero, while deteriorating forecasts are higher, with no upper bound.

The biggest error in the ten-year profile of BRITECCO is the Capital Stock in Investment Goods (CSIVG). Theil's inequality coefficient was calculated for CSIGV and found, for the ten year period 1974 to 1984, to be 0.045. Ash and Smyth's analysis of the United Kingdom Treasury and the National Institute for Economic and Social Research gave a best value of 0.29 (GDP, Treasury), while the NIESR was only marginally superior in its forecasts.

Material Standard of Living

This index is specific to ECCO, and is the sum of the manufactured goods available to the consumer, whether indigenously manufactured or imported, plus services. MSOL, as it is commonly abbreviated, was found to be useful for modifying many output and consumption relationships. For example, the output to capital ratio for manufactured goods would be expected to change through time with technical progress. The assumption is made that technical progress is reflected in rising MSOL, and the output to capital ratio modified appropriately. In Figure 4.5 one may see the difference this makes. The figure shows the actual value of a particular output of the economy, and BRITECCO forecast, based on 1974 initiation data, and the result without the use of the MSOL factor (No MSOL). In every case the MSOL factor improves the forecast.

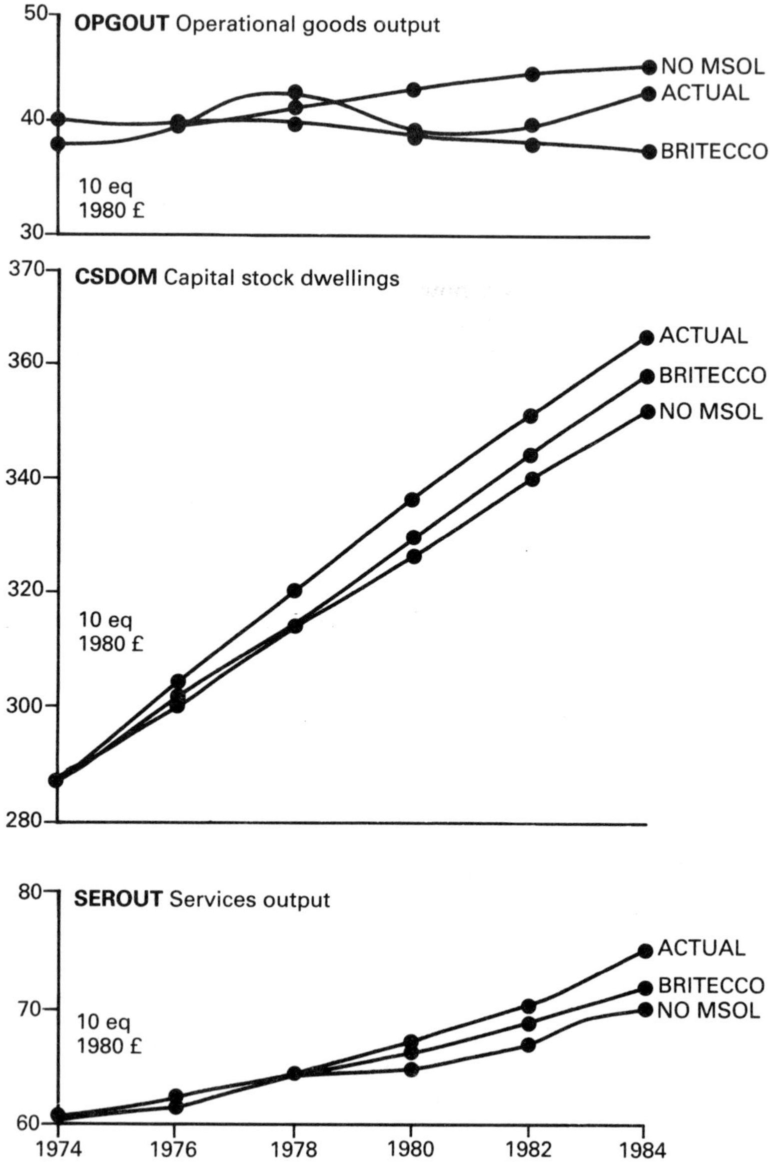

Figure 4.5 Comparison between BRITECCO and actual data, 1974–84. Operational goods output, capital stock dwellings and services output.

Potential for testing policy options

The validation of BRITECCO creates the temptation to explore some policy options. This is not done here for two reasons. Firstly, this is not a policy study. Secondly, policy objectives are essentially political. In Chapter 8, two of the tests are in effect policy options and reflect stated policies of at least one political party in the United Kingdom. But there is a third reason. BRITECCO is not complete. There are more data that can and should be inserted once research has established them. When that is done it is surely a powerful tool for policy analysis. The author therefore contents himself with offering the following partial list of some of the policy options that a fully developed model will be able to handle.

1 Agriculture – changes in land use policy
  – change in subsidies
  – de-intensification of arable farming with less fertiliser application to solve over-supply
  – reduction in agricultural areas
  – improved methods – affecting OCR
  – meat/cereal demand and consumer preference
2 Industry – investment policy
  – import policy
  – export incentives
  – consumption policy (e.g. 'buy British')
  – industrial efficiency – output to capital ratio
  – energy use in industry
  – subsidies
3 Domestic – construction rates
  – energy use
4 Services – profitability and output (OCR)
  – energy use
5 Energy supply – energy planning
  – rates of capital investment required
  – depletion policy
  – alternative energies – evaluation
  – coal/oil/nuclear options
6 Import/Export – targets
7 Pollution – outputs in relation to energy types used
  – CO_2, SO_2, particulate
8 Water – demand

– rates of investment
9 Forests – areas
– yields
– impact on imports
10 Employment – sectoral job opportunities
– employment/unemployment profiles

NOTES

1 This is an analysis made by M. Slesser in a report presented to UNESCO in 1984, unpublished.
2 Embodied energy is the sum of all primary energies taken from the earth and dissipated in the process of delivering a given good or service to the market place. Typically it is quoted in MJ/kg, GJ/tonne, GJ/$, etc.
3 Though solar energy is renewable, when that energy source is harnessed it is nevertheless dissipated as it is used.
4 The IFIAS conventions (see references) account for energy used in primary terms, and call this the Gross Energy Requirement (GER) of a good or service delivered to the market. When this good is itself fuel or energy, then the GER is the primary energy that is extracted in order to deliver a unit of fuel to the economy.

REFERENCES

Ascher, W. *Forecasting*. Johns Hopkins, Baltimore, 1978.
Baguant, J. *Mauritius 2000 – exploring the potential for enhanced national welfare through the use of ECCO*. Unesco, Paris, 1987.
Chapman, P., G. Leach and M. Slesser. 'The energy cost of fuels', *Energy Policy*, Vol. 3 (September), 1974, pp. 231–9.
Chapman, P., and F. Roberts. *Metal Resources and Energy*, London, Butterworth, 1983.
Colorado Energy Research Institute Report. *Net energy analysis*. PO Box 366, Golden, Colorado 80401, USA, 1976.
Cook, E. 'Limits to the exploitation of non-renewable resources', *Science*, Vol. 191, 1977, pp. 677–83.
FAO. *Agriculture towards 2000*. Food and Agriculture Organisation, Rome, 1982.
FAO and Unesco. *Carrying Capacity Assessment: with a pilot study of Kenya*. Report W/R8012, FAO, Rome, and Unesco, Paris, 1985.
Fleming, J. Thesis: 'The Energy requirement of the manufacture of ammonia'. University of Strathclyde, Glasgow, 1974.
Gilliland, M. *Energy Analysis: a new public policy tool*. AAAS Symposium series, Washington, DC, 1978.
IFIAS. Report 6 *Energy analysis conventions*. International Federation of Institutes of Advanced Study, Ulriksdal Slott, Solna, Sweden, 1974.

Kellog, H. Quoted in P. A. Bailey, *Mining Engineering*, January 1976.
King, J. *Beyond Economic Choice*. Centre for Human Ecology, University of Edinburgh and Unesco, Paris, 1987.
King, J. and M. Slesser. 'Resource accounting for development planning', *World Development*, April 1988.
Marchetti, C. *On a fifty year pulsation in human affairs: Analysis of some physical indicators*, International Institute for Applied Systems Analysis, Laxenburg, Austria, 1985, pp. 83–5.
Patten, C. UK Minister for Overseas Development. Reported in The *Guardian*, London, 1987.
Patterson, M. G. 'Estimation of the quality of energy sources and uses', *Energy Policy*, 1983, pp. 246–551.
Peckham, R., and K. Klitz. *Energy requirement of North Sea oil*. Ispra, Italy, Joint Research Centre, Euratom, 1978.
Philips, D. P., and W. G. Edwards. 'Metal prices as function of ore grade', *Resource Policy*, Vol. 1, 1976.
Redclift, M. *Sustainable Development*. Methuen, London, 1987.
Roberts, P. 'Energy and value', *Energy Policy*, 1982, pp. 171–80.
Schrattenholzer, L., and A. S. Manne. 'International Energy Workshop poll response', *The Energy Journal*, Vol. 5, 1984, pp. 45–64.
Sintunawa, C. *Carrying Capacity Assessment for Thailand*. Report to Unesco Population Division, 1986.
Slesser, M. In: *Energy in the Economy*, Macmillan, London, 1978, p. 52.
Slesser, M. *Energy analysis: its utility and limits*. RM-78-46, Laxenburg, Austria, International Institute for Applied Systems Analysis, September 1978, p. 52.
Slesser, M. 'Energy inflation and its effect on the viability of solar energy systems.' Paper presented at International Solar Energy Society Symposium, Birmingham, 1980.
Slesser, M. 'Can solar energy replace fossil-fissile energy sources?', *Solar Energy*, Vol. 25, 1980, pp. 425–8.
Slesser, M. *Resource accounting in development planning: a validation study of the United Kingdom*, Part 1 (financial model). Resource Use Institute, 1985. Copies of the report may be obtained from the author (price £10.50).
Slesser, M. 'Net energy as an energy planning tool', *Energy Policy*, June 1987, pp. 228–36.
Slesser, M., and J. Hounam. 'Perspectives for long-term energy policy', *Futures*, February 1979.
Theil, H. *Techniques of Economic Forecasting*. OECD, Paris, 1965.
Unesco. *Resource Accounting – an application to the assessment of carrying capacity*, December 1984.
United Nations. 'Recommendation number 1', UN Conference on Population, Mexico, 1983.
Weinberg, A., and H. Goeller. 'The age of substitutability ', *Science*, Vol. 191, February 1976, pp. 683–8.

Part II

ECCO PILOT STUDIES

5

THE INTEGRATED APPROACH TO LONG TERM RESOURCE PLANNING AND NATIONAL CARRYING CAPACITY ASSESSMENT FOR THAILAND

C. Sintunawa

5.1. INTRODUCTION

For some years the rate of growth of Thailand's economy has been below expectations. Continued population growth has increased pressure on domestic food supply, and the country's balance of payments has been exacerbated by the need to import energy, capital goods and agricultural inputs. The situation has become more serious despite control measures introduced in late 1970s; rural fuel-wood and construction projects have not been able to keep pace with growing demand.

Much useful research has been conducted on individual components of the country's natural resource base, such as forests, soil, water, or minerals. However, there is still very little understanding of how these components interact over the long term; how, for example, agriculture requires and affects water resources, and how tourist activities affect environmental quality. Above all there is no real understanding of the trade-offs, if any, between high productivity and long-term sustainability in resource use. The individual planning programmes to develop and use natural resources are thus forced to deal with each investment project on an ad hoc basis. They tend to concentrate on short-term output at the expense of long-term stability. They also ignore the ways in which the development of one resource may alter the productivity of others.

In 1984, Thailand had a population of 50 million with a net growth rate of 2.0 per cent; at this rate the population doubles in thirty-six years. If the present growth rates of population and food production are maintained, there will be no rice to export in the year 1996. The deficit between the value of food export products and goods-energy import products will worsen.

To resolve this approaching dilemma decisions have to be made to reduce the growth in the rate of consumption of food and imported goods through population control programmes, or programmes to increase food and industrial production not only to serve the rapid increase in domestic consumption but also to earn enough foreign exchange to pay for capital and energy imports. In order to obtain growth of the economic system, Thailand needs to apply both of the above-mentioned measures simultaneously, as neither can be carried out separately.

The repercussions of the energy crisis, increasing consumption of both energy and food, and a higher trade deficit all force Thailand to explore means and alternatives for population–resource management on a sustainable basis. Thus there is a need to study solutions for long-term carrying capacity in Thailand.

Carrying capacity may be defined as the number of people sharing a given territory which can, for the foreseeable future and in accordance with the socio-cultural values of that territory, sustain a given standard of living utilising energy and other physical resources as well as technology, enterprise and skills.

The primary objective of this study is to construct a system dynamics model which can represent the total complexity of interactions between socio-economic, agricultural, industrial, energy, service and forest factors of Thailand in order to gain insights into the population–resource system. The understanding gained will then be used to verify and explore the following aspects:

- the size of the sustainable population for Thailand given present and future national social and economic development plans;
- policy alternatives to reduce stress arising from the population–resource pressure that always accompanies conversion from growth to long-term and sustainable equilibrium.

5.2. THE METHOD

The methods used in this study are energy systems analysis and systems dynamics. This approach offers a framework within which population, resources, environment and development may be quantitatively interrelated and goals related to means over the long term. The method involves a system of resource accounting in which resource needs are matched with resource availability. Use is made of recent developments in energy analysis whereby goods and services may be expressed in terms of the energy required to produce them. As energy is, after a certain point, essential for the intensification of virtually all economic activity, it can serve as a common numeraire for quantifying inputs and outputs. It also provides a robust method of accounting which overcomes the problem of attributing energy values to economic activities in the long-term future.

It is clear that numerous social, economic, biological and physical factors are involved in the processes that govern man's impact on his natural surroundings. While one can perceive the individual elements of this complex system, the analysis of the total complex of their interactions over time is beyond the capabilities of man's unaided mind. Formal systems analysis tools are required to trace the long-term implications of all the factors and to evaluate alternative policies.

5.2.1. Energy systems analysis

Although food production depends on the renewable resources of solar energy, nutrients and water, it has shown an increasing reliance on the exploitation of non-renewable resources, especially energy resources. The energy crisis is expected to have a significant impact on food production technology. As a result, developing countries will not be able to solve their food problems without solving their energy problems; without a satisfactory solution to both, economic growth will be severely constrained. The centrality of the food and energy nexus calls for a comprehensive policy approach. Only through a clear understanding of this food–energy pivot can the situation be reversed. A systems analysis of all interrelated factors in the agricultural ecosystem is required to plan for successful food production strategies. One of these factors is energy, especially fossil fuel energy, which can be measured and its flow through biological and physical systems analysed (see Chapters 3 and 4).

5.2.2. Data collection

Food crop farmers in forty-eight provinces were interviewed and data from a total of 642 cases were collected from every region of the country. The cultivation of Thailand's major food crops such as rice, maize, cassava, sugar cane and soybean were studied in detail to determine correlations between energy input and yield of protein per hectare. The data were then converted to energy values on the basis of energy input in megajoules per hectare, using conversion factors as described by Sintunawa (1983). Energy analysis of food crops was made and the selected case of maize production is shown in Tables 5.1 and 5.2.

Table 5.1 Energy inputs in each activity of maize cultivation

Case	*Soil preparation* Time Hr/ha	*Soil preparation* Energy MJ/ha	*Seeds* MJ/ha	*Fert[ser]* MJ/ha	*Transp[t]* MJ/ha	*Thresh* MJ/ha	*Total* MJ/ha	*Protein* kg/ha
1	1.9	912.5	33.8	–	45.0	586.9	1575.6	181.9
2	2.5	1212.5	42.5	–	7.5	463.8	1727.5	181.9
3	3.1	1656.3	30.6	–	25.6	419.4	2131.3	165.5
4	1.9	1050.0	50.6	–	149.4	1015.0	2262.5	194.0
5	4.4	2400.0	33.8	–	–	493.1	2927.5	212.2
6	3.1	1862.5	39.4	–	673.1	1026.3	3600.0	234.6
7	6.9	3637.5	37.5	–	79.4	680.6	4437.5	258.3
8	3.1	1887.5	35.0	2931.3	46.9	608.8	5510.0	264.9
av.	3.1	1781.3	38.1	291.9	85.0	516.3	2712.5	210.4

Protein yields in Table 5.1 are changed in the same direction with energy inputs and in these selected cases, the use of fertiliser is only found in one case. Energy input in soil preparation is considered to be the major part of the total energy input in maize cultivation but in rice, cassava and sugar cane production, energy input in the application of fertilisers has an important impact on the overall energy input for crop cultivation. The direct energy use in Table 5.2 refers to level of fossil fuels required in the cultivation process of maize. This has significant impacts on the possibility of carrying out crop production.

Table 5.2 Direct and indirect energy uses in selected cases of maize cultivation

Energy Input (MJ/ha)	*Cases* 1	2	3	4	5	6	7	8
Direct energy	953.1	1033.1	1281.3	1465	1850.6	2314.4	2345	1645.6
Indirect energy	588.8	651.9	818.8	46.3	1043.1	1245.6	1965	895.6
Materials	33.8	42.5	30.6	50.6	33.8	33.4	37.5	2968.8
Total	575.7	1727.5	2131.3	2262.5	2927.5	3600	4437.5	5510
Protein Yield (kg/ha)	181.9	181.9	165.5	194.0	212.2	234.6	258.3	264.9

The analysis of mathematical relationships between the protein yield of crops and total energy inputs suggests the following equation (correlation coefficient of 0.48). The best-fit equation for 642 interviewed cases is:

$$Y = 4.62 * E^{0.42} \quad (1)$$

where Y = protein yield in kilograms per hectare, and
E = the energy inputs to food crop cultivations expressed as the sum of all the inputs in MJ/ha.yr.

In addition to the field data collection and analysis described above, data from a variety of other sources were also collected. Data in 1984 were used as input data to this study.

5.3. THE THAI ECONOMY

Thailand is traditionally an agrarian nation. Today it boasts a complex multi-faceted economy embracing industries which employ the most sophisticated technology. Several important factors have contributed to the country's enviable growth. Its principal comparative advantage has been the abundance and diversity of its natural resources. Thailand not only enjoys agricultural self-sufficiency but is also the only net food exporter in Asia and one of the largest food exporters in the world.

Growth and diversification into new industrial areas have, to a large extent, been initiated by a dynamic private sector. Innovative private enterprise broadened the nation's agrarian base by exploiting the value-added potential of basic staple crops, and at the same time expanded into new product areas in response to world demand. With the Government providing infrastructure and exercising relatively limited control over private industry, a free enterprise system has emerged which has allowed development to take place at a rapid rate consistent with the needs and resources available.

With its agrarian base, the economy has experienced steady, stable growth. The introduction of improved technology and marketing expertise has made Thailand one of the world leaders in the sale of staple commodities. It has also transformed the country into a fast-rising manufacturer of sophisticated products built to international standards, which find ready acceptance in world markets.

Thailand's primary money earners in the late 1970s were the crops grown on its land. Today agricultural products account for the bulk of its foreign exchange earnings and are produced in such quantities that in many commodities the country ranks as the world's number one supplier. Moreover, Thailand's industrial sector produces a wide number of goods ranging from textiles to integrated circuits, low price furniture and fibre-glass yachts. Its rich reserves of minerals are eagerly sought by the world's industries. In recent years, local factories have been established to manufacture industrial goods and thereby enhance their value.

5.3.1. Trade and GNP

Between 1973 and 1980, the Thai economy was hit hard by successive phases of the energy crisis. The seriousness of these impacts is indicated by the price of imported crude oil: US$ 2.5 per barrel in early 1973, US$ 21.5 per barrel in 1979. The rising price of crude oil led to massive increases in the oil import bill, from 11.0 per cent of the total value of imports in 1973 to 22.3 per cent in 1979. This resulted in an increase in the trade gap from 4.98 per cent of GDP in 1973 to 8.5 per cent in 1979. The rising oil prices also generated cost push inflation, since the cost of producing manufactured goods and transportation services was seriously affected, and led to the high average annual inflation rate of 9.9 per cent from 1973 to 1979.

During the early 1980s, the discovery of natural gas in the Gulf of Thailand and the subsequent discovery of oil led to a massive development programme in the eastern seaboard area. This ambitious programme is designed to spearhead the national drive towards new industrialisation.

5.3.2. Foreign trade and balance of payments

In Thailand's open economy, foreign trade accounts for a major portion of the national product. Its importance has grown substantially over the past twenty years as its share in the national income increased from 34 per cent in 1961 to 41.4 per cent in 1982. As the economy becomes more open, it is increasingly susceptible to changes in world economic conditions.

5.3.3. Exports

During the period from 1978 to 1982 total value of exports increased more than twofold or at an annual average of 18 per cent. More than half of this increase can be attributed to improvements in world prices for Thai export commodities, whereas the remainder was due to export diversification and increases in the quantity exported. Total value increased from about 22 per cent of the gross national product in 1978 to approximately 23 per cent in 1982.

There have been improvements in the structure of Thai exports, most notably the diversification of export commodities. The share in total exports held by the country's six major products (rice, tin, rubber, maize, sugar, kenaf and tapioca) declined from about 54 per cent in 1978 to 50 per cent in 1982. Meanwhile exports of garments, gems, prawns and various types of beans were 7,445 million baht in 1978 and 18,031 million baht in 1982, or an increase of 142.2 per cent. An impressive rate of export growth has also occurred for electronic equipment, frozen squid, canned pineapple, fish meal and canned marine products.

5.3.4. Imports

Thailand's import bill increased from 108,899 million baht in 1978 to 196,616 million baht in 1982. Most of the increase was experienced after 1973 when petroleum prices started to rise substantially. Between 1961 and 1973, the portion of the total gross national product spent on imports stood at between 18 and 21 per cent. Between 1973 and 1982, this ratio increased to 28 per cent as a direct result of substantial rises in the import price of petroleum.

Import structure between 1967 and 1982 indicates that the proportion of consumer goods in imports has continually declined from 23.7 per cent of total import value in 1967 to only 11.6 per cent in 1982 as a result of the Government's industrial development policy oriented toward import substitution. At the same time imports of raw materials and capital goods increased substantially to about 50 per cent of total imports by the end of 1982. The bill for imported fuels and lubricants also rose dramatically from 7.1 per cent of total imports in 1967 to 31 per cent in 1982.

5.3.5. Terms of trade

Until 1974, Thailand enjoyed favourable terms of trade. During the period 1973–4 and in spite of the rapid increase in oil prices, the world-wide shortage of food and raw materials boosted the price of many Thai commodity exports. With the continuing increase in fuel prices, world-wide inflation, and the decline in primary product prices on the world market since 1975, the terms of trade have become less favourable.

5.3.6. Balance of payments

Thailand's trade deficit has been increasing gradually over the past two and a half decades. During the First Development Plan (1961–6), the trade deficit averaged about 2,367 million baht per annum. The average deficit per year during the Second Plan (1967–71) increased to about 10,288 million baht or about four times the size of the deficit during the First Plan. During the Fourth Plan period, the average annual trade deficit climbed further to 42,648 million baht. Trade deficits of 66,025 million baht and 36,888 million baht were subsequently registered during 1981 and 1982 respectively.

A substantial increase in the trade deficit was thus recorded during the period 1978 to 1982. The main reasons for this deterioration were a sharp increase in the value of imports caused by external inflation, and the increasing value of the US dollar with which the baht was linked (in 1983, 22.90 baht buying and 23.05 baht selling = US$1); and the huge demand for imports of raw and semi-processed materials created by the expanding industrial sector. At the same time, the world price of many Thai export commodities continued to decline, resulting in a lower growth rate in export earnings. While the trade deficit increased, income from services and foreign capital inflows were not sufficient to offset the tremendous gap. Consequently, the balance of payments registered a record deficit of 13,298 million baht in 1978. In response, the Government significantly increased its foreign borrowing from traditional sources, as well as from new sources such as the Eurodollar market and the IMF.

5.4. CARRYING CAPACITY ASSESSMENT FOR THAILAND

Economic activities that are the driving force of GNP were categorised into ten sectors. In this study the criteria used to disaggregate GNP were the degrees to which agricultural and industrial activities deplete environmental quality and generate impacts on trade balance, resulting in changes in standard of living.

5.4.1. Population

The model of the carrying capacity assessment for Thailand contains numerous feedback loops representing demographic and technical-economic means of achieving a favourable balance between population size and supply of resources. These loops are intricately intermeshed, and operate with different speeds and efficiency. Since both the supply of and demand for each resource are always varying and since societal responses of either type are usually delayed, a perfect population–economic-resource balance is rarely attained. The system is usually in motion, compensating for a deficiency in one resource, depleting an oversupply of another, building up a greater demand for a third. The function of the population sector in this study is twofold:

1 it calculates the total population size, which is one determinant of resource demand; it also calculates the size of sustainable population which derives from the country's managerial strategies of population–economic-resource complex system; and,
2 it represents the demographic response of the population, through the birth rate and the death rate, to the changing standard of living and environmental quality.

5.4.2. Forest

The forest sector serves three important functions:

1 it interrelates forest resource, uses, demand and planting;
2 it calculates changes in forest resources, which is one determinant of resource supply in a tropical country; and
3 it also calculates impacts on environmental quality, agriculture and tourist service output of Thailand's system.

5.4.3. Agriculture

The fundamental assumption of the agricultural sector of the carrying capacity assessment for Thailand model (CCAT model), is that the total amount of food that can be produced each year is limited. It is clear that the allocation of more physical resources (land, water, fertiliser, chemicals, farm machinery, and seeds) to food production will increase the annual food output. However, it is postulated that the physical resources that can be allocated to food production are limited: the available agricultural land is limited, the amount of fertiliser and other agricultural inputs are limited by the resources available for investment in agriculture. Although technological innovations may lead to higher yields on a given land area, it is also postulated that there are decreasing returns to technology's ability to increase land yields by diverting limited resource inputs to the agriculture sector.

The implication of the basic assumption is that the investments in raising arable land area and annual output per hectare must exhibit decreasing marginal returns, until at some point additional investments yield no return. This assumption of decreasing marginal returns is consistent with real-world trends, although there is probably no current real-world example of zero marginal returns to agricultural investment.

5.4.4. Debt

The debt sector contains interrelations between total debt, the rate of borrowing, the rate of repayment and the interest accumulations, representing dynamic changes of causal links of these elements according to real conditions in Thailand. The debt submodel of this study calculates the country's debt situation each year, the rate of repayment and borrowing, the total capital available for investment and the total picture of relations between the sustainable population and debt per capita.

5.4.5. Service

Service output, the intangible component of GNP, is composed of activities that promote the population's health, education, culture, and so on. The utilisation of service capital to produce service outputs improves the population's standard of living.

5.4.6. Industry

Industrial output is composed of the total national stream of manufactured goods. The utilisation of industrial capital to produce industrial output both increases the rate of environmental quality deterioration and the total capital resource available for investment, resulting in growth of material standard of living.

5.4.7. Environment

The long-term behaviour of environmental quality changes is modelled in this environmental quality sector. Persistent material pollutants include industrial and agricultural chemicals, wastes from the service sector, etc. An aggregated model of environment cannot be used to make precise forecasts of the levels and impacts of specific materials, nor is it useful in describing the current 'quality' of the environment. Instead, the purpose of the environmental sector is to represent in general terms the dynamic characteristics of the physical processes governing their generation, and the impact on both agriculture and tourism. The primary objective was to provide a conceptual dynamic structure that could capture the qualitative behaviour of the environment in the Thai system.

5.5. MODEL SPECIFICS

5.5.1. Loops 1-2-3: population and trade balance

Loops 1, 2 and 3 are shown in Figure 5.1. They represent the fact that an increase in population results in an increase in total death rate as well as in agricultural product consumption. This consumption creates an increase in annual consumer demand and a decrease in exports of agricultural products, leading to a decrease in export value and negative trade balance. An improved trade balance supports better food distribution and consumption throughout the country leading to an increase in the total resource available for investment. The availability of resource for investment drives increases in outputs of both service and industrial sectors. This results in an improvement of the standard of living, leading to a decrease in total birthrate.

Traditionally, Thais preferred to have large families. More children meant more hands to till the fields and harvest the crops. Also, in the days when the kingdom's strength depended on the number of men it could field in battle, it was imperative that its adult subjects have as many children as possible. When a family became too large for the land to support, the landless sons cleared forest areas for cultivation. With plenty for all, the population could grow unchecked except by natural causes; extra people could easily be accommodated.

In the period between 1937 and 1947, the population growth rate stood at 1.9 per cent. Improvements in public health and rising income opportunities in the 1950s and 1960s raised that figure to over 3 per cent per year. In the thirty years after the Second World War, the population jumped from an estimated 17.5 million to nearly 45 million people in 1979, making Thailand one of the world's twenty most populous nations.

Had there been unlimited tracts of land, the population could

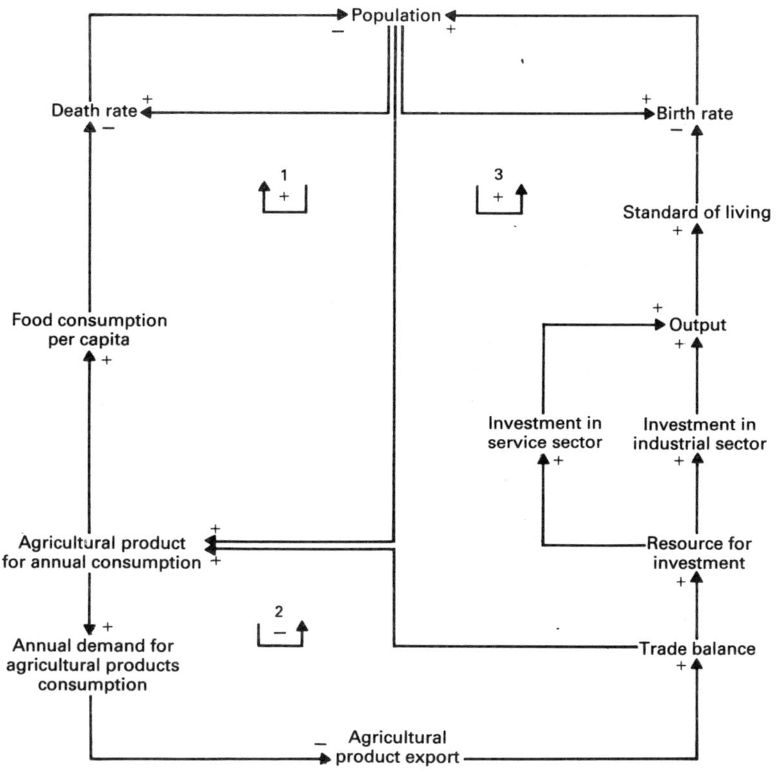

Figure 5.1 The population and trade balance loop.

have been absorbed. However, the available land was rapidly being used to accommodate the growing numbers. Virgin forests could no longer be felled without destroying valuable watersheds. Cities could absorb the overflow of landless sons but soon they too began to feel the pressures of over population. March 1970 saw the announcement of the National Population Policy which led to the incorporation of family planning programmes into the Third Five-Year Social and Economic Plan. Parents, hard-pressed to support their families, began to go to the district health centres for advice on contraceptives. By 1974, it was estimated that 25 per cent of all fertile married couples were using modern contraceptives, one of the highest percentages for developing countries. The result was that population growth was reduced to 2.7 per cent in 1976 and to 2.1 per cent by the end of the Fourth Plan in 1981. The success of the programme can be attributed to a number of factors. One was the existence of a well-developed network of state health centres, particularly in the central and lower northern regions where the programme had the highest response.

The Fifth Plan aimed to reduce further the population growth rate to 1.5 per cent by 1986. However it is necessary also to improve the quality of life of the population. Health and vocational training are two important measures in the Plan to achieve this. Thus the end result will be a stable and productive population that will allow the Government to make headway in its effort to bring improved standards of living to all. In this simulation model a fraction rate of birth normal (FROBN) in 1984 of 0.0286 and a fraction rate of death normal (FRODN) of 0.0077 in the same year were used. Changes in standard of living (SOLC) affect the birth rate fraction (BRF) while changes in the environmental quality (EQ) and food consumption per capita (FCPCYC) influence death rate portion (DRR).

5.5.2. Loop 4: forest regeneration loop

Loop 4 is shown in Figure 5.2 and is a positive feedback loop. A low-density forest or a young forest gives a high regenerative rate resulting in an increase in forest resource (FORRES). As forest density increases, this regenerative rate declines. Forest regeneration rate (FORREG) is derived from the relative change of forest (FORCH) multiplied by forest resource (FORRES).

5.5.3. Loop 5: change in arable land

Loop 5 (see Figure 5.2) represents the relationship between forest plantation and agricultural land. As forest plantation (FORPLN) rises, the total land available for agriculture (TLAFA) decreases. An increase in TLAFA creates a rise in agricultural production (AGPROD) and export (APEXP). The rise in the latter element creates an improvement of the trade balance (TBL), leading to an increase in the total capital resource available for investment (TCRAIN). When more resources

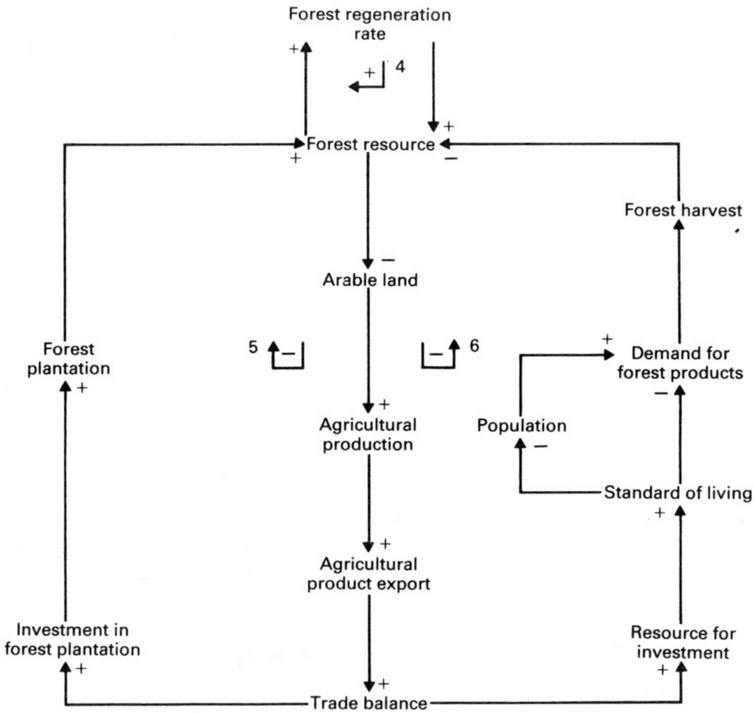

Figure 5.2 The forest-agriculture and standard of living loops.

are available, the investment in forest plantation (FORPLN) increases. Forest resource will become available for harvesting after a lengthy delay of twenty-five years from the date of planting.

5.5.4. Loop 6(a): decreasing demand for forest products

Loop 6(a) interrelates forest resources (FORRES), agricultural production (AGPROD), trade balance (TBL), population (P), demand for forest products consumption (DFFCW) and forest harvest (FORHAV). The change in TCRAIN drives the change in service output (SSOUT) and industrial output per capita (INOPCY) in the same direction, resulting in an improvement in standard of living (SOL). This leads to decreases in birth rate (BRF) and population (P). When population rises, the demand for consumption of forest products (DFFCW) increases leading to growth of forest harvest (FORHAV). This results in a decrease in forest resources.

The increase in standard of living causes a decrease in consumption of forest products due to technological improvements. Advanced technologies increase production efficiency and reduce waste from the production process. Thus wood use per capita (WUPPY) declines, resulting in a decrease in the demand for forest products.

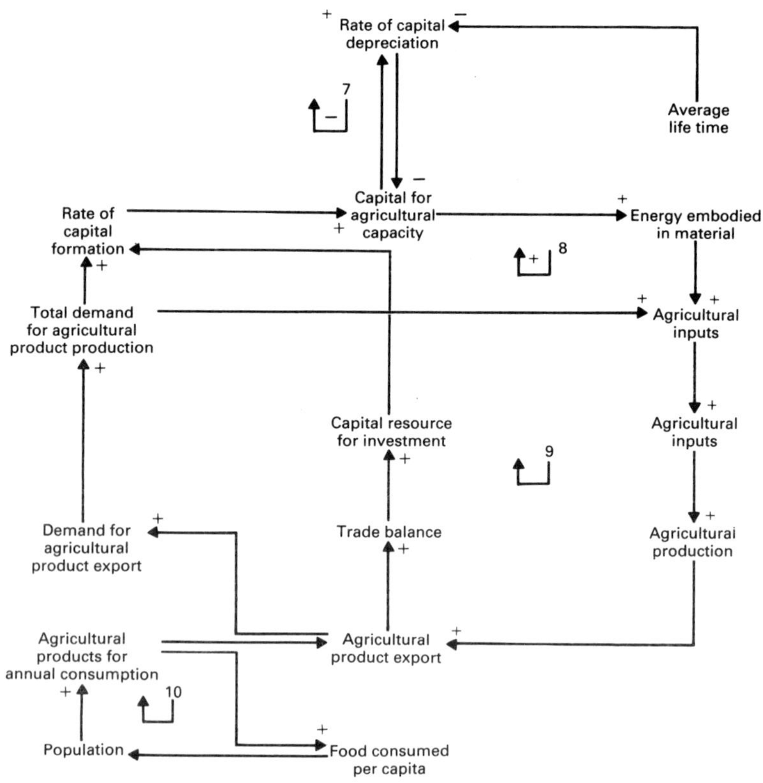

Figure 5.3 Causal relations of agricultural activities.

5.5.5. Loop 7: capital for agricultural capacity

Loop 7 (Figure 5.3) interrelates the level of capital for agricultural capacity (CAPFAC) and the rate of capital depreciation (ROCD). It is a negative feedback loop. The rate of capital depreciation becomes high as the level of capital for agricultural capacity increases and results in a decrease in capital for agricultural capacity. An average lifetime of twenty-four years for capital in agriculture is adopted.

5.5.6. Loop 8: food from investment in agriculture

Loop 8 (see Figure 5.3) is a positive feedback loop. The output of food can be raised in this model by increasing the intensity at which arable land is used. The land yield may indicate the process of increasing land yield, for example through the use of modern agricultural inputs such as improved seeds, fertiliser, pesticides, and farm machinery. As pressures for more food for export and consumption become greater, and more resources are invested in agriculture, investment in agricultural inputs will also increase.

An increase in agricultural inputs drives an increase in energy embodied in materials (EEBM) and results in an increase in agricultural intensification (EPPPH) which leads to an increase in agricultural production (AGPROD). The quantity of agricultural export (APEXP) depends on the total agricultural production (AGPROD) and both change in the same direction. A delayed agricultural products export serves as the demand for agricultural products export (APEXPD) and its increases drive an increase in total demand for agricultural product production (TDAPP). This high demand causes an increase in the rate of capital formation (ROCF) which leads to a higher level of capital for agricultural capacity (CAPFAC).

5.5.7. Loop 9: agricultural production and export

Loop 9 (see Figure 5.3) interrelates factors involved in agricultural products production and export. It has most factors in common with the previously described loop except in the passage through the energy embodied in materials (EEBM).

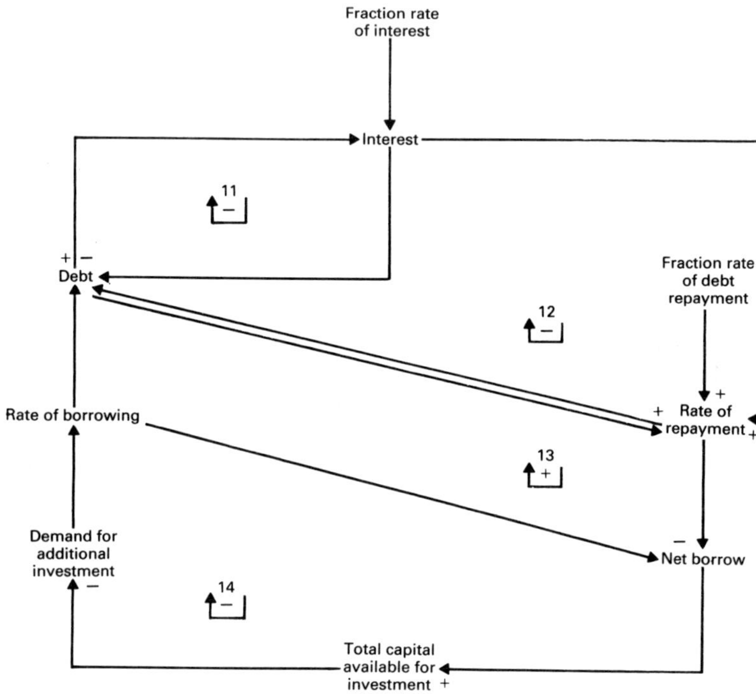

Figure 5.4 Causal relations of debt sector.

5.5.8. Loops 11–14: debt

Loops 11–14 of this sector are shown in Figure 5.4. Loop 11 interrelates an accumulation of debt and interest. As debt grows, annual interest (INT) increases at a fractional rate of 0.03 making debt accumulate even more. The increase of debt in this relation represents an exponential growth. The type identification of this loop is positive feedback. Loop 12 represents a negative feedback relationship between accumulation and rate of repayment. This loop regulates debt to a minimum level – the higher the rate of repayment, the smaller the debt. Loop 13 is a positive feedback loop representing causal relations between debt (DEBT), rate of repayment (RRP), rate of borrowing

(ROBR), total capital available (TCRAIN), and demand for additional investment (DADIN). Net borrowing will decrease as the rate of repayment rises. An increase in net borrowing per annum will result in an increase in the total capital available for investment. As this capital becomes available, the necessity to borrow money from abroad decreases. This results in a decrease in the rate of borrowing and debt. Loop 14 interrelates causal relationships between total capital available for investment (TCRAIN), demand for additional investment (DADIN), rate of borrowing (ROBR) and net borrowing (NETBR). It tends to regulate the level of borrowing from abroad. This loop is another negative feedback loop in the debt sector.

5.5.9. Loops 15–16: tourism

Loops 15–16 are shown in Figure 5.5 representing structural relations of the tourist sector. Loop 15 interrelates capital in the tourist service sector (TSCAP) and the rate of tourist service capital resource allocation to the tourist service sector (NCAPTS).

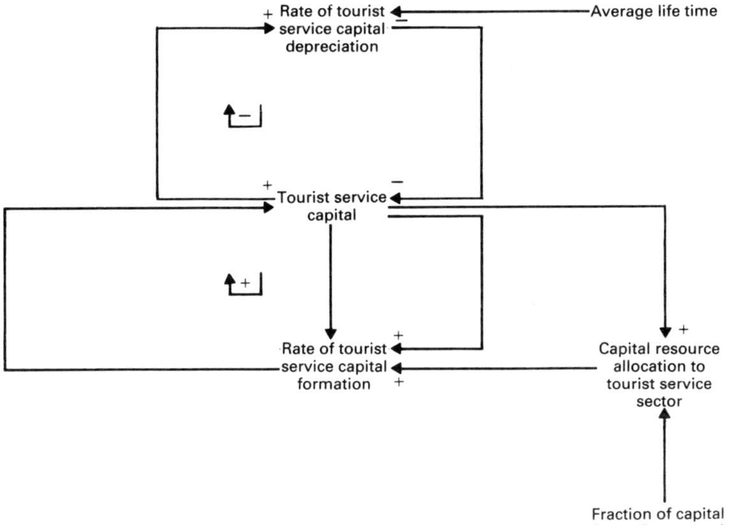

Figure 5.5 Causal relations of tourist service sector.

This loop is a positive feedback loop. The financial resources in this sector mostly belong to private owners and will continuously be maintained at least at the minimum rate to cover the annual rate of depreciation in order to offer services as usual. In addition, new investment will be made annually to support further the role of foreign exchange earnings. This new investment is proportional to the tourist service capital. Loop 16 represents the relationship between tourist service capital (TSCAP) and rate of tourist service capital depreciation (RTSCD).

This loop is a negative feedback loop tending to reduce the level of capital accumulation in this sector. The average lifetime of capital in this sector, fifteen years, is due to the type of services given to a great number of visitors all year round.

5.5.10. Loops 20–22: industry

Figure 5.6 depicts a causal-loop diagram and represents the causal relationships in the industrial sector.

Loop 20 is analogous to loops 15 and 17 previously described. The elements in this loop serve to moderate changes in the formation of industrial capital. The industrial output allocated to production is employed only to increase industrial capital stock. This serves to increase industrial production and, ultimately, to decrease investment in industrial capital. This is due to the fact that increased industrial output will reduce demand for additional investment in industrial capital stock.

Loop 21 represents interrelationships among five elements that influence the amount of investment available to industry. Increased demand raises the rate of capital formation, leading to growth in industrial capital stock and thus to increased total industrial output. As the industrial output increases, industrial output available for export increases. The elements in loop 22 are analogous to those in loop 21. They serve to moderate changes in investment to industrial capital stock. This loop is a negative feedback loop tending to regulate the level of additional investment in this sector. As the availability of industrial output for export increases, the total export value increases, resulting in an increase in the total capital resource available for investment. If this element increases, the demand for additional investment in industry tends to decrease, leading to a decrease in rate of investment.

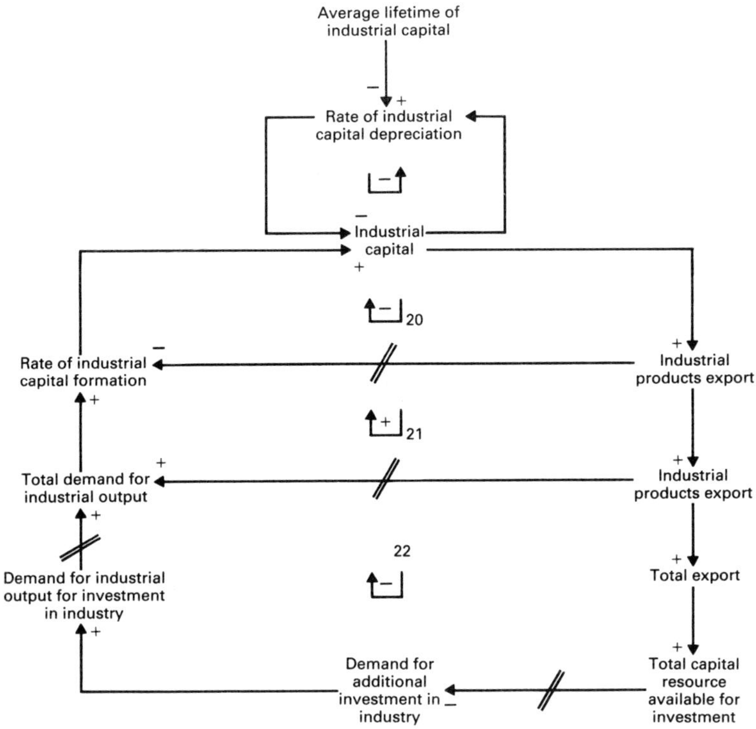

Figure 5.6 Causal relations in the industrial sector.

5.5.11. Capital sector

The total capital resources available to investment (TCRAIN) is derived from the total capital available delayed or from the previous year (TCRAID) and the net borrowing of the country before the previous year ended (NETBRD). The total capital resource available (TCRAI) is determined by the total export (TIM) and the local resource availability (RA). Exports in this study include agricultural products export (APEXP), industrial products export (INDEX), and output of the tourist service sector (TSOUT). Energy imports (EIMP) and the energy embodied in materials for production processes (EEBMT) dictate the total import (TLM). The local resource availability (RA) derives from industrial output allocated to investment (INOINV) and total energy supplies (TESUP).

5.5.12. Miscellaneous

The determination of the carrying capacity of a given system or country, the size of population that can be supported at a certain standard of living is studied. In this analysis the sustainable population is determined by the minimum population supportable by total food available (FPOPS1) and the population that can be supported at a given standard of living (SOLPOP).

5.5.13. Data inputs for this study

Initial values from the base year 1984 were used in the carrying capacity assessment of Thailand. These data were collected from various sources including field interviews and observation. The data collected were converted into energy values (explained earlier). However, some input values were only approximate, due to lack of reliable data. These values need further investigation.

Population: The round number of 50 million people was used as an initial 1984 value for the population sector. The fractional birth rate was 0.0286 while the fractional death rate in the same year was 0.0077 (Office of Prime Minister, 1984).

Forest: The Office of Agricultural Economics (1985) indicated that total forest cover was 15.7 million hectares. The rate of use of wood products (WUPPYN) was 0.2 m^3 per capita per year. New forest biomass per hectare (FORBPH-Wood): 372.4 m^3.

Capital resource requirement for forest plantation (CRRPH): 123.4 GJ/ha-yr.

Agriculture:

Total land available for agriculture: 18,478,000 ha.

Capital for agriculture: 12,935,000 GJ.

Food consumption per capita: 0.0298 tonnes protein per person per year.

Debt: In 1984 – US$ 6867.4 million. At GJ/US$, initial debt = 460.0 million GJ.

Service: Initial service capital in 1984: 2816 million GJ. Service output capital ratio: 0.057.

Industry: Initial capital in 1984: 25130 million GJ. Industrial capital output ratio: 0.019.

Environment: Initial environmental quality in 1984: 0.75.

5.6. ANALYSIS

The pressures applied to reduce foreign debt in this model were very high; debt decreases from 9.2 GJ/per capita in 1984 to 2.9 GJ/per capita in 2023, representing an average rate of 1 per cent per annum. The restriction in this sector aims to reduce the high debt to a minimum level, resulting in low total resources

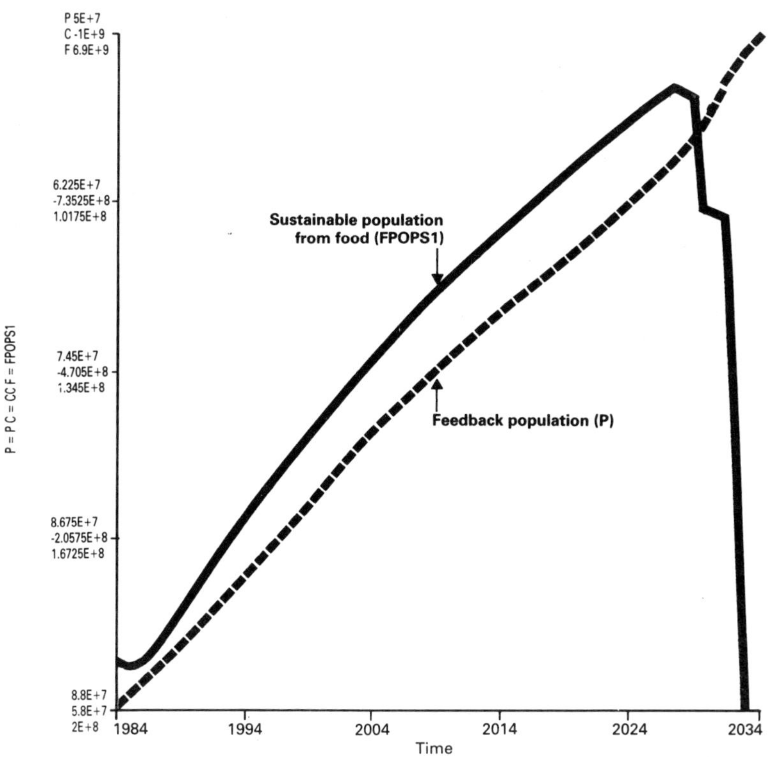

Figure 5.7 Feedback population (P), sustainable populations from food (FPOPS1).

available for annual investment. This causes minimum increase in sectoral outputs and material standard of living.

Figure 5.7 depicts levels of population, derived from feedback structure of the country's system (P), sustainable population or carrying capacity (CC), and sustainable population from total food available (FPOPS1). It is clear that the size of population (P) driven by internal feedback structures gradually increases from 1984 onwards to 2034 and passes the sustainable level (CC) in 1987 (three years after the simulation begins). This is due to the slight changes in standard of living since the model began to operate in 1984. In comparison to the size of sustainable

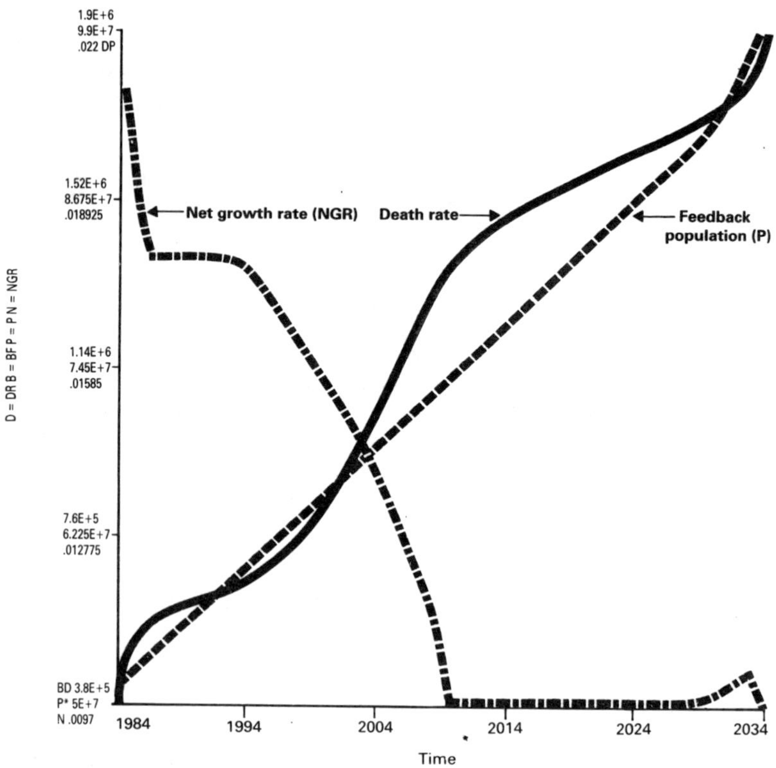

Figure 5.8 Relations of feedback population (P), net growth rate (NGR) and death rate (DR).

population from food surplus (FPOPS1), FPOPS1 is comparatively higher than the system's population (P) and sustainable population (CC). As Thailand is an agrarian country, the nation's agricultural potential is brought forward to produce food in sufficient quantity to meet the demand for annual consumption and export. In terms of food consumption, the total production each year is sufficient to feed a bigger population than CC and P, but in order to live comfortably other materials are also needed. These materials can only be attained through both local and international trade. This shows that the more stages of trading involved, the lower returns from agricultural product trading will be.

Figure 5.8 shows changes in population (P), death rate (DR) and net growth rate of population (NGR). The net rate of population growth decreases from 2 per cent per annum in 1984 to 0.9 per cent per annum in 2010. Population increases from 50 million in 1984 to 98.5 million in 2034, representing an average rate of increase of 1 per cent per year. If restrictions on debts and borrowing are removed, there will be more resources available for investment, leading to sectors' higher level of capital stocks and output. This means that the standard of living will rise, as will the size of the sustainable population.

REFERENCES

Bank of Thailand. *Quarterly Bulletin*, September 1984, Bangkok, Thailand.

Bishop, A. B. et al. *Carrying Capacity in Regional Environmental Management*. EPA-600/5-74-021, February 1974, EPA, Washington DC, USA.

Energy Studies Unit. *Methodology for Carrying Capacity*. Report to Unesco by Strathclyde University, Glasgow, UK, 1980.

Government of Thailand. *The Fifth National Economic and Social Development Plan (1982–1986)*. National Economic and Social Development Board, Office of The Prime Minister, Bangkok, Thailand, 1982.

IFIAS. *Methodology and Conventions*. Energy Analysis Workshop. Report No. 6, Int. Fed. Inst. Adv. Study, Stockholm, Sweden, 1974.

Meadows, D. L. et al. *Limits to Growth*, Universe Books, New York, USA, 1972.

Meadows, D. L. and D. H. Meadows (eds.). *Toward Global Equilibrium: Collected Papers*, Wright-Allen Press, Inc., Mass., USA, 1973.

Meadows, D. L. et al. *Dynamics of Growth in a Finite World*. Wright-Allen Press, Inc., Mass., USA, 1974.

Mellor, J. W. and B. F. Johnston. 'The World Food Equation: Interrelations Among Development, Employment and Food Consumption'.

Journal of Economic Literature, Vol. 22, June 1984, International Food Policy Research Institute, Massachusetts Avenue, Washington DC, USA.

Office of Agricultural Economics. *Agricultural Statistics of Thailand; Crop Year 1983/84*, Ministry of Agriculture and Co-operatives, Bangkok, Thailand, 1984.

Office of The Prime Minister. *THAILAND INTI 80s*. Royal Thai Government, Thai Watana Panich Press Co. Ltd., Bangkok, Thailand, 1983.

Pimentel, D. (ed.). *Handbook of Energy Utilization in Agriculture*. CRC Press, Baton Rouge, Florida, USA, 1973.

Sintunawa, C. 'Energy and Food Interaction and Alternatives for Thailand.' PhD. Thesis, Energy Studies Unit, University of Strathclyde, Glasgow, UK, 1983.

Slesser, M., and C. Lewis. *Biological Energy Resources*. Spon, London., UK, 1979.

Unesco and FAO. *Carrying Capacity Assessment, with a Pilot Study of Kenya, Final Report*, FAO, Rome, Italy, 1985.

World Bank. *World Development Report 1985*. Oxford University Press, London, UK, 1985.

6

EXPLORING THE POTENTIAL FOR ENHANCED NATIONAL WELFARE IN MAURITIUS USING ECCO 'ECONOMIC CO-ORDINATION MODEL'

J. Baguant and M. Slesser

6.1. INTRODUCTION

If the purpose of economic development be to increase welfare, a further purpose, now widely recognised, is that it be sustainable. This does not imply that a particular technology or practice, once introduced, should be permanent, but that whatever welfare is gained be maintainable. In the Mauritius 2000 study the University wishes to explore the many ways in which technological advance and the resources of the country can provide the population with enhanced, but sustainable, welfare.

To quote from the original paper of 1984 by Professor Manrakhan (1985), the Vice-Chancellor of the University of Mauritius, paragraph 3.12 (ii):

> A crucial objective ... is the evaluation of the possible outcomes for Mauritian society over the long run ... This will allow identification of required measures for favouring desired outcomes while also bringing out the dangers and opportunities facing the economy, will provide an opportunity for a more detached and long-term view than usually presented in a five-year plan and, more importantly, will allow policy makers a chance to view trends without the distortion of the immediate short run pressure that they face in day-to-day decision-making,

and paragraph 3.12 (iv):

> the identification of the limits, constraints and interactions across sectors of the economy, will enable policy makers to have a sense of possibilities and of the measures required to achieve desired objectives.

6.2. IMPLICATIONS FOR PLANNING

One policy currently under discussion is the intensification of sugar production, while maintaining present total output, thus releasing land for food production. This would improve Mauritian food self-sufficiency. What, however, are the consequences, in terms of balance of payments, energy considerations, water requirements, employment, provision of capital and so forth?

The planning implications of such a change in land use and intensification fall into three sequential parts, starting with the determination of what is physically possible, through economic evaluation, to presenting fiscal measures to encourage development in the appropriate direction.

The physical possibilities: this may be called physical economics. Its purpose is to determine the outcome over the longer term of introducing a policy and measuring its effect on all aspects of the economy. In this step, one is determining the possibilities, not the probabilities. The Ministry of Economic Planning and Development (MEPD) can use ECCO Mauritius (MECCO) to explore the consequences of the policy through the resource dynamics of the proposed intensification of sugar output. Table 6.6 (see the sugar sector) depicts the outcome for the sugar sector as cane output is intensified by gradual steps from the current 67 to 100 tonnes/ha over twenty years. Not only can the country become a net exporter of cereal and vegetable crops, but the contribution of bagasse to electricity production increases. It is for the decision maker to review the outcome and decide upon its merits, and perhaps ask for the effects, say, of a slower or faster rate of a change in land use. Once satisfied, the second stage is called into play.

The economic assesssment: the proposals and their outcome are now evaluated by economic methods to identify any likely impediments, and to determine whether changes in cost structure or taxes would be required to implement the proposed changes. An iteration between the physical and monetary economics of the proposed changes will very likely occur. Once a satisfactory policy has been identified, the next stage is implementation.

Fiscal measures: whether these changes are wrought by parliamentary decree, by economic incentives or by fiscal measures is now a matter for the MEPD to consider and advise. Moreover the proposed changes must be monitored. Tables presented at the end offer a mere fraction of the data that ECCO can provide to guide the policy maker. For example the water needs for irrigation will increase from 37 million m^3 a year to 46 million by the year 2000, bringing in its train further needs for investment in the water sector and the provision of more electricity. ECCO can provide information on whether the net effect, taking into consideration additional electricity from bagasse, is worthwhile. It can, for instance, be shown that beyond a certain intensity of output the net energy of the sugar system declines.

6.3. FEEDBACK STRUCTURE OF THE MAURITIAN ECONOMY

Though the structure of an economy is a reality, the structure modelled is a matter of perception. That offered here may be considered adequate or inadequate, according to one's knowledge and perception. It may therefore need modification as understanding proceeds. None the less it is a feedback model, and operates according to the principles of feedback. In other words the economy changes because of some causations. Whether this change may be considered good or bad is also a matter of perception, and ECCO attempts to offer a guide by providing an output of information to which the user can bring to bear his or her own value judgements.

As has been pointed out already, the structure changes somewhat according to the policies to be explored. For example, in the Reference Profile, it is an implicit policy that enough food is available to meet 1985 dietary and cultural needs, so that in the absence of a policy to increase food production, more is imported as population increases. Each sector is treated in aggregate. The inputs and outputs are treated as a whole, using mean values of relevant parameters. Thus, for example, in agriculture, no distinction is made between small plot holders and farms, and the arable system, apart from sugar cane, is treated as one aggregate whole.

Table 6.1 is taken from the published SNA for Mauritius for 1983. The sectors have been aggregated for the purpose of the present study.

Table 6.1 Inputs in Mauritius from published SNA for 1983

		Million Rupees
Food:	fish and animal protein	188.2
	animal feeds	36.0
	cereals, vegetables, oils and fats	1127
Consumer goods		1232
Inputs to sugar production		52.8
Raw materials		891.2
Transport		75.7
Fuel		1002.8

Source: CSO (1985, 1986, and 1987).

6.3.1. Capital stock

A key data element in each sector is the capital stock. A convenient device for determining the future rate of capital formation is to identify the desired capital stock needed to furnish a given level of output (say water or electricity), and to compare that with the actual capital stock in the previous year, and use the difference to drive resources into capital formation in the chosen sector.

6.3.2. Allocation of capital

The allocation of capital is analogous in physical economics to conventional economics. Where there is a choice to be made between competing options, it is made on the basis of the least marginal capital requirements, though in embodied energy terms. Where the objective is to explore some particular policy one need only declare the desired output as a function of time (or other parameter), and allow ECCO to make the necessary internal calculations. For example, in 1985 Mauritius was only 9 per cent self-sufficient in cereal and vegetable foodstuffs. Supposing one wishes to explore the consequences of raising this to (say) 70 per cent simply on strategic grounds, then it is enough to insert a statement in ECCO asking for certain levels of self-sufficiency through future time, coupled to the provision of some means of so doing. This might be extensification or intensification of existing agriculture, or some new proposal. The ECCO output would yield the time dependent consequences to all other aspects of the economy, imports and exports.

6.4. ECCO-MAURITIUS – MECCO

Figure 6.1 depicts the core of ECCO-Mauritius, or MECCO. The arrows do not indicate flows of money, goods or energy, but the direction of causation. For example, more manufacturing output requires more raw materials. The arrow goes from output to raw materials, not in the other direction, as in a flow diagram. These arrows carry either a positive or a negative sign. Taking the previous example, more output means more raw materials. An arrow from agricultural investment to total available for investment might be negatively signed, indicating that if more investment were to be made in agriculture, then less would be available for other sectors of the economy. A feedback loop exists when one can follow a series of arrows to arrive back at the point of departure. When the product of every arrow encountered is positive, then the loop is said to be positive and the elements within it have a tendency to grow larger. When the product is negative, the reverse is the case. Figure 6.1 is seen to have one of each type, so that the system has an in-built tendency to grow that is constrained by a negative feedback system. If at any time the negative loop becomes stronger than the positive, growth ceases. This can be occasioned by any one of the many feedback loops, and as time passes one may dominate another. For example, in the Reference Profile sustainability declines, due to the constraint on local firewood supply creating the need for more energy imports. In a run in which a forestry plantation programme is initiated, the eventual growth of new biomass sources overcomes the earlier decline, and sustainability starts to rise again. The time lag in these events is large – almost thirty years!

Feedback loops are a property of any system that does not have at least one positive and one negative loop, wherein at some state or at some time, the one will balance the other. One may

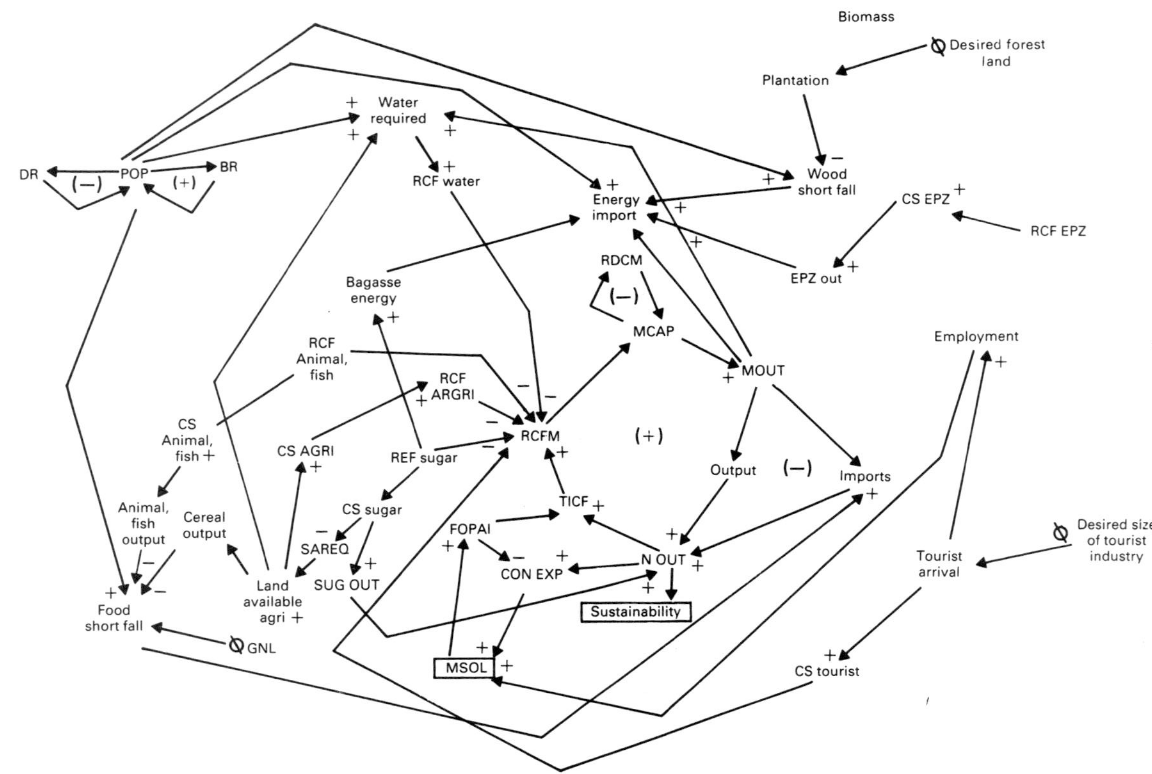

Figure 6.1 Causal loop diagram.

find examples everywhere one looks: the final height of a human being; body temperature; the water level in a domestic tank; the maximum speed of a car; the optimal size of a manufacturing plant, the economic demand/ supply intersection in the price of a good.

Since ECCO reflects a real economy there are many feedback loops. Only the two most significant are captured in Figure 6.1. The growth tendency permits the economy to put aside some output to create capital, which in turn, can generate output. The controlling negative feedback effect is stimulated by increasing cost per unit of output, created by such factors as increasing population density, high technology, rising expectations amongst the population, and many others. It is part of the task of economic management to make sure that growth matches or exceeds population growth. One function of MECCO is to identify whether current or envisaged policies can indeed achieve this objective over the long term, or whether these policies contain the seeds of their own destruction.

Each sector has one common feature – a capital stock. In the causal (sometimes called influence) diagrams that follow, the rate of capital formation is abbreviated to RCF, and capital depreciation is a function of capital lifetime, and may be expressed as RDC/lifetime. If capital stock was not renewed, this depreciation would be an exponential decay, as in real life. It is worth noting that this is different from common accounting practice, where depreciation is usually straight line. Since capital stock data comes from financial data produced by accountants which will have used straight line depreciation, this introduces yet another element of uncertainty.

6.5. KEY OUTPUTS

6.5.1. Output

With some 700 equations, each of which in a dynamic model can yield information through time, the amount of potential information is too great to put into a report. The user seeking a specific item of output not listed in the general output must obtain a fresh run of the model with a request for that output. The range of possible outputs may be viewed by examining the model program listing – see the technical report. Any term in the program may be listed to output.

Two MECCO models exist. One is a technical model for the benefit of the model designer or operator, and is expressed in resource accounting terms throughout. In this report the model used has outputs and inputs which are expressed in monetary terms where appropriate. It must be borne in mind that certain input/output relationships cannot be adequately quantified in money terms, and therefore within the model are dealt with in resource accounting terms.

6.5.2. Indicators

The outputs offered in this report reflect the policies to be explored, but offer a set of indicators which may help the user to decide on the merits of a policy. For ease of comprehension capital and outputs are expressed in financial terms where appropriate. The interpretation of indicators is left to the user, though the authors, as is explained later, do have their own opinions as to which are most relevant.

The program listing expresses all terms as acronyms, the definitions of which may be found in the technical report. The following acronyms are amongst the more important and are used in the program listing and in the tables that follow.

MSOL	Material standard of living	Rs/y
TLOAN	National debt outside Mauritius	Rs
INTI	Annual interest paid on debts outside Mauritius	Rs/y
SUST	The sustainability ratio for Mauritius	%
Agriculture:		
SSC	Self-sufficiency in cereal production	%
SSFP	Self-sufficiency in animal and fish protein	%
XPSUG	Sugar available for export	t/y
SAREQ	Sugar area under cultivation	ha
PCA	Land area for cereal agriculture	ha
Energy:		
EIMP	Energy imports	GJ/y
TELDM	Total electricity demand	kWh/y
AVWS	Available biomass energy	t/y
Water:		
WATDEM	Water demand	m^3/y

Production and output:

MOUT	Manufacturing output	Rs/y
ZOUT	EPZ output	Rs/y
SEROUT	Services output	Rs/y
TOA	Tourist arrivals	
NTORM	Tourist rooms in hotels, etc.	

Capital stocks and formation:

CSHOUS	Housing stock	Rs
CSXXX	Capital stocks all sectors	Rs
RCFXXX	Rate of capital formation all sectors	Rs/y

Population and employment:

POP	Population
PGR	Population growth rate
UNEMP	Unemployment
TOLEMP	Total employment
LFORCE	Available labour force

6.5.3. Abbreviations

The following abbreviations are widely used (the units are in 1985 rupees or GJ).

RCF	Rate of capital formation	Rs/y or GJ/y
RDC	Rate of capital depreciation	Rs/y or GJ/y
—LT	Average lifetime of capital stock	y
CS—	Capital stocks and formation	Rs or GJ
—CAP	Capital stock (when not using CS)	Rs or GJ
—OUT	Output of a particular sector	Rs/y or GJ/y
OCR—	Output to capital ratio	Rs/Rs or GJ/GJ

In general the alphanumeric acronyms used reflect the subject. For example 'water' is usually expressed as 'WAT'. It may help the readers of the program listing to appreciate that no acronym may be more than six characters long, and hence must sometimes be condensed. For example 'Water demand' is condensed to 'WATDEM'.

6.5.4. Criteria of success

As has been stated, judgement of the outputs must be left to the user. However, two indicators are offered which, however judged, are valuable indicators. MSOL (material standard of living) is a parameter that reflects the amount which the individual citizen may (on average) have available to spend after meeting basic needs. It includes that part of output which is consumed (as opposed to being invested) plus imported manufactured goods (but not raw materials) plus services output. Thus it is not a quality of life indicator. It is not an aggregate measure of national prosperity like GDP per capita. It is a measure of an individual's freedom to spend beyond basic needs. One would imagine that a politically successful set of policies for the country would create a rising MSOL.

SUST (sustainability ratio) seeks to express the degree to which the country is self-sustaining. This ratio allows one to look at the country as a whole and see the degree to which it is self-sufficient overall not in particular sectors. For example, in 1985 the country was only 9 per cent self-sufficient in cereal production, but 71 per cent sustainable, by virtue of other aspects of the economy and despite large food imports.

One way of interpreting SUST is to think of it in terms of resilience to external economic shock. The oil price rises of 1974 and 1978, for example, would have had less impact on a country with a SUST closer to 100 per cent. A change in the world marketing climate for, say, sugar could have a major impact on Mauritius, and if sustainability was assessed only in terms of the financial balance of trade, it could be masking the real situation due to price distortion. It is the underlying resilience of the economy one wishes to measure.

SUST is the ratio of the total energy generated in Mauritius divided by the total energy required to run the Mauritian economy, all energies being brought to a standard quality – see program listing for equation. The first term is the total energy (expressed as a standard quality) generated within the country. In the case of Mauritius this is effectively photosynthetically-derived energy (sugar, biomass, crops, etc.) and hydro-electric energy. In the future it might include photovoltaic, ocean thermal, waves, and even fossil, were oil or coal to be found.

The second term is the energy used (again expressed as a standard quality) to run the economy, less imports used to create exports, and exports. In the Mauritian case these effectively amount to the export from the Economic Processing Zone, the net benefit from the tourist trade and the export of sugar and molasses. Smaller items such as fish exports, remittance of capital overseas and so on, will need to be included in a fully detailed study.

To take a simple example of the manner in which sustainability will change, a decision to intensify sugar output through added capital and inputs will increase EIN, but also increase EOUT. The net benefit will accrue if the increase in output exceeds the input.

6.6. THE REFERENCE PROFILE – RP

The 'Reference Profile' is that evolution of the country through the next forty years to 2025 in which the present interrelationships in Mauritius are unchanged. That is, there is no change in current policies or trends. This, of course, will not occur. This version is MECCORV, where 'V' stands for running MECCO in 'value' terms not energy. New policies can be imposed on the RP to permit one to see the consequences.

Table 6.2 gives a profile of the country under such circumstances. In order to give meaning to the table, the reader will

Table 6.2 MECCO – Reference Profile – 1985 rupees

TIME	*POP* *E+06*	*PGR* *%*	*PERUNE* *%*	*MSOL* *E+03*	*SUST* *%*	*TEIMP* *E+06*
1986	0.9971	1.2	21.63	8.698	69.75	10.152
1988	1.0213	1.2	23.12	8.871	67.27	10.672
1990	1.0460	1.2	24.19	8.670	66.36	10.831
1992	1.0714	1.2	25.67	8.423	65.65	10.928
1994	1.0974	1.2	27.13	8.166	65.04	11.000
1996	1.1240	1.2	28.59	7.915	64.48	11.062
1998	1.1513	1.2	30.04	7.668	63.96	11.115
2000	1.1792	1.2	31.48	7.403	62.15	11.423
2002	1.2078	1.2	32.91	7.164	61.90	11.418
2004	1.2371	1.2	34.32	6.937	61.64	11.417
2006	1.2671	1.2	35.73	6.715	61.38	11.416
2008	1.2978	1.2	37.11	6.498	61.12	11.416
2010	1.3293	1.2	38.48	6.284	60.87	11.415
2012	1.3615	1.2	39.84	6.075	60.62	11.414
2014	1.3946	1.2	41.18	5.868	60.38	11.413
2016	1.4284	1.2	42.51	5.664	60.15	11.412
2018	1.4630	1.2	43.83	5.464	59.92	11.410
2020	1.4985	1.2	45.13	5.266	59.70	11.408
2022	1.5349	1.2	46.42	5.070	59.49	11.406
2024	1.5721	1.2	47.70	4.877	59.28	11.405

Table 6.3 MECCO – Reference Profile – GJ

TIME	*POP* *E+06*	*PGR* *%*	*PERUNE* *%*	*MSOL* *E+03*	*SUST* *%*	*TEIMP* *E+06*
1986	0.9971	1.2	21.72	8.839	69.07	10.174
1988	1.0213	1.2	23.42	8.598	68.42	10.305
1990	1.0460	1.2	24.46	8.308	68.07	10.375
1992	1.0714	1.2	26.17	8.017	67.71	10.425
1994	1.0974	1.2	27.87	7.730	67.40	10.463
1996	1.1240	1.2	29.56	7.451	67.12	10.492
1998	1.1513	1.2	31.23	7.180	66.85	10.513
2000	1.1792	1.2	32.91	6.770	65.70	10.680
2002	1.2078	1.2	34.57	6.524	65.66	10.657
2004	1.2371	1.2	36.22	6.291	65.57	10.641
2006	1.2671	1.2	37.84	6.062	65.49	10.623
2008	1.2978	1.2	39.44	5.836	65.40	10.605
2010	1.3293	1.2	41.01	5.614	65.32	10.588
2012	1.3615	1.2	42.56	5.394	65.23	10.570
2014	1.3946	1.2	44.09	5.177	65.14	10.554
2016	1.4284	1.2	45.59	4.963	65.04	10.538
2018	1.4630	1.2	47.07	4.751	64.95	10.524
2020	1.4985	1.2	48.53	4.541	64.84	10.513
2022	1.5349	1.2	49.96	4.333	64.74	10.504
2024	1.5721	1.2	51.38	4.126	64.62	10.498

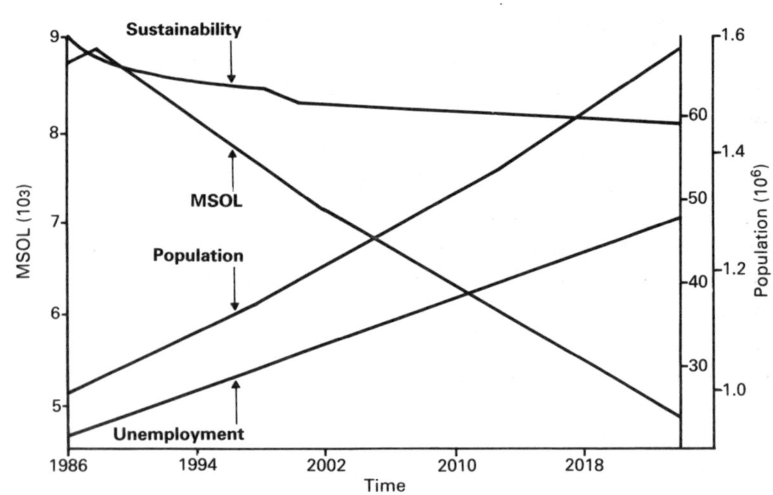

Figure 6.2 Output of Reference Profile.

wish to be aware of the trends incorporated (Figure 6.2). Table 6.2 gives monetary outputs in 1985 Rupee terms; Table 6.3 gives all output in tonnes and GJ.

The following summarises conditions in the Reference Profile:

Population: is held at the 1985 growth rate of 1.2 per cent.
Goal nutritional level: the cereal intake in 1985 is 14.8 kg of protein equivalent per year per capita (imported and indigenous), and an animal and fish protein intake of 6.9 kg of protein equivalent per capita per year.
Sugar cane output: no effort is made to increase sugar cane output or to release sugar land for food production. Output is maintained at 67 tonnes/ha.
Sugar manufacture: no investment is made to upgrade the manufacturing facilities in sugar from cane production, though existing facilities are maintained.
Sugar harvesting: techniques remain as in 1985, excluding possible improvements.
Export processing zone: the EPZ is maintained at its 1985 level.
Manufacturing: is allowed to grow at 2 per cent annually, with the option to borrow internationally in order to achieve such growth.
Water wastage: no investment is made to curb water wastage through leaks in the existing water-distribution system.
Tourist industry: the tourist industry grows at historical rates and does not exceed 200,000 tourist arrivals annually.
Biomass: no woody biomass plantations are created to offset the consumption of wood for fuel. Illegal cutting of forest reserves continues to meet the shortfall in fuel supply, but this cutting decreases in proportion to the remaining reserve area, and ceases altogether when only 50 per cent of the present 56,000 ha forest reserve remains. Wood demand to diminish as MSOL rises and vice versa. Unsatisfied wood-fuel demand creates an additional import of kerosene.
Industrial investment: ECCO contains a term FOPAI – fraction of output allocated to investment – which responds slightly to changes in MSOL. A fall in MSOL creates a rise in FOPAI in an effort to maintain the long-term growth of output. The 1985 value is 9 per cent. This is an example of a policy imposed on ECCO at this stage for want of definitive information on current government economic policy.

Water provision: all water demand is satisfied, even if it draws capital away from industrial investment.
Domestic energy provision: domestic energy demand rises in proportion to MSOL. The 1985 value for electricity is 137 kWh/capita. Thermal energy demand is 1.03 GJ/capita. This excludes use of wood fuel, which amounts to 3.1 GJ per capita (on average, for not everyone uses wood fuel). Wood energy in the home is reckoned to be 25 per cent as effective as kerosene.
Electricity provision: electricity is provided from bagasse, hydro-power and imported diesel fuel (Baguant, 1982). In the Reference Profile the bagasse (with some coal) remains constant at 103 million kWh and hydro-electricity is 115 million kWh. Hydro-power is, of course, a function of rainfall, and will be less in dry years.
Services: services change in proportion to changes in MSOL and population.
Employment: calculation of employment assumes 1985 levels of employment per unit of capital or, in some cases, per unit of output. The labour force is a function of population, and hence unemployment is calculated as the difference. In a more refined model, a disaggregated population sector would provide a better idea of the real labour force.

6.7. POLICY RUNS

Clearly there is an infinite range of possible policies. In due course some will be proposed by planners, politicians and others. For the purposes of demonstration, MECCO has taken nine straightforward policies and examined the long-term effect of each in turn. Chapter 6 reports the outcome where the sum of all attractive policies are collectively implemented and used to develop and test further policies thought to be beneficial to Mauritius.

It must be emphasised that the proposal of a policy is not the same thing as putting it into effect. MECCO indicates to the policy proposer the possible outcome of such a policy. If the proposer or decision-maker is satisfied with the outcome, then the 'Possible' has been identified. It is then the business of planners to determine how such a policy may be implemented. Each profile runs to the year 2025 from the base year 1985. Each policy run has a summary table which should be compared with Table 6.2.

6.7.1. Population growth reduction

Since 1950 there has been a trend towards reduced population growth rate. Let us suppose that the country's population policy and investment in birth control permits this trend to continue, so that by 2025 the population growth rate is 0.2 per cent. Table 6.4 depicts the outcome. The following may be noted for the year 2025:

Population: total 1.213 million (cf. RP 1.591 million), 2025 growth rate 0.2 per cent.
Unemployment: 31 per cent, a drop of 18 per cent from the Reference Profile (RP).
MSOL: much improved over RP, 7,391 (cf. RP 4,530).
Self-sufficiency in cereals: improves to 7.8 per cent (cf. RP 6 per cent).
Wood-energy: use falls by 50 per cent due to maintenance of MSOL.
Sugar export: less home demand allows exports to be 14,000 tonnes/y greater. Molasses exports up 9000 tonnes/y.

Table 6.4 MECCO – Policy Run P1: reducing population growth

TIME	*POP* *E+06*	*PGR* %	*PERUNE* %	*MSOL* *E+03*	*SUST* %	*TEIMP* *E+06*
1986	0.9969	1.2	21.61	8.699	69.76	10.151
1988	1.0197	1.1	23.01	8.880	67.31	10.665
1990	1.0415	1.0	23.86	8.704	66.44	10.820
1992	1.0620	0.9	25.01	8.499	65.78	10.914
1994	1.0809	0.8	26.02	8.303	65.23	10.986
1996	1.0982	0.7	26.91	8.130	64.73	11.049
1998	1.1135	0.6	27.65	7.982	64.27	11.106
2000	1.1266	0.5	28.24	7.834	62.54	11.421
2002	1.1378	0.5	28.72	7.732	62.36	11.428
2004	1.1476	0.4	29.10	7.654	62.15	11.444
2006	1.1561	0.3	29.40	7.593	61.95	11.463
2008	1.1639	0.3	29.65	7.544	61.73	11.488
2010	1.1710	0.3	29.86	7.503	61.52	11.516
2012	1.1774	0.3	30.02	7.470	61.30	11.545
2014	1.1831	0.2	30.12	7.445	61.08	11.577
2016	1.1880	0.2	30.18	7.428	60.86	11.610
2018	1.1927	0.2	30.22	7.416	60.63	11.649
2020	1.1975	0.2	30.26	7.408	60.39	11.691
2022	1.2023	0.2	30.29	7.400	60.14	11.734
2024	1.2071	0.2	30.32	7.393	59.89	11.779

National debt: 23.5 billion Rs, greater than with the higher population growth, and due to the demand for services and housing that is triggered by MSOL remaining at almost 1985 levels.

6.7.2. Raising nutritional levels

This is a normative policy in which cereal intake is taken to rise to 16.4 kg protein equivalent per capita by 2005, while animal and fish protein intake rises to 7.7 kg/capita. The effect of this policy (see Table 6.5) is to increase cereal imports by 2500 tonnes/y protein equivalent, and animal protein imports by 1300 tonnes/y protein equivalent. Such increased demand for imports depresses MSOL slightly to 4,240 in 2025 (cf. RP 4,530).

6.7.3. Intensification of sugar production to release land for food production

There is ample potential to increase sugar cane output per hectare, but little prospect in the present-day world of selling

Table 6.5 MECCO – Policy Run P2: improved goal nutritional level

TIME	*POP E+06*	*GNLC E−03*	*GNLA E−03*	*PERUNE %*	*MSOL E=03*	*SUST %*	*TEIMP E=06*
1986	0.9971	14.88	6.94	21.63	8.696	69.71	10.150
1988	1.0213	15.04	7.02	23.13	8.854	67.20	10.655
1990	1.0460	15.20	7.10	24.20	8.635	66.26	10.796
1992	1.0714	15.36	7.18	25.69	8.368	65.54	10.873
1994	1.0974	15.52	7.26	27.17	8.091	64.91	10.924
1996	1.1240	15.68	7.34	28.65	7.819	64.34	10.962
1998	1.1513	15.84	7.42	30.12	7.551	63.80	10.989
2000	1.1792	16.00	7.50	31.59	7.263	62.00	11.270
2002	1.2078	16.16	7.58	33.06	7.001	61.74	11.235
2004	1.2371	16.32	7.66	34.51	6.749	61.48	11.204
2006	1.2671	16.40	7.70	35.96	6.505	61.27	11.173
2008	1.2978	16.40	7.70	37.40	6.276	61.06	11.153
2010	1.3293	16.40	7.70	38.82	6.053	60.85	11.136
2012	1.3615	16.40	7.70	40.23	5.834	60.65	11.117
2014	1.3946	16.40	7.70	41.63	5.617	60.46	11.098
2016	1.4284	16.40	7.70	43.01	5.404	60.28	11.079
2018	1.4630	16.40	7.70	44.38	5.193	60.10	11.059
2020	1.4985	16.40	7.70	45.74	4.985	59.93	11.039
2022	1.5349	16.40	7.70	47.09	4.779	59.77	11.019
2024	1.5721	16.40	7.70	48.42	4.576	59.61	11.000

that enhanced output. This policy explores intensifying cane output per ha from 67 to 100 tonnes/ha, while constraining sugar output to 750,000 tonnes/y. The land released is allocated for growing traditional Mauritian cereal crops. The policy is very successful (see Table 6.6). The output of cereals rises to a level where self-sufficiency in cereals has reached 44.9 per cent (cf. RP 5.6). Sugar-growing land falls from 83,500 ha in 1985 to 65,200 ha by the year 2000. MSOL, instead of falling to the level of 4563 Rs in the Reference Profile falls only to 6560 Rs. However, the effect of enhanced intensification is to raise energy imports and other energy intensive inputs, while the maintenance of MSOL draws in energy for other aspects of the growing economy. Thus energy imports rise to 15,000 million GJ (cf. RP 11,700 million). One marked benefit is that unemployment is reduced from 49 per cent in the Reference Profile to 38 per cent.

Table 6.6 MECCO – Policy Run P3: intensify sugar and release land

TIME	*POP* *E+06*	*SAREQ* *E+03*	*TCO* *E+03*	*PERUNE* *%*	*MSOL* *E+03*	*SUST* *%*	*TEIMP* *E+06*
1986	0.9971	83.50	1.41	21.59	8.697	69.85	10.144
1988	1.0213	83.50	1.41	22.63	8.903	68.00	10.772
1990	1.0460	83.50	1.41	23.12	8.763	67.79	11.084
1992	1.0714	83.50	1.41	23.75	8.609	68.27	11.367
1994	1.0974	78.58	3.85	23.95	8.606	68.20	11.762
1996	1.1240	73.28	6.47	24.55	8.714	66.74	12.253
1998	1.1513	69.38	8.40	25.04	8.783	65.93	12.713
2000	1.1792	67.23	9.46	25.82	8.728	63.24	13.589
2002	1.2078	65.88	10.13	26.81	8.622	62.57	13.798
2004	1.2371	65.22	10.46	27.81	8.495	61.94	13.990
2006	1.2671	65.22	10.46	28.90	8.327	61.26	14.141
2008	1.2978	65.22	10.46	30.00	8.148	60.57	14.281
2010	1.3293	65.22	10.46	31.07	7.972	59.88	14.424
2012	1.3615	65.22	10.46	32.10	7.802	59.18	14.575
2014	1.3946	65.22	10.46	33.11	7.638	58.47	14.734
2016	1.4284	65.22	10.46	34.09	7.480	57.75	14.901
2018	1.4630	65.22	10.46	35.04	7.328	57.02	15.077
2020	1.4985	65.22	10.46	35.95	7.183	56.28	15.263
2022	1.5349	65.22	10.46	36.84	7.044	55.52	15.458
2024	1.5721	65.22	10.46	37.69	6.911	54.76	15.664

6.7.4. Better use of bagasse

In this policy investment is made in sugar manufacturing to improve combustion of bagasse, and make better use of steam (Baguant, 1984a and 1984b). The outcome is spectacular (see Table 6.7). The potential for generating electricity for distribution to the national grid rises from 103 (RP) to 270 million kWh/y. The effect is to reduce energy imports by 1.37 million GJ, or 163 million Rs/y at 1987 prices. This was achieved by investment in three stages up to 1998 of 150 million rupees (1985) per stage. The benefit to the nation, apart from the obvious virtue of a satisfactory return on investment, is that sustainability falls less, viz. 65.7 per cent (cf. RP 59.3 per cent) in 2025. MSOL benefits slightly over the Reference Profile.

6.7.5. Improved loading and transport arrangements in sugar harvesting

There is scope in sugar harvesting for improved technology and handling. The capital costs and outcomes are small, and

Table 6.7 MECCO – Policy Run P4: investment to improve Bagasse electricity

TIME	*POP E+06*	*KWHB E+06*	*TELDM E+06*	*PERUNE %*	*MSOL E+03*	*SUST %*	*TEIMP E+06*
1986	0.9971	103	411	21.63	8.698	69.75	10.152
1988	1.0213	103	423	23.12	8.871	67.27	10.672
1990	1.0460	159	428	24.18	8.729	68.83	10.299
1992	1.0714	159	430	25.64	8.495	68.06	10.411
1994	1.0974	215	433	27.08	8.299	69.84	9.957
1996	1.1240	215	434	28.50	8.062	69.20	10.038
1998	1.1513	271	435	29.91	7.856	71.08	9.548
2000	1.1792	271	436	31.30	7.622	69.17	9.896
2002	1.2078	271	436	32.68	7.395	68.82	9.908
2004	1.2371	271	436	34.04	7.174	68.47	9.923
2006	1.2671	271	435	35.39	6.959	68.12	9.937
2008	1.2978	271	435	36.72	6.748	67.78	9.951
2010	1.3293	271	435	38.03	6.541	67.44	9.965
2012	1.3615	271	434	39.33	6.338	67.11	9.980
2014	1.3946	271	433	40.62	6.138	66.78	9.995
2016	1.4284	271	433	41.89	5.941	66.45	10.009
2018	1.4630	271	432	43.14	5.748	66.13	10.024
2020	1.4985	271	430	44.39	5.557	65.82	1 .039
2022	1.5349	271	429	45.62	5.369	65.51	10.054
2024	1.5721	271	428	46.83	5.184	65.21	10.070

Table 6.8 MECCO – Policy Run P5: improved cane harvest and transport

TIME	*POP E+06*	*NSOL*	*PERUNE %*	*MSOL E+03*	*SUST %*	*TEIMP E+06*
1986	0.9971	112	21.63	8.699	69.77	10.144
1988	1.0213	111	23.13	8.868	67.06	10.736
1990	1.0460	111	24.19	8.657	65.89	10.980
1992	1.0714	111	25.67	8.398	64.96	11.161
1994	1.0974	111	27.15	8.131	64.14	11.315
1996	1.1240	111	28.62	7.868	63.38	11.454
1998	1.1513	111	30.08	7.612	62.67	11.583
2000	1.1792	111	31.53	7.314	60.14	12.195
2002	1.2078	111	32.99	7.063	59.83	12.225
2004	1.2371	111	34.43	6.828	59.49	12.267
2006	1.2671	111	35.85	6.599	59.14	12.312
2008	1.2978	111	37.27	6.373	58.80	12.360
2010	1.3293	111	38.67	6.151	58.46	12.411
2012	1.3615	111	40.06	5.932	58.11	12.466
2014	1.3946	111	41.43	5.716	57.77	12.523
2016	1.4284	111	42.80	5.503	57.43	12.585
2018	1.4630	111	44.15	5.291	57.09	12.652
2020	1.4985	111	45.49	5.082	56.74	12.724
2022	1.5349	111	46.82	4.875	56.39	12.803
2024	1.5721	111	48.14	4.670	56.03	12.889

ultimately show up as a very slight benefit to MSOL (see Table 6.8).

6.7.6. Economic Processing Zone grows 7.5 per cent annually

Over recent years the EPZ has been growing at 7.5 per cent a year due to government policies of tax holidays and other incentives. In Policy 6, the effect of continuing such a rate of growth is explored. The results are presented in Table 6.9.

In terms of unemployment the policy is so successful that by 2012 unemployment has fallen to 1.56 per cent, and thereafter such a growth policy would need labour to be imported, or taken from existing enterprises outside the EPZ. Of course, in reality an approach to low levels of unemployment alters the employment environment and affects wages and incentives. The following comments apply to the situation in the year 2012, and not 2025:

Table 6.9 MECCO – Policy Run P6: EPZ grows at 7.5% annually

TIME	*POP E+06*	*CSEPZ E+09*	*ZOUT E+09*	*PERUNE %*	*MSOL E+03*	*SUST %*	*TEIMP E+06*
1986	0.9971	3.127	1.345	20.78	8.732	69.59	10.229
1988	1.0213	3.397	1.461	20.51	9.110	66.28	11.043
1990	1.0460	3.691	1.587	19.68	9.168	64.34	11.568
1992	1.0714	4.010	1.724	19.12	9.204	62.52	12.080
1994	1.0974	4.357	1.873	18.42	9.255	60.72	12.615
1996	1.1240	4.733	2.035	17.54	9.337	58.88	13.197
1998	1.1513	5.142	2.211	16.47	9.455	56.99	13.835
2000	1.1792	5.587	2.402	15.20	9.588	53.87	14.802
2002	1.2078	6.070	2.610	13.71	9.789	52.05	15.544
2004	1.2371	6.594	2.836	11.96	10.050	50.12	16.394
2006	1.2671	7.164	3.081	9.92	10.374	48.06	17.366
2008	1.2978	7.783	3.347	7.55	10.770	45.90	18.485
2010	1.3293	8.456	3.636	4.78	11.255	43.61	19.782
2012	1.3615	9.187	3.950	1.56	11.846	41.19	21.298
2014	1.3946	9.981	4.292	−2.21	12.570	38.64	23.089
2016	1.4284	10.844	4.663	−6.69	13.464	35.96	25.233
2018	1.4630	11.781	5.066	−12.06	14.581	33.12	27.841
2020	1.4985	12.799	5.504	−18.65	15.999	30.13	31.080
2022	1.5349	13.906	5.980	−26.97	17.840	26.97	35.209
2024	1.5721	15.108	6.496	−37.91	20.306	23.64	40.656

Unemployment:	1.56% (RP 40.1)
National debt:	29.6 billion Rs (RP 23.25)
MSOL:	11,846 (RP 5,900)
Sustainability:	41.2% (RP 59.3)
Water demand:	1.02 billion m^3/y (of which EPZ 3.4 million)
Water use:	81.1% of average rainfall supply
Total energy imports:	Increase by 10.13 million GJ, or 1.2 billion Rs at 1987 prices

Interpretation of these perhaps surprising results is required. Firstly reduced unemployment enhances welfare and increases MSOL, bringing in its wake demands for housing, services and so forth. This creates demands for capital, and since in the Reference Profile non-EPZ manufacturing is maintained at a growth rate of 2 per cent, this may only be achieved by susbtantial borrowing. The EPZ draws in a high demand for imported manufacturing goods, as well as raw materials for its own processes. Its very size creates big demands for thermal energy, electricity and water, requiring substantial capital investment. Meanwhile the indigenous provision of energy is not enhanced (even though the net EPZ export/import is not counted in calculating sustainability). Thus national sustainability is eroded.

Thus while such a high growth rate does assist unemployment and MSOL, and may therefore be politically attractive, it creates steadily declining national sustainability or, in other words, a rather fragile economy. Clearly this sector has such a powerful effect on Mauritius that a much deeper study is called for than offered here.

6.7.7. Reducing water wastage

In Mauritius the fraction of the rainfall that must be collected to satisfy national water needs is relatively high. In 1985 it was 56.9 per cent of both underground and above-ground water sources (Harel, pers. comm.). It is known that there are substantial leaks and wastages in the system, the correction of which calls for

Table 6.10 MECCO – Policy Run P7: reduce water wastage

TIME	*POP* *E+06*	*WATDEM* *E+06*	*FWSU* *%*	*PERUNE* *%*	*MSOL* *E+03*	*SUST* *%*	*TEIMP* *E+10*
1986	0.9971	745	59.1	21.63	8.699	69.78	10.145
1988	1.0213	774	61.4	23.15	8.868	67.07	10.739
1990	1.0460	789	62.6	24.24	8.657	65.91	10.985
1992	1.0714	796	63.1	25.74	8.398	64.98	11.166
1994	1.0974	797	63.2	27.23	8.130	64.17	11.320
1996	1.1240	794	63.0	28.71	7.867	63.41	11.460
1998	1.1513	788	62.5	30.18	7.611	62.71	11.590
2000	1.1792	778	61.7	31.65	7.313	60.18	12.202
2002	1.2078	766	60.7	33.11	7.062	59.88	12.232
2004	1.2371	753	59.7	34.56	6.827	59.54	12.274
2006	1.2671	746	59.1	36.00	6.598	59.19	12.319
2008	1.2978	744	59.0	37.41	6.372	58.85	12.367
2010	1.3293	743	58.9	38.80	6.150	58.51	12.418
2012	1.3615	742	58.8	40.19	5.931	58.17	12.472
2014	1.3946	741	58.7	41.56	5.715	57.83	12.530
2016	1.4284	739	58.6	42.92	5.501	57.48	12.592
2018	1.4630	738	58.5	44.27	5.290	57.14	12.659
2020	1.4985	736	58.4	45.61	5.081	56.79	12.731
2022	1.5349	735	58.3	46.94	4.874	56.44	12.810
2024	1.5721	733	58.1	48.25	4.669	56.09	12.896

Table 6.11 MECCO – Policy Run P8: tourist increases to 500,000

TIME	*POP* *E+06*	*TOA* *E+03*	*NTORM*	*PERUNE* %	*MSOL* *E+03*	*SUST* %	*TEIMP* *E+06*
1986	0.9971	154	2630	21.63	8.699	69.78	10.145
1988	1.0213	154	2630	23.13	8.868	67.07	10.739
1990	1.0460	200	3419	24.19	8.657	65.91	10.985
1992	1.0714	200	3419	25.67	8.398	64.98	11.166
1994	1.0974	246	4208	26.75	8.143	64.16	11.332
1996	1.1240	246	4208	28.22	7.890	63.37	11.482
1998	1.1513	293	4997	29.31	7.647	62.64	11.625
2000	1.1792	293	4997	30.77	7.360	60.09	12.247
2002	1.2078	339	5786	31.87	7.123	59.76	12.292
2004	1.2371	339	5786	33.32	6.897	59.38	12.344
2006	1.2671	385	6575	34.41	6.681	59.02	12.404
2008	1.2978	385	6575	35.83	6.467	58.63	12.464
2010	1.3293	431	7364	36.92	6.258	58.27	12.529
2012	1.3615	431	7364	38.32	6.050	57.88	12.595
2014	1.3946	477	8153	39.39	5.848	57.52	12.668
2016	1.4284	477	8153	40.77	5.645	57.13	12.742
2018	1.4630	524	8942	41.83	5.448	56.76	12.822
2020	1.4985	524	8942	43.18	5.250	56.37	12.905
2022	1.5349	524	8942	44.53	5.048	56.00	12.988
2024	1.5721	524	8942	45.86	4.848	55.63	13.077

investment. In this policy, investment in water services is spread over twenty years from 1985, and is reckoned to cost about 1 billion Rs (1985). The effect is to reduce the fraction of water availability that must be harnessed from 70.4 per cent in the Reference Profile to 58 per cent, a very significant reduction, and allowing room for economic and population expansion in the future (see Table 6.10).

6.7.8. Increasing tourist investment and attraction

Tourism is perceived as a way of increasing employment. In this policy run, tourism may expand above an annual intake of 500,000. This requires the construction of hotels and draws in the need for many inputs, including food. The outcome is not encouraging (see Table 6.11). Unemployment falls only marginally to 43 per cent (cf. RP 49 per cent). By 2025 the number of tourist rooms needed is 8940 (cf. 2630 in 1985). MSOL is scarcely affected (cf. 4600 Rs), while sustainability is slightly reduced (55.8 per cent). Self-sufficiency in foodstuffs also falls slightly due to tourist demand for food. There is scarcely any effect noticed on the national debt.

6.7.9. Creating biomass plantations

In 1985 there were 56,000 ha of forest reserves. It is government policy to maintain this forest, and contain harvesting rate to growth rate, thus maintaining a steady-state forest stock. In fact there is a great deal of illegal cutting – estimated in 1985 to be 150,000 tonnes per year. It seems it is almost impossible to control. In the policy introduced here, land otherwise incapable of supporting crop production is used for biomass plantations. The driving force for investment is the degree to which there is a reduction in forest reserve stock and demand for wood fuel. This demand is set to rise when MSOL falls, and vice versa.

In the policy run, biomass plantations are planted at the rate of 200 ha/y initially, rising to 500 ha/y as experience is gained. They will consist of fast growing acacia, harvestable in five years. As may be seen in Table 6.12, by 2025 the plantation area will be

Table 6.12 MECCO – Policy Run P9: forest plantation programme

TIME	*POP* *E+06*	*FPA* *E+03*	*WOODSF*	*FRHNL* *E+03*	*MSOL* *E+03*	*SUST* *%*	*TEIMP* *E+06*
1986	0.9971	202	132	137	8.700	69.87	10.122
1988	1.0213	584	133	123	8.873	67.34	10.672
1990	1.0460	956	140	111	8.668	66.35	10.876
1992	1.0714	1321	149	100	8.415	65.57	11.018
1994	1.0974	1689	157	90	8.153	64.91	11.131
1996	1.1240	2069	166	81	7.896	64.31	11.229
1998	1.1513	2467	175	73	7.645	63.76	11.315
2000	1.1792	2887	183	0	7.354	61.39	11.881
2002	1.2078	3329	190	0	7.108	61.26	11.862
2004	1.2371	3794	197	0	6.879	61.10	11.853
2006	1.2671	4278	204	0	6.657	60.94	11.845
2008	1.2978	4783	212	0	6.439	60.78	11.838
2010	1.3293	5306	220	0	6.224	60.64	11.832
2012	1.3615	5850	229	0	6.013	60.49	11.826
2014	1.3946	6414	239	0	5.805	60.36	11.822
2016	1.4284	7001	250	0	5.600	60.22	11.819
2018	1.4630	7613	262	0	5.397	60.10	11.818
2020	1.4985	8251	275	0	5.198	59.98	11.819
2022	1.5349	8919	289	0	5.000	59.86	11.822
2024	1.5721	9618	304	0	4.804	59.75	11.828

9690 ha. This will reduce the wood shortfall (normally satisfied by importing kerosene) from 477,000 (RP) to 311,000 tonnes/y. This has the effect of reducing energy imports by 1.2 million GJ/y or 143 million Rs at 1987 prices. There is a slight improvement in sustainability – 62.3 per cent (cf. RP 59.3). MSOL rises very slightly.

6.7.10. Conclusions

In the policies explored above, those that are most effective (in isolation) at enhancing sustainability are:

- intensification of sugar cane output, releasing land for food production;
- falling birth rate;
- improved use of bagasse and steam in sugar manufacture;
- introduction of biomass plantations.

Those most effective (in isolation) in reducing unemployment are:

- the EPZ growth;
- falling birth rate;
- sugar intensification and release of land for food.

Those that are most effective (in isolation) in increasing MSOL are:

- expansion of EPZ;
- sugar intensification;
- improved bagasse use;
- falling birth rate.

Of these the EPZ alone stimulates large international borrowing.

6.8. COMBINATIONS OF POLICIES

One cannot define a desirable policy without applying some criterion or criteria. In the following the authors have applied their criteria of what represents a desirable outcome. Briefly, a desirable outcome is one in which sustainability and MSOL are both enhanced. This may not be the view of others.

Table 6.13 MECCO – Combined Policy Run C1:
P1+P3+P4+P5+P7+P9

TIME	*POP E+06*	*PGR %*	*PERUNE %*	*MSOL E+03*	*SUST %*	*TEIMP E+06*	*KWHB E+06*	*SSC %*	*NSOL*
1986	0.9969	1.2	21.59	8.697	69.90	10.137	103	9.54	112
1988	1.0197	1.1	22.54	8.919	68.42	10.665	103	9.33	114
1990	1.0415	1.0	22.82	8.878	71.16	10.306	162	9.14	124
1992	1.0620	0.9	23.10	8.798	72.00	10.479	165	8.96	129
1994	1.0809	0.8	22.79	8.945	74.89	10.182	230	24.04	148
1996	1.0982	0.7	22.74	9.173	73.52	10.630	230	39.79	159
1998	1.1135	0.6	22.40	9.420	75.52	10.391	295	50.96	177
2000	1.1266	0.5	22.17	9.581	73.42	11.013	297	56.74	183
2002	1.1378	0.5	22.00	9.672	72.69	11.228	298	60.17	186
2004	1.1476	0.4	21.74	9.755	72.03	11.421	298	61.57	189
2006	1.1561	0.3	21.45	9.812	71.31	11.583	299	61.12	189
2008	1.1639	0.3	21.09	9.871	70.54	11.746	299	60.71	189
2010	1.1710	0.3	20.63	9.945	69.74	11.924	299	60.34	189
2012	1.1774	0.3	20.05	10.038	68.89	12.119	299	60.01	189
2014	1.1831	0.2	19.35	10.151	67.98	12.336	299	59.73	189
2016	1.1880	0.2	18.51	10.289	67.02	12.578	299	59.48	189
2018	1.1927	0.2	17.56	10.448	65.99	12.849	299	59.24	189
2020	1.1975	0.2	16.49	10.627	64.88	13.152	299	59.01	189
2022	1.2023	0.2	15.30	10.828	63.70	13.489	299	58.77	189
2024	1.2071	0.2	13.94	11.054	62.43	13.866	299	58.54	189

6.8.1. Combination of policies 1, 3, 4, 5, 7 and 9

In this combination policy 1, continued development of the EPZ and tourism are excluded. The outcome is presented in Table 6.13, and summarised below.

Sustainability:	rises, peaking at 75.5% in 1998, falling slowly to 63.3% by 2025
Unemployment:	reduces progressively to 15.3%
MSOL:	rises steadily to 10,519 Rs.
Self-sufficiency:	cereal self-sufficiency rises to 58.5% (cf. RP 5.9%)
National debt:	rises to 52.7 billion Rs (5.2 billion in 1985 and 25 billion in the Reference Profile)

Thus almost the same level of MSOL is achieved as with 7.5 per cent annual growth of the EPZ (policy run 6), yet the sustainability has been enhanced rather than the system being rendered more fragile.

6.8.2. Above policy with EPZ growth

In this run the combined policy run 1 above is combined with an EPZ growth of 7.5 per cent annually, explored in policy run 6. The outcome (see Table 6.14) is a very rapid drop in unemployment reaching 1.5 per cent by the year 2002, by which time the capital stock of the EPZ has doubled in real terms. National debt has already reached 31.7 billion Rs, and energy imports have risen to 15.8 million GJ (cf. RP 11.07). By 2002 sustainability has fallen to 41 per cent. The policy is impossible because the entire labour force is used, and there is a serious question as to whether debt can be allowed to rise so fast. A logical development of this policy is to control the growth of the EPZ in such a way as to maintain low unemployment. This is done below in section 6.8.4.

Table 6.14 MECCO – Combined Policy Run C2: P1+P3+P4+P5+P7+P9+P6

TIME	*POP* *E+06*	*PGR* *%*	*PERUNE* *%*	*MSOL* *E+03*	*SUST* *%*	*TEIMP* *E+06*	*KWHB* *E+06*	*SSC* *%*	*NSOL*
1986	0.9969	1.2	20.75	8.731	69.74	10.214	103	9.54	112
1988	1.0197	1.1	19.92	9.158	67.41	11.036	103	9.33	114
1990	1.0415	1.0	18.29	9.381	69.01	11.048	162	9.14	124
1992	1.0620	0.9	16.49	9.594	68.60	11.644	165	8.96	129
1994	1.0809	0.8	13.93	10.077	69.93	11.840	230	24.04	148
1996	1.0982	0.7	11.40	10.699	67.07	12.871	230	39.79	159
1998	1.1135	0.6	8.30	11.403	67.16	13.312	295	50.96	177
2000	1.1266	0.5	4.97	12.100	63.39	14.731	297	56.74	183
2002	1.1378	0.5	1.29	12.812	60.69	15.869	298	60.17	186
2004	1.1476	0.4	−2.96	13.628	57.89	17.149	298	61.57	189
2006	1.1561	0.3	−7.84	14.563	54.84	18.603	299	61.12	189
2008	1.1639	0.3	−13.53	15.685	51.54	20.325	299	60.71	189
2010	1.1710	0.3	−20.26	17.069	48.01	22.411	299	60.34	189
2012	1.1774	0.3	−28.39	18.809	44.21	24.990	299	60.01	189
2014	1.1831	0.2	−38.40	21.046	40.14	28.252	299	59.73	189
2016	1.1880	0.2	−51.15	24.000	35.77	32.503	299	59.48	189
2018	1.1927	0.2	−68.05	28.032	31.09	38.262	299	59.24	189
2020	1.1975	0.2	−91.98	33.787	26.10	46.455	299	59.01	189
2022	1.2023	0.2	−129.37	42.555	20.81	58.954	299	58.77	189
2024	1.2071	0.2	−197.30	57.200	15.27	80.047	299	58.54	189

Table 6.15 MECCO – Combined Policy Run C3: P1+P3+P4+P5+P7+P9+P8

TIME	*POP E+06*	*PGR %*	*PERUNE %*	*MSOL E+03*	*SUST %*	*TEIMP E+06*	*KWHB E+06*	*SSC %*	*NSOL*
1986	0.9969	1.2	21.59	8.697	69.90	10.137	103	9.54	112
1988	1.0197	1.1	22.54	8.919	68.42	10.665	103	9.33	114
1990	1.0415	1.0	22.82	8.878	71.16	10.306	162	9.14	124
1992	1.0620	0.9	23.10	8.798	72.00	10.479	165	8.96	129
1994	1.0809	0.8	22.39	8.958	74.87	10.195	230	24.04	148
1996	1.0982	0.7	22.34	9.196	73.46	10.654	230	39.79	159
1998	1.1135	0.6	21.61	9.457	75.44	10.431	295	50.96	177
2000	1.1266	0.5	21.37	9.630	73.29	11.065	297	56.74	183
2002	1.1378	0.5	20.81	9.736	72.53	11.298	298	60.17	186
2004	1.1476	0.4	20.53	9.831	71.82	11.505	298	61.57	189
2006	1.1561	0.3	19.86	9.905	71.06	11.687	299	61.12	189
2008	1.1639	0.3	19.48	9.978	70.24	11.868	299	60.71	189
2010	1.1710	0.3	18.62	10.070	69.39	12.068	299	60.34	189
2012	1.1774	0.3	18.01	10.178	68.47	12.285	299	60.01	189
2014	1.1831	0.2	16.89	10.313	67.52	12.529	299	59.73	189
2016	1.1880	0.2	16.00	10.470	66.48	12.796	299	59.48	189
2018	1.1927	0.2	14.61	10.654	65.38	13.101	299	59.24	189
2020	1.1975	0.2	13.46	10.856	64.19	13.436	299	59.01	189
2022	1.2023	0.2	12.17	11.076	62.95	13.800	299	58.77	189
2024	1.2071	0.2	10.70	11.321	61.61	14.208	299	58.54	189

6.8.3. Combination policy 1 with tourism

This combination policy serves to reduce unemployment further, but only by 2 per cent (see Table 6.15). Very little other change is introduced, though of course the model cannot demonstrate the physical impact of further hotels on the Mauritian coastline.

6.8.4. Controlled rate of EPZ growth to maintain low unemployment

In this policy the rate of capital formation in the EPZ is related to unemployment levels, so that as unemployment falls, so does investment in the EPZ, tending towards a balance. Table 6.16 presents results.

The outcome is surprising, in that it requires only a 50 per cent increase in EPZ capital over 1985 levels to bring unemployment down to a steady value of 1.5 per cent. Sustainability rises for a while, peaking at 70.1 per cent in 1998, and thereafter falls

Table 6.16 MECCO – Combined Policy Run C4 (see text for details)

TIME	*POP E+06*	*PGR %*	*PERUNE %*	*MSOL E+03*	*SUST %*	*TEIMP E+06*	*KWHB E+06*	*SSC %*	*NSOL*
1986	0.9969	1.2	20.94	8.723	69.78	10.196	103	9.5	112
1988	1.0197	1.1	20.57	9.100	67.65	10.946	103	9.3	114
1990	1.0415	1.0	19.53	9.248	69.57	10.849	162	9.1	124
1992	1.0620	0.9	18.58	9.353	69.60	11.285	165	9.0	129
1994	1.0809	0.8	17.14	9.683	71.58	11.253	230	24.0	148
1996	1.0982	0.7	16.08	10.087	69.51	11.960	230	39.8	159
1998	1.1135	0.6	14.82	10.503	70.71	11.973	295	51.0	177
2000	1.1266	0.5	13.79	10.821	68.09	12.828	297	56.7	183
2002	1.1378	0.5	12.89	11.053	66.83	13.256	298	60.2	186
2004	1.1476	0.4	11.96	11.268	65.70	13.646	298	61.6	189
2006	1.1561	0.3	11.08	11.446	64.54	13.989	299	61.1	189
2008	1.1639	0.3	10.19	11.618	63.38	14.321	299	60.7	189
2010	1.1710	0.3	9.24	11.797	62.22	14.654	299	60.3	189
2012	1.1774	0.3	8.24	11.986	61.05	14.991	299	60.0	189
2014	1.1831	0.2	7.14	12.190	59.87	15.338	299	59.7	189
2016	1.1880	0.2	5.95	12.413	58.67	15.698	299	59.5	189
2018	1.1927	0.2	4.67	12.653	57.41	16.081	299	59.2	189
2020	1.1975	0.2	3.27	12.909	56.12	16.488	299	59.0	189
2022	1.2023	0.2	1.72	13.186	54.76	16.928	299	58.8	189
2024	1.2071	0.2	−0.04	13.492	53.32	17.414	299	58.5	189

to 53 per cent in 2025. The serious aspect of the policy is that by 2025 the national debt has reached 58 billion Rs (cf. RP 25.5). It would seem that if the EPZ concept were to be successful in assisting the development of the Mauritian economy, there would have to be a higher element of indigenous input. In the next policy run, this possibility is explored by way of reducing the fraction of output allocated to consumption, leaving more for industrial development.

6.8.5. Feedback from borrowing to indigenous investment

In MECCO total indigenous capital formation (TICF) is a function of the product of net output (i.e. output less raw material imports to support output) times FOPAI, the fraction of industrial production allocated to investment. If growth is to occur without incurring ever-increasing loans, a larger proportion of output must be invested and less consumed. In order not to create a situation of declining standard of living which would be politically embarrassing, a feedback loop is added in which

Table 6.17 MECCO – Combined Policy Run C5 (see text for details)

TIME	*POP* *E+06*	*FOPAI* *%*	*TLOAN* *E+09*	*PERUNE* *%*	*MSOL* *E+03*	*SUST* *%*
1986	0.9969	11.6	5.692	20.95	8.618	70.23
1988	1.0197	12.3	6.741	20.63	8.789	68.98
1990	1.0415	12.6	7.908	19.67	8.875	71.29
1992	1.0620	13.0	9.334	18.78	8.943	71.58
1994	1.0809	14.1	10.612	17.42	9.188	74.11
1996	1.0982	15.3	11.309	16.45	9.445	72.75
1998	1.1135	16.6	11.713	15.32	9.701	74.85
2000	1.1266	17.5	11.625	14.44	9.870	72.92
2002	1.1378	18.2	11.248	13.72	9.997	72.25
2004	1.1476	18.9	10.715	12.99	10.117	71.67
2006	1.1561	19.4	10.027	12.32	10.213	71.03
2008	1.1639	20.0	9.264	11.67	10.306	70.36
2010	1.1710	20.6	8.455	10.99	10.402	69.72
2012	1.1774	21.2	7.606	10.30	10.501	69.09
2014	1.1831	21.8	6.720	9.57	10.603	68.48
2016	1.1880	22.5	5.798	8.80	10.709	67.89
2018	1.1927	23.2	4.886	8.04	10.816	67.30
2020	1.1975	23.9	4.001	7.28	10.921	66.70
2022	1.2023	24.7	3.115	6.51	11.028	66.09
2024	1.2071	25.4	2.242	5.70	11.136	65.47

FOPAI increases as MSOL rises, thus attenuating the rise in MSOL. This yields the equation:

$$\text{FOPAI} = (\text{MSOL}/\text{MSOL85}) * 0.09$$

where 9 per cent is the 1985 value of FOPAI in Mauritius.

This reduces national debt significantly by the year 2025, from the figure of 58 billion Rs to 32 billion Rs (see Table 6.17). By 2025 FOPAI has risen to 16 per cent, yet MSOL has scarcely dropped. However this is also considered to be too high a figure. The fact that a rise in FOPAI has little effect on living standards, yet serves to reduce national debt, encouraged the authors to explore the impact of FOPAI further. A feedback loop was introduced by which increases in borrowing pushed FOPAI higher. Table 6.17 shows that it is perfectly possible to maintain growth and living standards while actually reducing national debt. National debt rises to 11.7 billion Rs in 1998, at which point FOPAI has risen from the 1985 figure of 9 per cent to 17 per cent. Thereafter, FOPAI continues to climb reaching 25 per cent in 2025, but national debt actually declines, dropping to

2.42 billion Rs by 2025. This is half the 1985 value. Sustainability is then 65.1 per cent (cf. RP 59.3).

The modification to the programme was as follows:

FOPAI = 0.09 * (MSOL/MSOLI) * (RCFM2/RCF85)

RCFM2 is the rate of borrowing necessary to maintain 2 per cent annual growth in Mauritian manufacturing industry (MCAP).

6.8.6. MECCO review

This study has revealed MECCO to be a highly interactive model, readily responding to changes in policy. Unfortunately validation is not possible given that the base year for the model's initiation is 1985. None the less, where the outcome is a physical consequence one can be confident of the numerical result. To ascribe to any one policy the word 'best', would be to assume a value judgement that the authors would rather leave to the user. It is worth noting, since the authors have spent a considerable time on this study, that they still regard MSOL, Sustainability, Unemployment and National Debt as the key criteria for judging the merits of a policy.

6.8.7. Scope for further study

There is always scope for further study, both in testing model structure, and improving and disaggregating the data base. For example in MECCO, animal and fish protein sectors have been treated as one sector, whereas it is obvious that they are entirely different. This approach was taken in response to time and data constraints. However, the greatest challenge remains to explore policies that will enhance Mauritian sustainability. We mention below some ideas that may be worthy of study.

Fishing : Mauritius has an enormous fishing zone, largely unexploited by Mauritian boats. Effectively this extends the area for solar capture (one basis of energy provision), but also extends the potential for export. The present policy of leasing rights to foreign boats should be examined by MECCO to evaluate where future policy could lie.

Import substitution: A major factor in the comparatively low sustainability of the country is the fact that so much is imported in the way of raw materials – reflected in the terms RMI and IMPGD in the program listing. Enhanced use of indigenous materials would raise sustainability. MECCO could be used to establish the sort of effect this might have on unemployment and MSOL.

Further development of sugar cane: Genetic advances in sugar cane could provide higher levels of intensification, higher sugar yields and higher fibre yields. It is unlikely to be able to do all three to the same degree. The first two offer a means of producing more sugar (if there is a market), a substrate for biochemical transformation to high value products or the release of more land for indigenous food production. The last offers additional bagasse and hence indigenous electricity generation.

There is also a cultural factor that could assist sustainability. Today there are substantial imports of rice, which could be substituted by less costly local cereals. This requires acceptance of these products by the population.

ACKNOWLEDGEMENTS

This chapter is an extract from the final report – *Exploring the Potential For Enhanced National Welfare through the Use of 'The ECCO – Economic Co-ordination Model'* commissioned by Unesco in May 1987.

The authors would like to thank Unesco for financial support and the University of Mauritius and its Vice-Chancellor, Professor J. Manrakhan, for moral and financial support. Thanks are also due to the organisers of the International Workshop/Seminar – Modelling for Population and Sustainable Development, The Netherlands – who enabled us to present our study. Finally thanks are due to the University of Edinburgh in general and to the Centre for Human Ecology in particular for providing facilities to develop the final model.

REFERENCES

Baguant, J. *Energy data book: Mauritius*, University of Mauritius, Reduit, 1982.

Baguant, J. 'Electricity from the sugar industry', *Biomass Journal*, 1984a.

Baguant, J. 'The sugar industry as a major supplier of energy', Bioenergy Conference, Gothenburg, Sweden, 1984b.

CSO. Bi-annual statistical reports, Port Louis, 1985, 1986, 1987.

Harel, P. Water resource assessment (SIGMA, Mauritius), private communication.

Manrakhan, J. *Mauritius 2000: a generalised framework for academic activities*, University of Mauritius, Reduit, 1985.

7

MODELLING FOR POPULATION AND SUSTAINABLE DEVELOPMENT IN KENYA

B. K. Njoka

7.1. INTRODUCTION

ECCO, Enhancing Population Carrying Capacity Options, is a modelling approach developed by Professor M. Slesser of the Resources Use Institute, Scotland. The approach relates the dynamics of, and the potential for population growth.

The methodology involves a resource accounting approach to assessing the long-term options for national development. It could be used as a means of exploiting the long-term consequences of key policy options particularly those pertaining to population growth.

7.1.1. Background information

The United Nations has been concerned about population, resources, environment and economic development for many years. This led to the creation of a trust fund in 1982 to encourage joint research among the different organisations of the United Nations system. In the same year a project put forward by the Food and Agriculture Organisation of the United Nations (FAO) and the United Nations Education, Science and Cultural Organisation (Unesco) was approved.

FAO had already carried out some work through its Agro-Ecological Zone Project. Methods had been developed to estimate the population that could be fed at various levels of agricultural input. This was achieved by assessing the productivity potential and quantity of inputs required to meet self-sufficiency in food.

Kenya was one of the countries where this study was carried out and in fact from the study a Kenyan Agricultural Data Base was developed. Unesco for its part had evolved means of assessing, in quantifiable terms and including all aspects of the economy, how national carrying capacity could be enhanced through time. This, as described in the introduction, involved the development of a methodology designed to help governments identify possible long-term outcomes of policy options. A pilot study to experiment with the methodology was carried out in Kenya where much prior investigation had been carried out, and where there was also the high population growth rate.

A working group including Professor Slesser and Mwenge International Associates carried out the pilot study. Additional data was collected, and a number of illustrative scenarios were run.

7.1.2. Methodology

The methodology involves a system of resource accounting in which the demand for resources is matched with their availability. The resource accounting approach involves quantification in terms of energy; for example, goods and services are expressed in terms of the energy required to produce them.

Energy serves as the numeraire for quantifying inputs and outputs and provides a method of accounting which overcomes the problem of attributing money values to economic and related activities. The energy analysis sets out to assess the energy that has to be sequestered in order to make goods and/or services available. It includes factors such as the energy required to provide energy; for example, the energy required to process and transport a barrel of oil, or the energy required to produce a kilogramme of pesticide from raw materials. This energy is termed as Gross Energy Requirement (GER) and is measured in megajoules or gigajoules per kilogramme of product or unit produced.

The ECCO model was developed to manage the complexity of data and interactions involved in this methodology of dynamic resource accounting.

7.2. A REVIEW OF THE KENYAN ECCO MODEL

Kenya was chosen for the initial pilot study as the country already had a significant data base arising from FAO's agro-ecological study on population supporting capacity in Kenya. The country's high population growth rate was another reason. Additional data were generated with the assistance of Mwenge International Associates of Nairobi, and these were then recast into energy terms. Time and finance for the pilot study were limited and the results obtained could only be regarded as tentative.

The following sectors were included in the pilot study:

- Population Sector
- Area Sector
- Industrial Sector
- Services Sector
- Tourist Sector
- Borrowing and Aid Sector
- Agricultural Sector
- Energy Supply Sector
- Solar Sector
- Hydro and Geothermal Sector
- Biomass Sector
- Water Sector
- Trade Sector
- Oil Refinery Sector
- Non-Food Crop Sector

The following seven scenarios were run to test the Kenya ECCO Model:

Run 1 This was the reference scenario where conditions prevailing in 1980 were sustained under the following conditions:

population growth rate: 3.8 per cent;

birth rate in the reproductive age groups continued to grow at 11.5 per cent and the death rate in the three major population sub-divisions remained unchanged;

loans continued to be provided at a rate equal to 1980 per capita rate;

four planned hydro-power and geothermal facilities were introduced and a proposal regarding fuel wood was implemented.

Run 2 The birth rate was reduced to 1.9 per cent by 1995 but other conditions remained as in Run 1.

Run 3 Fiscal change: Run 2 plus, as from 1985, a rise in industrial output from a fraction of 0.248 to 0.5, remaining at that level thereafter.

Run 4 Enhanced borrowing: Run 3 plus a rise in the rate of borrowing to 2.5 times the previous year between 1985–95.

Run 5 Run 4 plus self-sufficiency in energy as an objective.

Run 6 Stringent birth control to yield a 1 per cent population growth rate plus improved land management; further modification to Run 4 by having a firmer birth-rate policy reducing population growth to 1 per cent by 2020 and introducing better agricultural management leading to an input/output yield relationship found in the subsistence agricultural sector.

Run 7 Run 6 plus an interest rate of zero; instead of borrowing, aid is granted at a rate equal to the 1980 borrowing per capita rate.

In the reference scenario, the results were disastrous: falling output, a huge population by 2020 (75 million) depending on food imports to survive, and a very sharp drop in biomass output due to the exhausting of standing biomass.

In Run 2, even after reducing population growth rate to 1.9 per cent by 2000, it was found to be insufficient to solve Kenya's impending crisis, unless accompanied by greatly enhanced loans. This is tested in Run 3, where the effect is significant and positive except that the loans need to be repayed. The borrowing eventually undermines the gains in the years up to 1995; problems involve exports to meet debt repayment, and imports of energy and cereals while also creating a capital base for industry.

The result of Run 5 was to draw capital from industrial growth, but provided no long-term solution. In Run 6 the policy adopted seems successful in that living standards rise, the country moves towards self-sufficiency in energy, and maintains 95 per cent self-sufficiency in food. In Run 7, significant advances are made as the country achieves a high measure of both energy and food self-sufficiency. The population requires twice the 1980 level of cereal imports, but only imports 30 per cent of energy, industrial output per capita is three times as high in 2020 as in 1980, and the standard of living rises, being 2.2 times 1980 levels with a population of 32 million.

A conclusion of the study was that the model indicated strongly the need to plan over the longer term. Within five years of any policy change, very little change was observed, and even after fifteen years the impact may not be evident. Short-term trends may even be contrary to long-term trends.

Further work in Kenya has highlighted that greater sustainability could be achieved by simply reorganising the relative roles of agriculture and cash crops.

7.3. ECONOMIC PROJECTION TO THE YEAR 2000

7.3.1. Population

Kenya's population continues to grow at a rate of 0.4 per cent per year, the highest in the world. It is projected that by the year 2000, Kenya will have a population of 35 million, about 80 per cent more than in 1984. The population will include a work force of about 14 million people (already born), an increase of 100 per cent. The urban population may actually increase to about 9–10 million people by the end of the century, and constitute a very high proportion of the whole.

The great challenge that now faces Kenya is to reduce the population so that the economy can provide adequately for all Kenyans. To achieve this the Kenyan fertility rate should be reduced and it is hoped that the family planning programme will be instrumental in reducing population growth rate to about 3.7 per cent per year. Economic growth and urbanisation could also encourage reduced family sizes, as is the trend everywhere in the world. Nevertheless measures that may be taken to control the population growth rate may not effectively reduce the size of the population by the year 2000, and Kenya must plan to accommodate it. This can only be achieved by expansion of the economy. Kenya's production capacity should expand at the same rate as the population. A projection of GDP growth has been set at 5.6 per cent per year for the purpose of economic development, but the question is whether such a rate can be achieved, and if so, how?

7.3.2. Agriculture

Kenya is an agricultural country with few mineral resources (soda ash, fluorspar, gemstones, limestone) and at present no oil or coal deposits. It is therefore only through agriculture that the country can provide food security for its increasing population, create farm family income and off-farm jobs, and above all supply export crops. However, scarcity of arable land in Kenya is the central concern for agricultural development, which could cause competition for land between the various agricultural enterprises.

Kenya's land area is about 44.6 million ha, and only 8.6 million ha have medium to high potential; this represents about one-fifth of the total land area. Of this, 5.2 million is allocated to crop and milk production, while the rest is devoted to beef and stock rearing (national parks and forest reserves). Unfortunately no means have been found to increase land available for agricultural use. About 540,000 ha could possibly be put under irrigation, and according to the FAO inventory survey about 600,000 ha of land is potentially reclaimable by drainage and flood protection. These irrigation and drainage potentials are not yet developed, and this means that the country will have to depend in the short term on the existing agricultural land.

Kenya is self sufficient in maize, beans, potatoes, vegetables, milk, beef and meat products, but this may not continue because of the population increase. The challenge is therefore to increase production of these commodities on the land already devoted to them by intensification. Farmers should start using high-yield varieties and more modern methods to increase production per unit area. The country will no doubt then invest more in agriculture and introduce incentives to farmers to achieve this. Although at present the country imports wheat and rice, incentives (e.g. good prices, seasonal loans, etc.) to farmers could improve self-sufficiency in these commodities.

Although non-food or cash crops are very important to the Kenyan economy, only 5 per cent of agricultural land is devoted to growing them. To achieve the required economic development, production of cash crops must also grow. This would mean intensifying production and expanding the area devoted to these crops. However, care should be taken not to encroach on land devoted to food crops or food self-sufficiency may be affected. Use of high-yield coffee varieties which are also disease-resistant would be a major aim. Replanting the existing coffee area with new varieties and improved coffee management could double output by the year 2000.

The country does not aim to expand the area presently under Arabica coffee, but there is still a lot of potential for expansion of Robusta. The Government hopes to expand this area to twice the present hectarage by the year 2000. The projection is to have foreign exchange revenue growth rates of 7 per cent per year on average.

Similarly the country hopes to intensify tea production and expand the amount of land at present planted to tea by 50 per cent; the hectarage should increase from 83,200 ha to about 124,000 ha by the year 2000.

Kenya is at the moment self-sufficient in fruits and vegetables, but this may not be the case in the future, given change in diet (consumption of more fruits and vegetables) and population increase. These crops have some advantages over other food crops in that they can be exported and are high-value crops. The country should therefore grow enough to meet local demand and leave a surplus for export, while at the same time supplying raw materials to agro-based industries.

7.3.3. Ways to increase production in agriculture

The Government has laid great emphasis on the intensification of agricultural production by the use of high-yield, improved crop varieties and modern chemicals. The high-yield varieties are better converters of fertiliser but still require substantial amounts to give maximum yields. At present fertiliser has been used at much less than recommended levels. Farmers should be encouraged and advised on use of fertilisers, to achieve the Government's goal of intensification of production as well as to avoid environmental problems.

Another very important area is farm mechanisation. Fifty per cent of total production cost is used in land preparation. For increased production, the Government should continue to ensure availability of farm machinery, and encourage efficient use of these costly resources. On small farms use of draught animals should be encouraged. It has been noted that the use of the ox-plough reduces land preparation time by 40 per cent compared to preparation using hand tools.

Though irrigation is seen to be a costly undertaking, especially where pumped irrigation is involved, it is a way to expand agricultural production to areas where agriculture would otherwise not be possible. Other options include use of drought-resistant crops (e.g. cassava, cow peas, etc.), or rain-harvesting methods.

According to a survey carried out by FAO on Land Resource Inventory, the irrigation potential in Kenya was estimated at 540,000 ha, with a further 600,000 ha of land potentially reclaimable by drainage and flood protection. Only about 26,000 ha of land have been put under irrigation, while only about 1 per cent of reclaimable area has been developed. FAO has projected that by the year 2003 about 123,000 ha of land should be under irrigation, and about 56,000 ha reclaimed. Although irrigation is seen as a means to make new agricultural land available, it could also be used in existing areas to increase crop production and the quality, for example, of fruit and vegetables.

7.3.4. Kenya's industrial sector

Kenya is an agricultural country but the Government is encouraging industrial development. In 1964 the manufacturing plus construction utilities accounted for over 13 per cent of GNP whereas in 1984 they accounted for over 19 per cent. Industry is expected to increase its contribution to the national economy and is projected to grow at a rate of 7 per cent up to the year 2000. To achieve this, the domestic market for manufactured goods is expected to expand markedly, and this will only be possible if there is rapid growth in agricultural production to create non-farm job expansion in the rural areas. The Government should invest in modern industries so that they become highly productive and capable of competing on the world market. Industrialisation in Kenya should also help to expand and diversify the country's export base. Industrial growth, such as expansion of agro-based industries, must support and promote the development of agriculture in rural areas. Developments in the canning industry could lead to new export markets being opened for Kenyan fruit and vegetables;

the textile industry would also provide a domestic market for cotton and the export of finished goods.

7.3.5. The energy sector

Table 7.1 shows expected energy requirements for Kenya to the year 2000.

Table 7.1 Energy requirements, 1985–2000 ('000 tons)

	1985	*2000*	*Growth rate 1985–2000 (% p.a.)*
Fuel wood	14,972	23,480	3.0
Wood for charcoal	8,754	17,513	4.7
Commercial wood	1,077	2,588	6.7
Biomass	1,112	2,177	4.5
Petroleum	2,080	3,821	4.1
Coal/Coke	97	180	4.2
Electricity:			
– production (kWh)	2,480	6,077	6.2
– capacity (MW)	586	991	3.6

There will be a greater demand for fire wood in rural areas and charcoal in urban areas. Demand for electricity will increase, particularly with distribution to rural areas to substitute for wood and petroleum-based energy sources.

Afforestation programmes are needed to meet the projected demand for wood. Three million ha must be developed for agro-forestry in medium- to high-potential areas where it does not interfere with food production. Afforestation programmes will also offer some environmental protection.

Electricity demand is projected to grow at 6.2 per cent. A national electric-power master plan is being prepared to provide the balance capacity for the year 2000.

The demand for petroleum is projected to grow at the rate of 4.1 per cent per year. This assumes that industry will switch from use of petroleum products to electricity and/or biomass, with road transport becoming more efficient. Oil imports will continue given the absence, so far, of domestic reserves.

7.3.6. Rural–urban balance

It is projected that by the year 2000 the urban population will reach 9–10 million people compared to 3 million in 1984. Accommodation of this larger population means the construction of six more cities like Nairobi. It is the Government's policy to promote smaller urban centres throughout the country, facilitating a dispersed pattern of urban development. This aims to divert rural migration to the big urban centres, but would require government investment in infrastructure to make such small urban centres attractive.

7.4. ECCO KENYA – PHASE II

It has been observed that even with the Kenyan FAO Agro-Ecological Zone Study, the overall Kenyan data base used in the pilot study was not adequate and further work is required to improve and update it. There is a need to reformulate ECCO and create an agro-industry sector. This sector would include cash crops and an agro-bank to allocate foreign exchange, giving priority to agro-industry capital formation. This would specify foreign currency flows (earned from cash crops and providing capital for the acquisition of bulk capital (goods) as well as an important component of the Kenyan industrial sector.

Other sectors which need to be specified are housing and rural–urban migration. These sectors require urgent planning on short- and long-term bases.

In Phase II, the Kenyan ECCO model will be adapted to fit the current national situation, requiring detailed data analysis. The data base required for all the major sectors will include:

- population projection;
- profile of food output and demand with food balance sheets;
- profile of total agricultural output and its utilisation in terms of domestic consumption and export;
- land resources and utilisation which include agricultural land use, non-agricultural land use and forestry;
- profile of energy output and demand;
- profile of housing and its demand on land and other resources;
- profile of industrialisation;
- profile of water availability and use, which includes estimates

of available resources and their uses for all types of economic activity (e.g. irrigation, power, domestic use, etc.);
- rural–urban migration – to deal with environmental problems and other stresses that could occur;
- profiles of tourism, and others.

7.5. CONCLUSION

This paper is based on Kenya's Sessional Paper I – 1986 on economic management for renewed growth. It outlines the Government's economic projection and policy strategies to meet certain set goals by the year 2000. The Kenya ECCO Phase II could be used to assess and explore the long-term consequences of these key policies. It could then be used as a planning tool to look at the overall national strategy for sustainable development, given relationships between population, natural resources and the environment.

Part III

FUTURE ECCO APPLICATIONS

8

NATIONAL STUDIES

8.1. RESEARCH ON POPULATION AND SUSTAINABLE DEVELOPMENT IN CHINA

(*Li Wenhua*)

This section briefly describes the current status of studies in the field of population carrying capacity and its modelling for sustainable development in China. Special emphasis is placed on the introduction of the methodology for study of the Potential Productivity and Population Carrying Capacity of Land Resources (PCLR). This work is sponsored by the Bureau of Land Resources' Regionalisation and is co-ordinated by CISNAR with the joint efforts of scientists from different institutions. This work is carried out for the whole of China and for nine agricultural regions. Twenty-seven key areas have been chosen for detailed trial studies. Population growth is estimated by an exponential growth model and matrices transfer model. The potential productivity is estimated by the Thornswaite and Wageningen models and the method of exponential means with consideration of the further improvement of agricultural structure and investment. The carrying capacity is estimated from the balance between resource requirement and resource availability.

This research was completed in several regions. The simulation model for the entire PRED study will be started as from 1988, being the second phase of our work.

The relationship between population, resources, environment and development (PRED) is one of the major preoccupations of humanity at the present time. It is particularly acute in China because of the large population combined with rather limited natural resources and rapid development.

Since the mid-1970s, a number of studies have been launched to consider the population problem in China using a quantitative approach. In the first stage, dynamic population models were introduced to study the relationship between population growth, fertility and mortality, etc. The results are striking: the rate of mortality has sharply decreased while the birth rate has remained at a very high level. The Chinese population is facing a very critical situation. On the basis of the above-mentioned studies a dynamic model for population development was established. The scientific definition and method for estimation of a series of parameters have been developed, such as population size, mortality, fertility, growth rate, life expectancy and index of labour force, etc. Different indices of future population (1980–2080) are also a subject of intensive research and debate. The problem of stabilisation is studied both from the theoretical and policy making points of view.

Along with the revival of the national economy, culture and science during 1980–90, the new population policy based on quantitative population analysis has been implemented. The population control policy and the family planning programmes have met with great success. Along with these, of course, a series of economic and social problems have occurred which need to be solved. The team of quantitative population researchers is strengthened from year to year. A group of scientists has started to study age distribution, the dynamic process of mortality, and population projections for different regions and different times so as to provide the necessary information for preparation of the new population policy. The central population information system has been established and plays an active role in working out national policy for regional development. The Markov population migration model and random diffuse model have been established. In accordance with the characteristic features of the distribution of natural resources and population, simulation of the role of migration between Eastern and Western China and the approach for controlling this process has been developed.

During the last two years quantitative population research in China has paid great attention to the study of the relationship between population, resources and environment. One kind of such research is to study the dynamic relationship between population, employment, economic growth and its modelling.

Another important field of research is the so-called population regional planning model based on conditions of expected economic growth, social development, reasonable rises in living standards and feasible investment to decide the population target as well as strategy for controlling this process. Such a model has been implemented on a trial basis in several countries.

On the other hand, natural resource scientists who used to study the physical aspect of this complex problem are becoming more aware of the inextricable links between population, resources, environment and development and have started to work in close co-operation with economists and decision-makers. One of these studies is known as the PCLR project (Potential Productivity and Carrying Capacity of Land Resources), which is co-ordinated by the Commission for Integrated Survey of Natural Resources (CISNAR) under the sponsorship of the Bureau of Land Resources' Regionalisation with the active participation of scientists from different institutions.

The objectives of this project are as follows:

1 the potential productivity of food, fodder, cotton, sugar, oil, meat, milk, eggs, skins, timber, fuel, etc., in different periods and regions with different input and output conditions;
2 prediction of per capita productivity and living standards at different times and in various regions;
3 forecasting environmental change in different regions and at different periods under various conditions of exploitation of natural resources;
4 policy making towards sustainable development.

A series of resource accounts based on past, present and projected population, 1:1,000,000 land resources map of China, water-resource and climatic-resource data, existing policy and strategy for development and conservation of natural resources, etc., have been used. The temporal horizons are 2000 and 2025. Potential primary productivity is estimated on the existing system as well as on the basis of reform. There is a great potential for regulation of the agricultural structure and system in China; for example, regulation of the distribution and proportion of crop land, forests, rangeland, animal husbandry, etc., in space and time both between and within sectors.

Three different methods are used to estimate potential

primary productivity: the Thornswaite and Wageningen models and the method of exponential means.

Through the compensation of the resource requirements and their availability by 2000 and 2025, we could obtain the carrying capacity region by region as well as for the whole of China. Based on this study, a series of proposals towards sustainable development are expected to be made, which will in turn be submitted to the relevant decision-makers for further development, for example, of the strategy of land resource management and investment.

According to agricultural regionalisation, nine regions have been delineated and provide the basis for carrying-capacity studies. These regions are the north-eastern region, the semi-arid region of Inner Mongolia, the north plain, the Loess plateau, the north-western region, the south China region, the south-western region and the Chinghai Tibetan plateau. Within these regions, twenty-seven smaller areas have been selected for detailed studies.

So far we have completed the potential carrying capacity of land resource study for China as a whole, and for the north plain, the Xingjong autonomous region, and Province of Shangxi. Some interesting results have been obtained. For example, it is estimated that the total annual primary productivity for the whole of China is approximately 72×10^8 tonnes per year according to the Thornswaite model and 100×10^8 tonnes according to the Wageningen model. While current productivity is 32×10^8 tonnes it is predicted that this figure will reach 25×10^8 tonnes in 2000 and 40×10^8 tonnes in 2025 under medium investment. If we take 400 kg of crops per person per year as the minimum living standard for food, then the population carrying capacity will be 1.16 billion in 2000, and 1.48 billion for 2025, while the potential population carrying capacity estimated on the basis of the Thornswaite and Wageningen models will be 1.68 and 2.5 billion, respectively.

Another example is the study for the north plain of China. It has been found that the agricultural structure in this region is not reasonably organised. After the regulation of the agricultural structure with consideration of the balance between different crops and water resources, 9.7 million tonnes cereal productivity could be expected. The population carrying capacity is therefore about 243 million. To obtain such results, the necessary input (in particular of fertiliser) is estimated.

According to family planning projections, the total population figure will be 221 million. Consequently agricultural productivity could not only meet the requirements in cereal crops, cotton, oil and vegetables but could export 8.53 million tonnes of commercial crops, 2.38 million tonnes of cotton and approximately 1 million tonnes of oil to support other regions.

From the above-mentioned example it is easy to understand that our work is characterised by its integrated features. It combines forecasting with practical reforms in agriculture; it integrates the general assessment with concrete compensation of natural resources between and within sectors. We also aim not to limit ourselves to seeking out questions but to try to point out the strategy for solving them. Although our work is still a PCLR rather than ECCO, it will provide a good basis for the forthcoming ECCO studies.

From 1988 onwards, we shall set up a new project which will cover not only agricultural production but also the entire economy in a holistic manner. It is to be expected that the ECCO model could be used in further studies.

References

Cheng Baiming. 'A review of the methods of the study on carrying capacity of land resources', 1987.

Cheng Sikong. 'The methods for prediction of cereal productivity', 1987.

Li Lishian. 'Dynamic analysis of the carrying capacity of three districts of south Xingjong autonomous region', 1987.

Li Lishian. 'The estimation of the potential productivity in land resources carrying capacity studies', 1987.

Shi Yuling. 'The potential productivity and carrying capacity studies of land resources of the north plain of China', 1987.

Zheng Weichii. 'Estimation of the potential productivity of land resources in North Xingjong autonomous region', 1986.

8.2. INTRODUCTION TO THE ZIMBABWE CARRYING CAPACITY ASSESSMENT PROJECT (*A. M. Ruboko*)

8.2.1. Project background

The association of the Zimbabwe Institute of Development Studies (ZIDS) with the Unesco-sponsored Carrying Capacity

Assessment programme began with ZIDS' participation in the Carrying Capacity Assessment Course held in 1987 at the University of Edinburgh.

Although this was ZIDS' first contact with the ECCO model, the concepts of carrying capacity assessment, systems dynamics, and energy analysis have been used by researchers at the Institute. This prior familiarity with the guiding concepts of ECCO made the Institute readily interested in the model. Subsequently ZIDS devoted some time to understanding ECCO and recently obtained assistance from Unesco and Professor Malcolm Slesser to develop a Zimbabwe version. Variables used in the present version of ZIDSECCO are shown on pages 149–53.

8.2.2. Country profile

ECCO, in the first instance, is an approach to the modelling of population, resources, environment and development. Some modifications are expected in the construction of national ECCO models, responding to conditions unique to each user country. Below we outline some of the conditions prevailing in Zimbabwe.

Zimbabwe historically has had food-grain surpluses, exporting mainly to Zambia and South Africa. Total food-grain exports from Zimbabwe were about 500,000 tons for 1983.

The agricultural sector can be broken down into six subsectors:

1 large-scale commercial farms;
2 state farms (Arda Estates);
3 small-scale commercial farms;
4 resettlement areas;
5 communal areas;
6 co-operative farms.

Each of these agricultural systems exhibits a very distinct energy demand, water demand, agrochemical and capital characteristics, and falls within specific agro-ecological zones. The large-scale commercial farms and state farms have a high capital, energy, and agro-chemical intensity. State farms, however, exhibit a much higher irrigation content than the large-scale commercial farms. Small-scale commercial farms fall between

Table 8.1 Food-grain production: commercial farm sector versus communal farm sector (1970–1983)

Table 8.1a Maize production in tonnes

	Commercial	*Communal*
1970	839,627	245,700
1971	1,400,000	455,000
1972	1,762,067	555,000
1973	810,358	145,000
1974	1,634,356	470,000
1975	1,328,075	435,000
1976	1,287,752	550,000
1977	1,213,285	400,000
1978	1,178,234	450,000
1979	721,916	420,000
1980	910,739	600,000
1981	1,833,395	1,000,000
1982	1,213,376	595,000
1983	624,786	285,000

Table 8.1b Sorghum production in tonnes

	Commercial	*Communal*
1970	6,876	65,338
1971	7,583	136,500
1972	19,930	120,120
1973	27,886	22,750
1974	14,048	150,000
1975	5,581	125,000
1976	14,267	120,000
1977	15,199	36,000
1978	16,177	57,000
1979	18,883	30,000
1980	16,299	66,000
1981	25,131	100,000
1982	17,335	50,000
1983	7,356	44,000

Table 8.1c Wheat production (commercial farms only)

	Commercial
1970	54,127
1971	87,184
1972	82,037
1973	83,921
1974	97,383
1975	121,083
1976	141,433

Table 8.1c (cont.)

	Commercial
1977	164,340
1978	203,052
1979	152,990
1980	154,993
1981	183,316
1982	191,880

the communal areas and the large-scale commercial farms in these characteristics.

The communal farming sub-sector, historically the least productive (in terms of its coefficients of performance) produces basically for subsistence purposes, selling on surpluses. The significance of this sector lies in the fact that it directly supplies food-grain for approximately 70 per cent of the population and is not a food importer. Recently the trend has been for this sector to engage more in commercial oil-seed crops and cotton for cash; this has occurred with the encouragement of Government. Since 1980, food-grain production levels for this sector have been increasing, peaking at 50 per cent of total national grain output in 1984.

The output of the communal vs. commercial (large scale) sector is indicated in Table 8.1. As can be seen, the commercial sub-sector has historically produced the bulk of grain and commercial crops in the country. This sector was exclusively large-scale commercial farming with very high yields amid massive land under-utilisation. About two-thirds of arable land in this sector is presently unused for crop production, but has maintained its indigenous forest cover, unlike the communal sector which has suffered serious loss of forests and massive soil erosion due to population pressure and poor land husbandry. As a corrective measure, the Government has begun a programme of resettling communal farmers in the commercial farm zones alongside a reforestation programme. This has not been as successful as hoped and high rates of tree losses are readily noticeable features of resettled areas.

Zimbabwe otherwise enjoys a relatively well-balanced economy with an established industrial sector. This is based primarily on the processing of agricultural products with limited exploitation

Table 8.2 Sectoral contribution to GDP (at constant 1980 prices)

Sector	*1986* *$ million*	%
Agriculture and Forestry	540	13.9
Mining and Quarrying	285	7.3
Manufacturing	915	23.5
Electricity and Water	108	2.8
Construction	60	1.5
Distribution, Hotels and Restaurants	415	10.7
Transport and Communication	244	6.3
Finance and Insurance	241	6.2
Public Administration	391	10.0
Education	106	2.7
Domestic Services	57	1.5
Other Services	252	6.5

Note: All data in Table 8.2 relate to marketed output only.

of its diverse mineral products. The sectoral contributions to GDP shown in Table 8.2 provide an indication of the present structure of the economy.

This economic stability, however, is likely to be upset by a number of adverse factors. These include frequent occurrences of drought, unfavourable balance of payment conditions, strains on foreign currency due to debt repayment (currently 35 cents in every dollar earned in foreign exchange goes towards debt repayment), and an increasing demand by sectors competing with industry. From an ecological perspective the increasing tendency towards desertification, and above all the increasing pressure on land of a population currently growing at an annual rate of 3.0 per cent, poses a serious threat to any economic gains that the current development trend may stand to achieve, and despite the fact that Zimbabwe has a relatively low land/population ratio.

The energy sector is 40 per cent wood fuels, 13 per cent electricity, 12 per cent liquid fuels, 0.4 per cent ethanol, and 23 per cent coal. Total energy demand was estimated at 238.77 PJ in 1982.

Zimbabwe has vast deposits of coal, over 1500 MW installed capacity in electricity with a large domestic expansion and import potential. All refined oil products are imported, costing the country about 25 per cent of total foreign exchange in 1984.

Investment in electricity has been massive. Besides competing for foreign currency with the industrial sector, the thermal electricity programme has cost very strategic industries millions of dollars in increased tariffs which have grown by over 200 per cent since 1980. The most affected industries are the ferrochrome smelters, the fertiliser producers (electrolytic) and steel works. The two ferrochrome smelting complexes together demand close to 200 MW. The iron and steel plant alone has a demand of 60 MW, while the ammonia fertiliser plant has a demand of 90 MW. Any electricity development or pricing structure will affect not only the well-being of these major consumers but also will have a significant effect on the terms of trade for the export goods produced in these industries.

8.2.3. Objective

This project seeks to acquire a capability for evaluating or assessing the relationships between population dynamics, natural resources, the environment and the various national economic activities in Zimbabwe (it assumes that population is the prime mover of all economic activity). In this regard ZIDS aims to produce a working model constructed on the ECCO approach. Once successfully established and validated the model will be adopted for use at the institute and introduced in relevant government departments.

8.2.4. Method

In this project, ZIDS will work around the present version of ZIDSECCO to develop a full Zimbabwean version of ECCO. Although ECCO has not been validated for Zimbabwe, there is the desire at ZIDS to begin using systems simulation methods alongside other methods of economic analysis. For this reason ECCO will be refined and validated.

8.2.5. Scope of work

Work on the project will fall under three categories. The first is model development/improvement. The second is data collection. The third category is model validation and operationalisation.

8.2.6. Model development

The equations in ZIDSECCO are at present very basic. In some cases they achieve the desired purpose in this form. In others there is need to make the equations more sophisticated. In most cases this improvement involves determining coefficients and adding extra variables to incorporate the effects of as many factors as possible.

In the present ZIDSECCO a number of parameters are excluded which, if included, would make the output of the model more meaningful. These include:

1 CFS (commercial farming sector – non food);
2 Housing;
3 Separate mining and separate industrial sectors (these two are presently aggregated);
4 Drought/output relationship in agriculture;
5 Biomass energy;
6 Industrial forestry;
7 Ethanol – from sugar – liquid fuels;
8 Tourism;
9 Electricity distribution.

8.2.7. Data collection

Most of the data used in the current ZIDSECCO are inaccurate. Values for some parameters are borrowed from the Kenyan model.

Data collection will thus constitute a major project activity. A considerable amount of these data can be found in official statistics but for most of the items in the model, fresh surveys and in some cases studies/research will have to be conducted.

Variables or parameters for which these activities are relevant are indicated below.

Population

POP	Population
RPOP	Rural Population
URBPOP	Urban Population
RBR	Rural Population Increase
UBR	Urban Population Increase
RPGR	Rural Population Growth Rate
URBPGR	Urban Population Growth Rate

Area		
TLA	Total Land Area	
FA	Forest Area	
SFA	Communal Farms Areas	
CFAF	Commercial Farms	
CFACC	Commercial Farms Cash Crops	
NONCL	Unusable Land	
RANGEL	Range Land	
Industry		
CSIND	Capital Stock In Industry	D
RCFI	Rate of Capital Formation in Industry	
RDCI	Rate of Capital Depreciation in Industry	
RCFD	Rate of Capital Formation Delayed	
ICC	Industrial Capital Life Time	R
INDOUT	Industry Output	
OCRI	Output Capital Ratio in Industry	D
INPPP	Industry Production Per Person	
CONSE	Consumption and Exports	
FOPAI	Fraction of Industry Output Allocated to Investment	D
TICF	Total Indigenous Capital Formation	
CONS	Consumption of Industry Output	
RIMP	Resource Imports	D
RIPR	Resources required per $ of output	
Services		
CSSER	Capital Stock In Services	D
RCFS	Rate of Capital Formation in Services	RD
SCFD	Rate of Capital Formation in Services Delayed	
RDCS	Rate of Capital Depreciation in Services	
SCLT	Services Capital Life Time	R
SEROUT	Services Output	
OCRS	Output Capital Ration in Services	R
DCSSER	Desired Capital Stock in Services	
Thermal energy demands		
TEDIND	Thermal Energy Demand In Industry	
TEDI	Energy Consumed/$ of Industry Output	R
TEDSER	Thermal Energy Demand in Services	
TEDS	Energy Consumed/$ of Services Output	
TEDCFS	Thermal Energy Demands in Commercial Farms	

EDA	Energy Consumed/$ of CFS Output	D
Agriculture		
CSCFS	Capital Stock in Commercial Farms	D
RCFCFS	Rate of Capital Formation in Commercial Farms	
RDCCFS	Rate of Depreciation of Capital in Commercial Farms	
CFSLT	Capital Life Time in Commercial Farms	D
AOCFS	Actual Output in Commercial Farms	
DROUTH	Drought	
CCOUT	Commercial Farm Cereal Output	
DSTOCK	Desired Food Stock	
GNL	Goal Nutrition Level	R
RNCP	Rural Non-Cereal Protein	R
CPERG	Energy Required for Commercial Food Production	R
CERSUP	Cereal Supply	
FOODXP	Food Exports	
ANIMF	Animal Feed	R
CPP	Capital Stock Required to Produce Food in Communal/Rural Sector	R
RCSSFS	Energy Required to Produce Food in Rural Sector	D
RCFSFS	Rate of Capital Formation in Communal Areas	
RDCSFS	Rate of Capital Depreciation in Communal Areas	
LTRUR	Life Time Rural Capital	R
SFD	Rate of Capital Formation Delayed	D
RCFA	Rate of Capital Formation in Rural Agriculture	
VPPH	Vegetable Protein Produced	
RURFD	Rural Food Demand	
GNLR	Goal Nutritional Level in Rural Sector	
ENDAG	Energy Demand In Rural Agriculture	
SFSECP	Rural Food Export	
PERG	Energy Required for Cereal Production	R
PO	Zero Input Integrity	R
CERDEM	Cereal Demand (urban)	
GNLU	Goal Nutritional Level in Urban Sector	
CERIMP	Cereal Imports	D

GERIMP	Gross Energy Required for Cereal Imports	
GERC	External Energy Requirement	
APROT	Animal Protein in Commercial Farms	
Energy		
CSCOAL	Capital Stock in Coal Mining	D
RCFCL	Rate of Capital Formation in Coal	
RDCCL	Rate of Depreciation of Capital in Coal	
ECLT	Energy Capital Life Time	D
COLOUT	Coal Output	
OCRCOL	Output Capital Ration in Coal	
GJCOAL	Thermal Energy Content of Coal	R
CVCOAL	Calorific Value of Coal	
Thermal energy demand		
REDX	Thermal Energy Demand	
ERI	Primary Energy Required/Unit of Energy Delivered	
ENDD	Energy Demand in Domestic	
ENDPP	Energy Demand Per Person	
EIMP	Energy Imports	
TEDEL	Thermal Energy Demand for Generation of Electricity	
Thermal electric capacity		
ELCPY	Electricity Capacity	
RP	Rate of Building of Capacity	
RD	Rate of Depreciation of Capacity	
AELSUP	Total Available Electricity Supply	
THEDEL	Thermal Energy Demand	
CELSUP	Available Thermal Supply	
HYSUP	Available Hydro Supply	
TELCPY	Total Available Electricity Capacity	
RCFE	Rate of Capital Formation in Electricity	
MCE	Marginal Capital Stock	R
Electrical energy demand		
EEDIND	Electrical Energy Demand in Industry	
EEDI	Electrical Energy/Unit	R
EEDSER	Electrical Energy Demand in Services	
EEDS	Electrical Energy/Unit in Services	
EEDAGR	Electrical Energy Demand in Agriculture	
EEDA	Electrical Energy/Unit in Agriculture	R
EED	Electrical Energy Demand	
ELDD	Electrical Energy Demand in Domestic	D

Hydro sector		
HYCPY	Hydro Electric Capacity	
RBH	Rate of Building (maintenance only)	
RDH	Rate of Depreciation of Hydro Sector	
HLT	Hydro Life Time	
Water sector		
WATIND	Water Demand in Industry	D
WTDI	Water Demand/Unit Industry	R
WTDSER	Water Demand in Services	D
WDA	Water Demand in Agriculture	D
WDE	Water Demand in Energy	
WDEF	Water Demand/Unit of Coal Produced	R
WDCC	Water Demand in Cash Crops	D
WDD	Water Demand in Domestic	D
WATDER	Total Water Demand	D
DWCAP	Desired Water Capital	R
WGF	Water Demand Growth Factor	R
WCFD	Water Capital Formation Delayed	R
CAPW	Marginal Capital Requirement	R
WCAP	Water Capital	D
RCFW	Rate of Capital Formation in Water	R
RWCD	Rate of Depreciation of Capital in Water	R
LTWC	Water Capital Life Time	R
WSUP	Water Supply	D
EWS	Energy for Water Supply	R
PERWS	Energy Required/m^3 of Water	R
Borrowing and aid		
DEBT	International Debt	
NETBOR	Net Borrowing	
RP	Rate of Repayment of Debt	
RPD	Delay before Repayment	R
INT	Interest	
ANINT	Real Interest Rate	
MSOL	Material Standard of Living	R
IMPORT	Imports	
IMPGD	Imported Manufactured Goods	D

D – data refinement required
R – additional research required to determine value of this parameter

Outputs

The expected outputs of the project are:

1 a working computerized carrying capacity model;
2 a report on the systems dynamics of Zimbabwe's economy as observed from simulations in ECCO.

Inputs

Inputs into the project have been broken down thus:

1 financial,
2 physical aids,
3 human,
4 time.

A detailed budget of these is being prepared.

8.3. INTEGRATION OF POPULATION, RESOURCES AND ENVIRONMENT (*P. Twagiramutara*)

8.3.1. Introduction and background

The population

Rwanda's population growth rate was estimated at 3.6 per cent in 1978 and 3.7 per cent for the period of the third Five-Year Economic, Social and Cultural Development Plan for 1982–6. The country's total population was estimated at 4,831,527 in 1978 and 6,574,958 in 1987. It could reach 11,300,224 in the year 2002.

In 1987 there was a labour force of 3.4 million out of a total population of 6.57 million: 93 per cent of this labour force worked in primary production; 3.0 per cent and 4.0 per cent in the secondary and tertiary sectors respectively.

In 1978 it was recorded that 4.5 per cent of the population lived in the country's twelve urban districts and 95.5 per cent in rural areas. It is estimated that by the year 2000, the urban population could account for 17 to 25 per cent of the total population.

Material and energy resources

The impact of this population pressure is felt through a set of factors defining the state of the land's material and energy resources:

- the small size of family farms in relation to the number of people living off each unit;
- the need to import food;
- the country's poverty in terms of the resources needed for external payments;
- poor development of infrastructures (storage, processing and conservation) which might help improve trading channels between regions in surplus, and those in deficit or other centres of consumption;
- the low level of production of non-agricultural goods and services based on labour-intensive, low-capital technologies that consume little foreign exchange for imported raw materials and equipment;
- the still embryonic state of inter-city communications;
- the high level of foreign currency expenditure on acquisition of energy and imports of hydrocarbon fuels;
- the low level of technological development, and poor use made of domestic energy resources (new and renewable) which could create more local non-agricultural jobs.

The high population growth rate and low level of development of available resources have the following effects on the rural environment: deforestation tendencies, over-exploitation of the land, degradation of soil fertility, increase in infectious diseases in rural households reduced to using polluted river water. Effects on the urban environment are firstly, an increasing tendency for the population to concentrate in districts without sanitation in the capital, Kigali, and in towns of secondary size; and secondly, the concentration of refuse and polluted water in residential areas.

Socio-cultural factors

The following socio-cultural factors should be taken into account in developing Rwanda's partial capacity to withstand population pressure:

- adoption of behaviour, attitudes and mentalities favourable to family planning;
- advances in socio-demographic knowledge;
- establishment of appropriate family-planning services in each prefecture;
- adoption of more effective cropping techniques, use of higher-yield seed and use of fertiliser on a large scale;
- adjustment of attitudes to the development and promotion of technological innovations and job-creating synergies capable of generating additional income.

Spatial distribution of population

Policies are needed regarding the spatial distribution of the population, in particular the urban–rural balance. These policies should take due account of demographic changes and their medium- and long-term prospects. Statistical data important to such policy development and analysis are summarised below.

Population estimates for the year 2000 range between 9.3 and 11.6 million, an increase of between 2.8 and 5.1 million between 1987 and the year 2000. Estimates of the urban population in 2000 range between 1.7 and 2.4 million, or even (though this is an extreme case regarded as unlikely) 1.7 to 4.8 million, that is, an additional 1.44 to 2.17 or 1.44 to 4.59 million people by the year 2000. Consequently,

- planning and development of the capital, Kigali, should prepare to house one-third of the country's urban population;
- the eleven other major urban centres will have to house one third of the total urban population; and
- the remaining, smaller settlements currently springing up and expanding in the Rwandan countryside could in their turn house a third of the total urban population.

On this hypothesis the rural poulation would range either between 7.6 and 6.9 million, or between 9.2 and 9.9 million, or again between 4.7 and 7.0 million.

8.3.2. Modelling for population and sustainable development

Available data in various services and establishments throughout Rwanda are not sufficient for the development of an ECCO model. Moreover, available data on the central elements of ECCO (population, resources, environment and development) are not always reliable.

On the basis of these limitations and insufficiencies, it would be desirable and advisable that a study be carried out to expand and refine the available data. Such a research study would permit collection of data on the main interrelated axes of the ECCO approach. Such research would also highlight those socio-cultural factors crucial to sustainable development.

Propositions

The proposed research study applying the ECCO approach to Rwanda would take place through a diagnostic analysis of concrete situations on the macro and micro socio-economic levels, and from a dynamic simulation of an integrated and participative land plan model. This would be essentially directed towards the reinforcement of various interrelated development poles (e.g. capital city: Kigali), secondary towns, small towns and rural centres, and fundamentally centred on the food self-sufficiency strategy in accordance with the economic, social and cultural fourth five-year plan in preparation.

Data relating to population, material and energy resources, and socio-cultural factors, which are interrelated with the spatial environment, would thus be integrated from that dynamic simulation. This, in turn, would be achieved following the ECCO approach and within that land plan modelling. This would involve:

- a land plan modelling essentially conceived within the national, regional or local sustainable development perspective;
- a land plan modelling specially based on and supported by the overall food self-sufficiency strategy which underlies the fourth five-year plan's preparatory works.

In short, in the Rwandan context, the setting up of an ECCO model suitable for integrated resources planning and which takes demographic features into account, requires (as mentioned above) additional research studies that would be carried out by a multidisciplinary team. Further, these studies would complement a short exploratory study aiming to define concisely the major interrelationships between resources, environment and development.

The major axes of the proposed research study are as follows:

1 To conduct research into each development option to determine its demographic impact on the basis of reliable estimates of the changes in tendencies of the long-term urban population growth.

This research would especially deal with the problem of small towns and rural centres which begin and expand throughout the country.

2 To conduct research into development options and their impacts on the urban–rural distribution of the population.

Of interest here are changes in non-agricultural occupation.

3 To conduct research to estimate changes in the present and future productivity of cultivated lands.

This would be achieved by taking into account various predominant conditions in terms of inputs (existing cropping and animal husbandry practices, level of intensification, other inputs, investments) and in terms of outputs (yield, surplus for sale, newly acquired production factors, e.g. equipment, infrastructure, services, etc.).

4 To conduct research into the carrying capacity of rural land in order to test both current and potential capacity.
5 To conduct research into the various energy inputs and outputs.

Interest will be focused on energy required for the liberation of resources and the production of goods and services.

9

SECTORAL STUDY – EXPLORING THE POTENTIAL OF CARRYING CAPACITY ASSESSMENT, POPULATION GROWTH AND SELF-SUFFICIENCY IN KENYA USING ECCO

J. D. Owino

9.1. BACKGROUND ISSUES FOR KENYA

9.1.1. Economic growth

There has been little in the way of good news for the Kenyan economy. Tourism and manufacturing sectors are healthy, and the rains have been good, but the outlook for tea and coffee prices has become more pessimistic with each passing month. There is no longer any talk of the 1986 boom in commodity prices being sustained. The 5.5 per cent growth rate reportedly forecast for 1987 in the Government's Economic Survey thus appears too optimistic. GDP growth of the order of 4 per cent for 1987 appears more likely, suggesting that national income per capita will remain broadly static.

9.1.2. The balance of payments

The balance of payments deficit on current account is expected to deteriorate sharply from the estimated 1986 level of about $70 million. The fall in tea and coffee prices will reduce export revenue, and at the same time the expansion of consumer demand, which was stimulated by the 1986 coffee boom, will continue to augment imports. These are expected to rise from an estimated $1.4 billion (fob) in 1986 to around $1.5 billion in 1987. At the same time exports may fall from $1.2 billion in 1986 to about $1.05 billion. The resulting trade gap (fob/fob) of $450 million will only be partially closed by a surplus on services, in particular because tourist revenues are not growing in line with the Government's projections. The current account deficit is likely to return to a level of about $250–300 million, or possibly even more, in 1987.

9.1.3. Longer-term problems

Inflation is expected to rise from 4 per cent in 1986 to about 9 per cent in 1987, as price controls are removed and the excessive monetary growth of 1986 feeds through into consumer demand. Kenya's debt service ratio is currently just about manageable at around 25 per cent, but the sudden fall in the price of major export crops will frustrate the Ministry of Finance's attempt to reduce this. The 1987 budget has cut direct taxation as a means of sustaining growth in the private sector, but the net effect on revenue is likely to be neutral. The financial outlook will be even worse if the USA implements its threat to cut development aid as a consequence of alleged human rights abuses in Kenya.

Kenya's intermediate position between the least-developed and middle-income nations also means that the phase of easy development options is over. There is little new land to be made available by subdivision and irrigation, few businesses to be taken over from expatriates, and few imported consumer goods that can easily be replaced by local production. Tourist revenues, though still buoyant, are no longer growing at their former rate. Even the incremental sources of overseas aid recently tapped in the Middle and Far East are reaching the limit of their potential. Growth henceforward will have to come from export expansion, which implies a long and painful process of cutting costs and seeking new markets inside and outside Africa.

9.1.4. Population growth

Kenya has a shortage of rain-fed, arable land (one-fifth of its surface) as well as few mineral resources (soda ash, fluorspar, gemstones and limestone), although an oil exploration programme started in early 1986 may ultimately locate economic reserves. Without doubt, the greatest barrier to self-sufficiency is population expansion. By the year 2000, planners anticipate there will be some 37 million people to feed, house, educate and employ.

The estimated annual income growth of 6 per cent over the period 1990–2000 to stave off adverse effects on the economy is unlikely to be met. In real terms, living standards are declining and provision of adequate social services is straining state infrastructure. For instance, at the onset of the 1987 school year, over half Nairobi's 40,000 primary school beginners were unable to find places. Already parents are called upon to assist free state schooling through harambee (let us pull together) contributions. Planners are considering turning free state health clinics into fee-paying institutions. This widening gap between public expectation and Government delivery presages future civil unrest and higher crime rates.

More than 300,000 school leavers enter the labour market annually, many of them only primary-school graduates. There is a labour pool of 7 million, expected to double by the turn of the century, but only 1 million people draw wages. No more than 20,000 jobs are created each year, most of which are provided by the manufacturing sector. The Government would like to implement an expansion of job opportunities on smallholder farms and in rural market towns. Regardless, demand for work in the future will accelerate rather than abate as half of Kenya's 21.1 million population is under fifteen years old. Greatest pressure on industry to adopt labour intensive methods and increasingly vocal trade union movements are expected. The need to defuse this potential time bomb has been recognised by many members of Government. The national Council on Population and Development has targeted a reduction of population growth to 3.3 per cent by 1988. Donors, led by the World Bank and the United States, have stepped up contributions to family planning programmes, but public enthusiasm, inhibited by traditional values, lags behind.

This study attempts to link the population factor to overall development needs over a period of time taking into consideration the availability and utilisation of both physical and human resources as well as social and cultural goals to which human effort is directed. It will also estimate Kenya's population changes with reference not only to economic resources and environmental appraisals, but also to socio-cultural ends expressed in terms of quality of life. This requires a deep comprehension of Kenya's demographic factors for long-term development strategy in relation to natural resources, industrialisation, environment quality, socio-cultural environment and skills. The study will be based on a balanced approach within which the final result would be a symbiosis of descriptive assessment and refined assessment based on statistical analysis.

9.2. USE OF ECCO

9.2.1. Background

In 1981, with financial support of UNFPA, a small group comprising participants from Egypt, Sri Lanka and Kenya met at Unesco to discuss how the relationship between population, resources and environmental factors might be assessed and quantified in such a way as to indicate realistic options and policies for long-term development, particularly with regard to population change. The ECCO approach developed by Professor Slesser was discussed. This approach concentrates on the requirements of population change in relation to food production and associated energy needs for intensification of agriculture. It was agreed that the concept of carrying capacity was a useful means of comprehending population–resource–environment relationships by providing a physical framework within which shorter-term economic objectives might be met. It was proposed that the approach be extended to cover all sectors of the economy in more detail. The approach was evaluated by a second working group held in Unesco in May 1984, with participants from Thailand, Kenya, Jordan, Sri Lanka and Burundi. The group decided to adopt the methodology 'as a common basis for the assessment of carrying capacity and the development of a new and more holistic approach to long-term planning'.

9.2.2. Objectives

This study is not concerned with issues regarding the feasibility of certain prospects of economic growth. It is concerned with carrying capacity – the total resource system and its potential –

and identifies the critical areas of stress and imbalance related to certain levels of growth and development. It also attempts to indicate where the pattern of growth is likely to exceed the limits of sustainable development. As such its objectives span both the short and the long term.

Immediate objectives are:

1 as a component of an inter-country programme co-ordinated through Unesco, to contribute to the search for, and refinement of, methods for evaluating and quantifying the relationships between population, resources and the environment in the context of long-term development planning in Kenya;
2 to stimulate the utilisation of inter-disciplinary approaches to population/development issues in both Government sectors and the research community;
3 to increase cognisance of the social choices to be made including family-size changes in Kenya;
4 to investigate long-term results of Kenya's population policy options with reference to the growth of the national system as a whole and to the rate at which it can generate satisfactory standards of living on a sustainable basis; and
5 to search for long-term policy alternatives for Kenya with respect to the growth of the national system and to its capacity to maintain the population on a sustainable basis.

Long-term objectives are:

1 to guide Kenya's economic development towards that which can be sustained over the long term and which bestows a fair standard and quality of life within the relationships between population, natural resources including energy, and the environment;
2 to establish a quantifiable basis for assessing long-term strategies for Kenya's national development;
3 to assess compatibility between Kenya's population growth, and the rate of economic growth which can generate an adequate standard of living maintainable over the long term;
4 to formulate a basis for incorporating Kenya's population into long-term development planning considering the interaction between population, resources and the environment.

9.3. METHOD

The methodology involves a system of resources accounting in which resource needs are matched with resource availability. Use is made of recent developments in energy analysis whereby goods and services may be expressed in terms of the energy required to produce them. As energy is essential for economic activity, it can serve as a common numeraire for quantifying inputs and outputs and can provide a robust method of accounting which overcomes the problem of attributing monetary values to economic activities in the long-term future.

In order to manage the complexity of the data and interactions involved, a dynamic resource accounting model will be used, viz. ECCO – Enhancement of Carrying Capacity Options. For each set of policy options and for a given assumption of population growth, the model assesses the evolution of the economy as a whole in such a way that each sector satisfies the overall resource needs of all the other sectors. Once an acceptable outcome is found it provides a framework and long-term target for the balanced sectoral development of the country and for determining the degree of change in family size necessary for the well-being of the present and future population.

The envisaged approach works within a holistic framework in which population, resources and environmental factors may be quantitatively interrelated and objectives related to means over the long term. Such an approach assists in determining policies by examining the needs of the population (incorporating both size and consumption levels) and the economy's ability to meet such requirements on a continuing basis without any impairment to the environment. Through this approach the possibility exists to put into effect the concepts of sustainability, self-reliance and enhanced carrying capacity.

The result is a community (nation-state) where means exist to utilise accessible resources (physical, human, intellectual, cultural, infrastructural, capital, etc.) to release untapped or partially-tapped resources, or resources being inefficiently used, at a rate sufficient to maintain the per capita material standard of living, or better, indefinitely. If national development cannot be sustained, for whatever reason, a country will eventually exceed its carrying capacity. A sustainable economy requires that agricultural practices do not degrade its soil, that forests be renewed and that a country maintain its industry and provide food for its population indefinitely. Enhancement of a nation's carrying capacity implies, as far as possible, the provision of its own needs through its own resources, whether human or physical.

9.4. CONSTRUCTION OF KENYA'S ECCO MODEL

The first task will be to adapt the ECCO model structure to the national situation. The type, character, quality and coverage of the data base will be determined for all major sectors. This is imperative for the preparation of demand and resource availability for all the key resources which are important for developing the total resource balance for the economy and the stresses on the carrying capacity. Data and information needs include:

- a projection of population;
- b the profile of food supply and demand;
- c the profile of total agricultural output and its utilisation in terms of domestic consumption and exports;
- d land resources and use (including agriculture, non-agricultural land uses, forestry);
- e the profile of energy supply and demand;
- f the profile of housing and its demand for land and other resources (housing will be a major component of total investment, and its demand on all types of materials as well as on land will be one key factor in determining the stresses on the resource system);
- g the profile of industrialisation;
- h transportation (including all systems of transport and their impact on the expansion of the infrastructure; projections should include marine traffic having implications for marine pollution);
- i water availability and use (estimates of available resources and their uses for all types of economic activity with special attention to the river system and how it is affected by development, population growth, urbanisation, and so on);
- j urbanisation trends and the links between population, agriculture and environment.

Some of the data are readily available but a very considerable amount may have to be obtained from special surveys and investigations.

REFERENCES

Fitzgerald, Mary-Anne. *The Africa Review*, Kenya, 1987, p. 114.
Frohburg, H. and M. M. Shah. *Nutrition Status – Rural and Urban*, Kenya, 1980.
Kenya. Growth and structural change. Vol. II, The World Bank Report, 1983.
Kenya. Country report – Economic Intelligence Unit, no. 3, 1987.
Mwenge International Associates. Unesco Contract – Ken 13–287, no. 387702.4, Nairobi, 1984.
Slesser, Maud, C. Lewis, W. Edwardson (1977). *Food Policy*, no. 3, 1977.

Part IV

OTHER MODELLING APPROACHES

10

SUSTAINABLE DEVELOPMENT AND ECOLOGICAL MODELLING

L. C. Braat

10.1. INTRODUCTION

Economic development has acquired a new face. Until the 1980s it was generally taken to mean introduction and acceleration of industry and technology to achieve continuous and increasing economic or GNP growth. Recently the concept has obtained the adjective 'sustainable', implying a continuity of economic activity, and a change of focus from GNP growth to selective growth, substitution, diversification and increased quality of life.

The confrontation with worldwide problems of environmental degradation and resource depletion has undoubtedly contributed to the introduction of the concept of 'sustainable economic development'. In many of the sustainable development discussions, however, a number of issues remain largely neglected, for example:

1 What is sustainable economic development in terms of concrete goals, indicators, necessary conditions, constraints and policies?
2 What is the ecological basis of sustainable development? and
3 Which models are adequate, useful and effective in the planning and management of sustainable development?

In this chapter I shall briefly address the first and second questions and more extensively discuss the third.

When a new objective, that is, sustainability, is introduced in economic development, it is quite natural that shortly after the introduction several definitions of sustainable economic development still co-exist. Aside from an intuitive understanding of the meaning of 'sustainable' by both laymen and professionals, the implications are still quite unclear.

Laymen may take sustainable development as literally meaning indefinitely continuing economic growth, ever expanding welfare, wealth and well-being. Scientists and policy makers who are aware of the laws of thermodynamics and other constraints to productive processes, but who are also optimistic about man's capabilities to deal with such impediments, may interpret the concept as forever continuing expansion and change of economic activities due to technological innovation. Pessimistic professionals may fear that it implies limited economic activity and zero economic growth.

Although a generally accepted, formal definition may never exist, the concept is none the less widely used to argue the need for anything of interest to developing regions and countries, ranging from installation of nuclear plant to schemes of game cropping.

In this study we shall employ a definition which includes the possibility and occasional necessity of real growth and expansion of production volume, but implies an overall levelling off of the growth curve at a regionally specific maximum level, which is in tune with the carrying capacity of the natural resource base and which can be sustained for an indefinite period of time.

Implicit in the question about the meaning of sustainable development is the question about the conditions under which it may happen and exist, and about the factors which determine its realisation. These questions are only dealt with occasionally. There appears to be a lack of scientific knowledge of the way in which the sustainability of economic development in a certain region, country or even the world is dependent on and determined by acknowledged economic development factors such as political structure, level of technology, education of the labour force and ecological conditions and constraints on a regional, national or global scale.

Production of goods and services involves, next to labour, technology and capital, the use of resources from geological stocks (non-renewable or depletable) and ecological systems (renewable resources). In a closed regional or national system, indefinitely sustained economic activity would require a continuous supply of goods and services from renewable resource systems. Depletable resources can only contribute to the maximum long-term achievable sustainable economic activity level with the fraction which, using flow energies (sunlight, wind, water power), can be recycled.

In an open system, the maximum achievable level can be influenced through outside resource systems which can be exploited by means of political or economic acquisition. Trade exchange rates then determine the maximum level. In both cases, however, sustained economic development implies a sustainable rate of use of renewable resources.

Evidently, to analyse sustainable development options and constraints one needs to assess the actual levels of use which can be sustained by the renewable resource systems. To determine this in any specific region one needs to study both the complex population dynamics and the even more complex ecosystem flows and cycles in that region. This is the field of renewable resource ecology.

This discipline comprises the study of populations, communities and ecosystems under harvesting and performance of services such as absorption and decomposition of waste. Traditionally population biologists have determined the contents of the discipline. Most published studies therefore deal with single population dynamics under harvesting regimes. Attention to multi-species situations, foodweb implications and competition and predator–prey relationships has been growing in the past decade. More recently the performance of the resource-regenerative (reproductive) ecosystem has attracted interest. It involves the study of the ecological production processes, nutrient cycles, environmental quality, etc., needed to guarantee the continued supply of the harvestable part of the ecosystem. Systems-ecological principles have slowly gained recognition in this area, especially in the analysis of highly dynamic and variable environments.

The assessment of sustainable use levels is further complicated by the fact that most renewable resource systems are used in a number of ways, often simultaneously. For example, a mixed pine/oak/birch forest ecosystem on sandy soils may be used for timber production, aquifer recharge, outdoor recreation and genetic stock conservation.

Renewable resource management involves a wide score of activities. Next to traditional day to day supervision and repair, it now includes the application of the theory and models from renewable resource ecology.

The questions facing resource managers are essentially of two kinds. First there are the practical questions relating to the direct achievement of desired goals; secondly, the implications of the practical questions, that is, the more fundamental questions about underlying principles, optimal levels, effective methods, etc. For answering both types of question models, and especially computer simulation models, are considered useful instruments. In the next section potential and limitations of ecological models for analysing sustainable multiple use of renewable resources are discussed.

10.2. ECOLOGICAL MODELS OF SUSTAINABLE USE

Models in any form ranging from diagram to computer program have been used in economic development planning and resource management for several decades. Their potential has been demonstrated in many analytical studies, through forecasting, creating insight into complex relationships and data organisation. The limitations have been made clear by critical users and by the model builders themselves. They include misrepresentations of real world problems, costly studies, and unintelligible output in analyses and forecasts. In the last three decades ecological modelling has gone through an exponential growth phase. The pioneer activities of Lotka (1925) and Volterra (1931) in population biology, of Lindeman (1942) and Odum (1983) at the ecosystem level have been followed by extensive efforts to obtain more insight into the complexities of environmental and resource systems by means of statistical, econometric, simulation and analytical modelling techniques.

The development of ecological methods and models for the analysis and management of renewable resources and environmental quality has followed a dichotomy. Ecological modelling of renewable resources has focused on conditions for and impacts of harvesting plant and animal populations in forestry, fisheries, wildlife, range and pest management (Watt, 1968; Walters, 1985). Environmental biology on the other hand has become an established field dealing mainly with air, water and soil pollution aspects, both eutrophication (excess nutrients) and ecotoxicology (toxic micro-pollutants), and to a lesser extent the impacts of physical disturbance and noise (Jorgensen, 1979; Van Steenkiste, 1978; Rinaldi, 1982).

The population model

The basis of most renewable resource ecology models is constituted by the equation describing the dynamics of harvestable populations. Figure 10.1 shows the diagram of the example chosen, a dryland cattle population in Botswana. The future size of the cattle population in these models is determined by the size of the initial population and the intrinsic growth rate (which together lead to exponential growth) and the environmental carrying capacity (which causes the exponential growth curve to level off and form a sigmoid or logistic growth curve). An extensive body of literature exists analysing relationships between these model variables and examining explanatory models for birth, mortality, biotic and abiotic factors determining carrying capacity, etc. A theoretical average sustainable harvest can be calculated from the excess reproduction in the population which under average conditions exists as long as the population remains under the carrying capacity level.

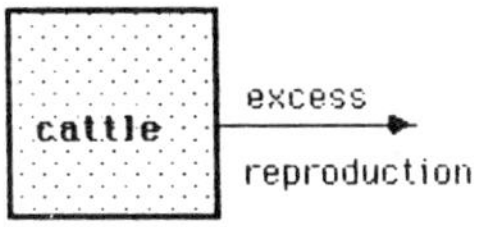

Figure 10.1 Population model.

Predator–prey

If the harvester is modelled as well, the model becomes an ecological-economic variant of the biological predator–prey model. In Figure 10.2 the cattle population is linked to the user/harvester: a human population. Cattle are used non-consumptively (i.e. without direct mortality) as providers of milk, dung for fertiliser and fuel, and draught-power in ploughing and pulling loads and/or used consumptively for meat and hides. The model shows man investing some energy in the size

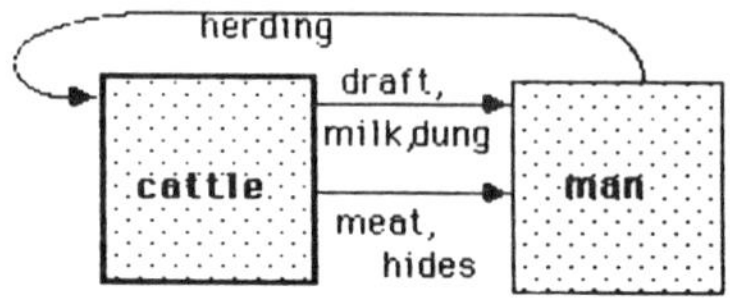

Figure 10.2 Predator–prey.

and quality of the cattle herd, for instance by providing water and protection against wild predators. The survival of human families in Botswana may not be fully dependent on the cattle they own but cattle herding is definitely the most important basis of existence for most families. Sustainable use in this model is determined by both the biological aspects of the population and the intensity of investment by the human users.

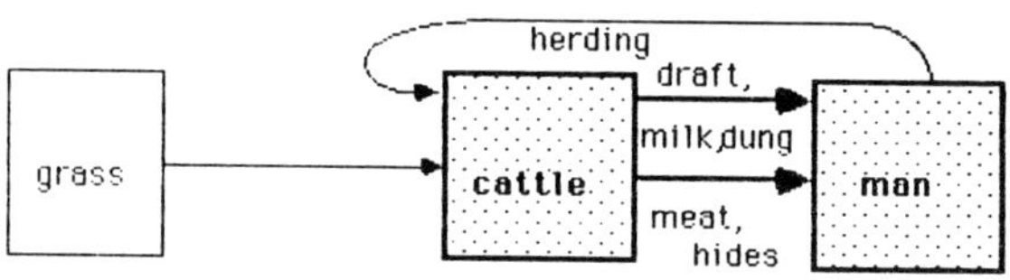

Figure 10.3 Food for cattle.

Food for cattle

Figure 10.3 depicts a first extension of the simple predator–prey model. The range as forage supplier to the cattle is modelled. In this way one aspect of the environmental carrying capacity is made explicit. Sustainable use of the cattle population is now related to the availability (rate of excess production) of grass biomass. The behaviour of the grass cover on the range can again be approximated by an abiological growth equation to which a term is added representing the intensity of grazing. In this way the sustainable rate of use of the cattle population is linked to a sustainable rate of grazing of the range.

Rainfall as driving variable

The intensity of grass production in drylands such as Australia, southern Africa and the Sahel region is very much determined by the amount of rainfall. The logical extension of the model therefore is a further explication of the environmental carrying capacity by modelling rainfall. In Figure 10.4 the rainfall pattern of Botswana (southern Africa) is therefore added. The rainfall time pattern influences the grass productivity over time, and subsequently the maximum sustainable herd size. The sustainable rate of cattle use is now no longer simply derived from the biological properties of the herd and the controllable investments of the users, but has become the much more complex result of these factors plus erratic environmental conditions. A further step towards reality is introduced by a feedback loop between cattle and grass, representing the impact of trampling (e.g. erosion).

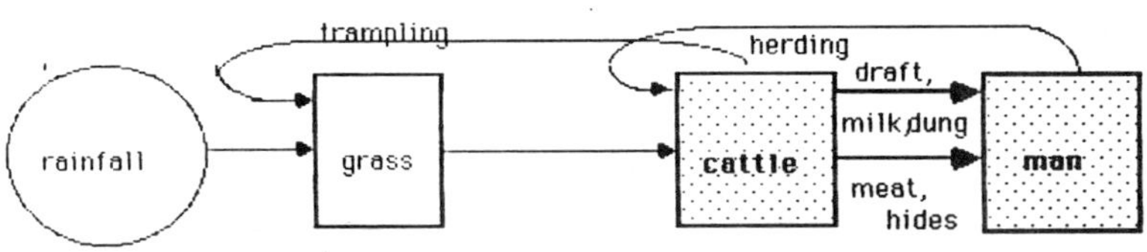

Figure 10.4 Rainfall as driving variable.

Food alternatives for cattle

In periods of drought, the mortality of cattle does not increase proportionally with the decreasing availability and quality of forage. This is due to the availability of food alternatives, such as crop residues and bushes which the cattle browse (see Figure 10.5).

Man in the ecological foodweb

The relief from starvation which food alternatives provide during drought needs to be put in perspective. The last extension diagrammed (see Figure 10.6) includes the other populations

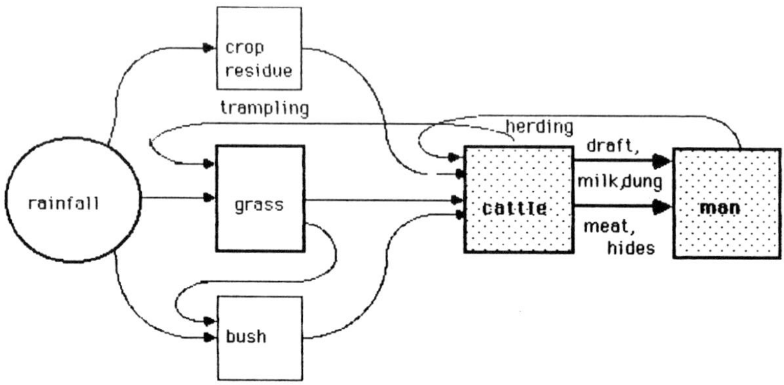

Figure 10.5 Food alternatives for cattle.

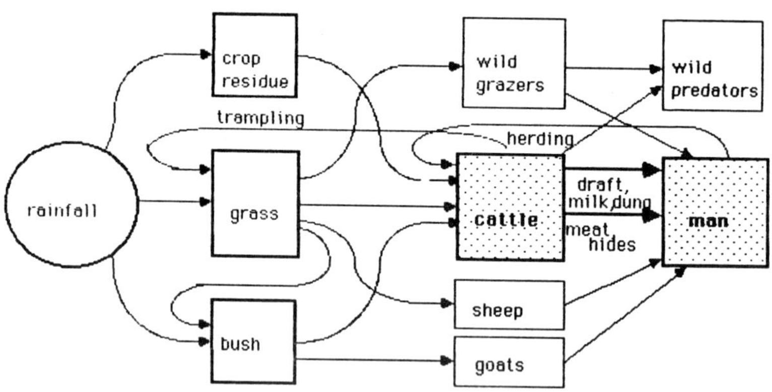

Figure 10.6 Man in the ecological foodweb.

of animals which are part of the dryland savannah system. In some areas cattle compete with wild grazers such as zebra and wildebeest. Sheep may offer competition for grass as well, while goats are tough competitors the moment the cattle herd turns to browsing.

Man may diversify his basis for the provision of his non-consumptive and consumptive needs by hunting wild grazers and keeping sheep and goats. In some parts of the semi-arid range he may find wild predators competing with him in harvesting wild grazers and cattle.

The model can of course be extended and detailed in many ways. The crucial scientific question is which factors are of greatest importance in determining the sustainable rate of using the primary renewable resource. The crucial management questions are then how to minimise the risk associated with the factors which cannot be manipulated; and how to maximise the long-term returns on investments in those factors which can be influenced. In the next section a case study is presented (see Braat and Opschoor, 1988) which deals explicitly with these management aspects.

10.3 CATTLE MANAGEMENT IN BOTSWANA: A CASE STUDY

Botswana is a land-locked country in semi-arid southern Africa. Historically, cattle farming has been the major source of rural income. A relatively simple dynamic ecological simulation model, comparable to the model shown in Figure 10.4, is used to present preliminary and tentative overview assessments of the sustainability of alternative management strategies.

The management problem

The key problem in managing a healthy and sustainable cattle herd is to match cattle stocking rates with the grazing capacity of the range. The majority of cattle in Botswana grazes under a traditional farming regime on the open, unfenced range. Essentially, two factors can limit herd expansion in a given area: food and water availability. Historically, water supply has been the limiting factor as cattle had to rely on rainfed pools and dongas. Since the 1930s, and in particular since the mid-1950s, diesel driven boreholes have penetrated the eastern part of Botswana and by now much of the western part. Therefore forage supply is currently the limiting factor. Hay stocking has never been part of the traditional system, so livestock survival and quality depend on the immediate availability of forage on the range. Overgrazing can in fact be observed in many areas, particularly in the eastern districts but also around the boreholes in the west. In other parts deterioration may not be visible yet but is suspected to approach threshold levels.

Long term average yearly rainfall, soil quality, slope and exposure are instrumental in determining the potential carrying capacity (PCC) of the range. The actual grazing capacity in a given year generally differs from the potential levels as a combined result of the actual rainfall and impacts of the stocking rate over the past two (or three) years.

Estimates of PCC run from 100 ha required to feed one livestock unit (LSU) in parts of the south-west (Kgalagadi district) to 1 ha/LSU in some parts of the Chobe district in the north-east. A national average PCC has been estimated as 11.5 ha/LSU.

Rainfall is a necessary requirement for grass biomass production. Average annual rainfall is low in the south-west and high in the north-east, and highly variable over time. Rainfall data are available from 1910 onwards. Analysis of temporal dynamics has generated hypotheses about a cyclical pattern, with an estimated period of sixteen to twenty years (Vossen, 1986; Tyson, 1980).

The stocking rate is defined as the number of hectares available per head of cattle, requiring the available grazing area and the herd size to be known. To calculate the available grazing area the number of boreholes and hand dug wells has been estimated. One borehole generally makes accessible 6400 ha of grazing land. At present a total grazing area of 150,165 km^2 is available in Botswana. Based on expected quality of deep groundwater, rough estimates have been made of potential expansion of the total grazing area by future borehole development. It is thought that in this way a maximum of 57,520 km^2 can be added in the next ten years.

Cattle herd data are available from several sources (see Arntzen and Veenendaal, 1986). In 1966 the total national herd in traditional farming numbered around 1,060,000 livestock units. A steady growth, only slightly slowed down by the mid-1960s drought, has brought the total to a peak value of more than 2,500,000 units in 1982, after which the drought of the early 1980s began to show effects.

Browsing, crop residues, and the relatively high availability of water points (rivers, boreholes and ponds) in the eastern districts have made continuous high stocking rates possible. In the western sandveld the overall density of cattle is relatively low, but around the water points and villages stocking rates have already reached critical levels.

With estimates for potential carrying capacity, rainfall and stocking rates, the actual grazing capacity per year can be calculated. The actual grazing capacity in an area may differ (yearly) from the PCC of that area as a result of the influence of rainfall and stocking rates. This deviation may be estimated using the potential carrying capacity at national, long-term mean rainfall (set at 450 mm), 2.5 times the PCC at the minimum rainfall (200 mm) and 67 per cent of the PCC at maximum rainfall (700 mm) (DHV, 1980; see Figure 10.7).

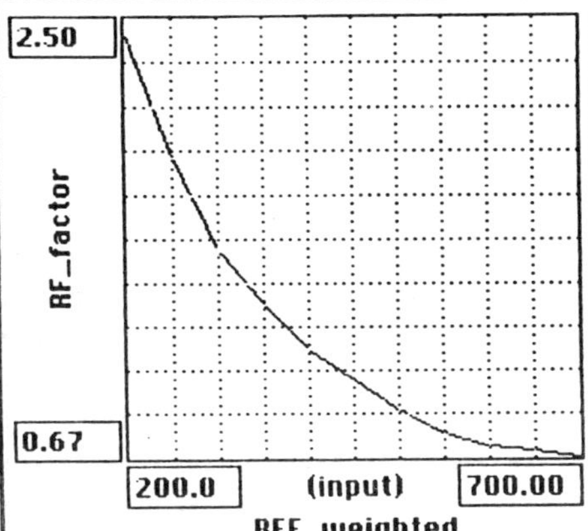

Input	Output
200.00	2.43
250.00	1.92
300.00	1.54
350.00	1.31
400.00	1.13
450.00	1.00
500.00	0.87
550.00	0.77
600.00	0.72
650.00	0.70
700.00	0.67

Figure 10.7 Influence of rainfall on grazing capacity.

The stocking-rate factor has been estimated in a similar way. At low intensities of grazing, grass production is known to be stimulated. In theory there is a balance between grazing and grass production at the stocking rate which matches the potential carrying capacity of the area. Where the stocking rate exceeds the actual grazing capacity, the latter is expected to decrease. This may be because grass seedlings are being trampled, because

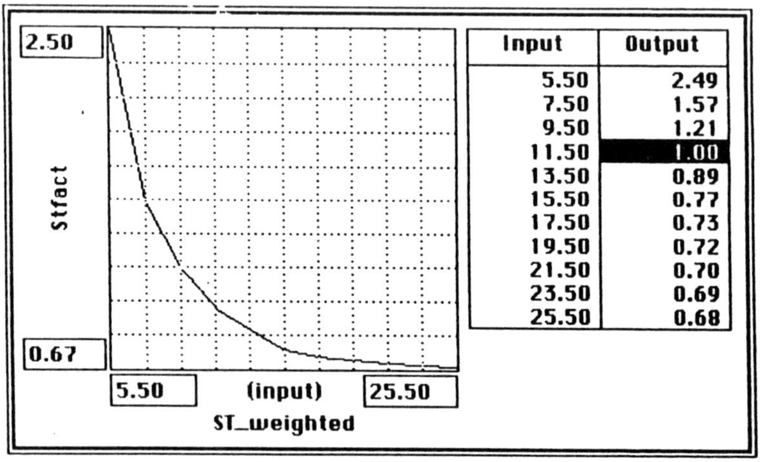

Figure 10.8 Influence of stocking rate on grazing capacity.

the top soil has been compacted or eroded and because the seed stock has disappeared (see Figure 10.8).

The cattle herd development equations in the simulation model have been based on Agricultural Statistics (1980–4) and National Development Plan data. Births and natural deaths (including home slaughter) are affected by the condition of the range. Data for estimating functional relationships between the condition of the range (the actual grazing capacity) and birth rate and death rate respectively were derived from agricultural statistics, using data from 1980 and 1981 as normal years and 1982, 1983, and 1984 as drought years (see Table 10.1).

The birth-rate influencing factor (R1, see Figure 10.9) is 1.0 if the grazing capacity equals the PCC of 11.5 ha/LSU. Limited empirical data allow for restricted curve fitting. The extension of the curves beyond the data range is completely hypothetical. The death-rate influencing factor has been constructed in a similar way (R2, see Figure 10.10).

Table 10.1 National cattle herd dynamics (x 1000) (traditional farms only)

Year	*Cattle*	*Births*	*Deaths*	*Off-Take*	*Purchase*
1980	2455	582	404	190	40
1981	2495	586	359	194	32
1982	2504	604	450	205	53
1983	2407	521	455	205	37
1984	2306	502	484	169	31

Source: Agricultural Statistics (1980–4).

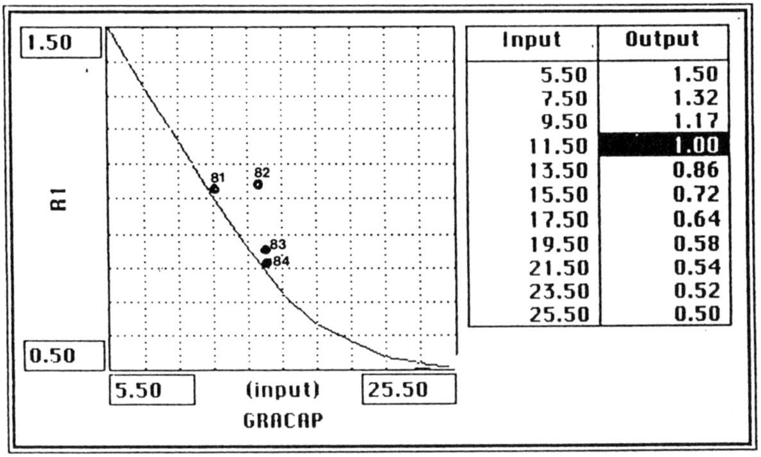

Figure 10.9 Influence of grazing capacity on birth rate.

Structure of the simulation model

A diagram of the range–cattle model developed in this study is presented in Figure 10.11. The diagram shows the range submodel with grazing area (RANGE-AREA), the stocking rate (ST-rate), rainfall (RainFall) and the grazing capacity (GRACAP), and the cattle submodel, with births (Births), natural deaths including home slaughter (NatDeath), commercial off-take (Off-Take) and purchase (PUrchase) determining total herd size (CATTLE).

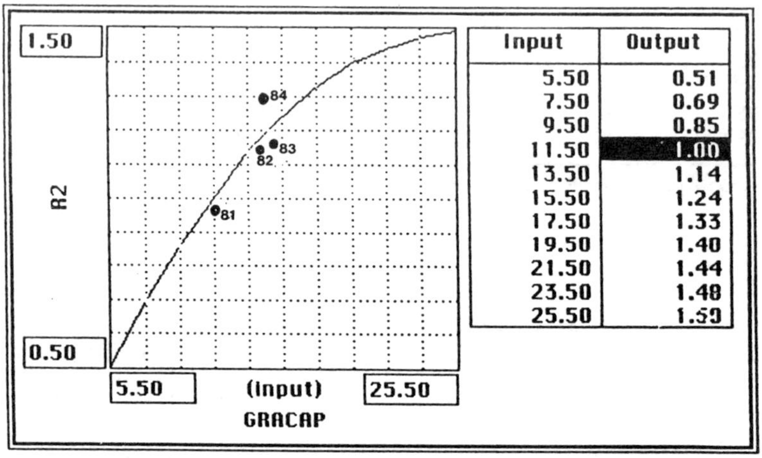

Input	Output
5.50	0.51
7.50	0.69
9.50	0.85
11.50	1.00
13.50	1.14
15.50	1.24
17.50	1.33
19.50	1.40
21.50	1.44
23.50	1.48
25.50	1.50

Figure 10.10 Influence of grazing capacity on death rate.

The two sub-models are linked by:

1 the impact of annual grazing capacity (independent variable) on birth rate – BI-rate – and death rate – ND-rate – (dependent variables) via table functions R1 and R2, respectively; and
2 the stocking rate which affects the annual grazing capacity. The effect of the stocking rate is averaged over two years. This represents the assumption that last year's stocking rate DEL-STrate has an impact which lasts one extra year (ST-weighted).

Rainfall, the main independent driving variable, is modelled by the combination of a sine wave (sine) and a yearly draw from a normal distribution (erratic) with 450 mm as the mean, representing a seventeen-year-cycle with deviations from the long-term mean for the country. Last year's rainfall (DELAYED-Rain) is taken for half its value to represent a moisture buffer in the soil (RFF-weighted).

An historical simulation has been conducted, using historic rainfall data from 1966 through 1986 as driving input. Initial

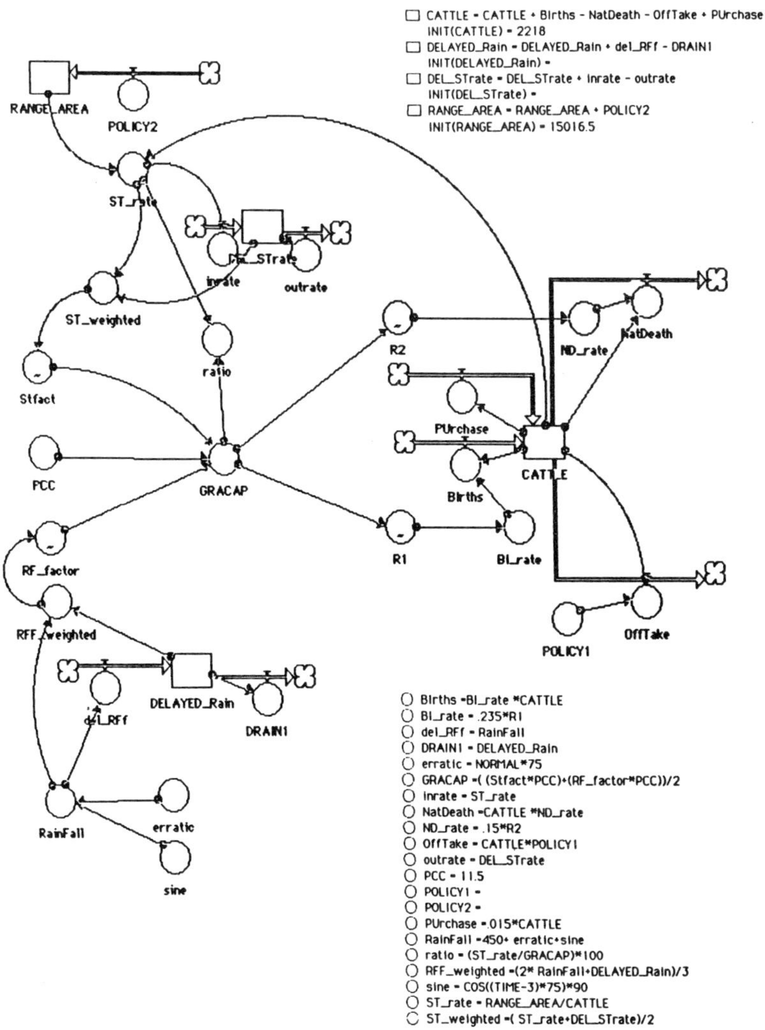

Figure 10.11 Structure of the model.

	SIMULATED DATA		FIELD DATA	
Time	RainFall	CATTLE	RainFall	CATTLE
1966	600	1060	600	1060
1967	505	1241	392	
1968	410	1434	415	
1969	423	1501	369	
1970	435	1541	438	
1971	344	1594	577	1650
1972	253	1590	254	
1973	428	1513	693	
1974	603	1506	600	
1975	591	1728	554	2162
1976	580	2008	577	
1977	464	2288	600	
1978	348	2401	323	
1979	449	2361	485	
1980	550	2344	554	2455
1981	478	2450	300	2495
1982	405	2533	406	2504
1983	356	2519	360	2407
1984	308	2455	309	2306
1985	291	2346		
1986	275	2218		

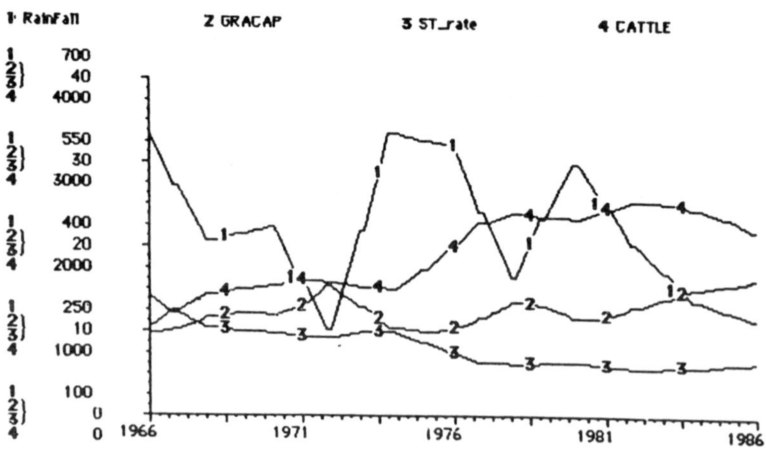

Figure 10.12 Historical simulation (1966–86).

conditions for this test simulation were: 1,060,000 cattle units in 1966, a 1977 national average PCC, and 1980/1981 values for birth, death, off-take and purchase rates. The range is assumed to be understocked between 1966 and the early 1980s.

Results are shown in Figure 10.12. Even though several initial conditions are not known and the rainfall table function can only generate historical data every other year, the simulated herd development follows historical cattle data rather closely.

Simulation for sustainable use management

Figure 10.12 shows the rapid development of the cattle herd over the period 1966–86. The model which has been used to mimic the history of the range–cattle system has been applied to explore its future as well.

In Figures 10.13 to 10.16, results of simulating the range–cattle system from 1986 to the year 2086 are shown. The graphs suggest that after the drought of the early to middle 1980s – with the commercial off-take rate held constant at 8 per cent per year – the herd size will oscillate around an average of 2.3 million livestock units, reaching a maximum of about 2.8 million and a minimum of about 1.8 million units.

The regularly returning drought periods cause decreases in the herd of around 450,000 livestock units, almost a quarter of the total herd. The constant 8 per cent commercial off-take leads to a hundred-year average of 185,000 cattle per year, with a minimum of 145,000 and a peak of 200,000. An indication of the stress on the range and consequently of the physical condition of the cattle is given by the stocking rate/grazing capacity ratio. If they match, then the ratio equals 100 per cent. If there are more cattle on the range than would be warranted by the grazing capacity, the ratio becomes less than 100, implying hungry cattle. If there are few cattle on a good quality range, the ratio goes over 100 and the cattle have plenty of forage. In the case of a fixed 8 per cent off-take rate, the long-term average ratio value becomes 55 per cent, implying a range under continuous heavy stress.

These values then represent the mean long term carrying capacity of Botswana and the variation as a consequence of rainfall patterns and stocking rate impacts.

The future generated by the following simulations may not be

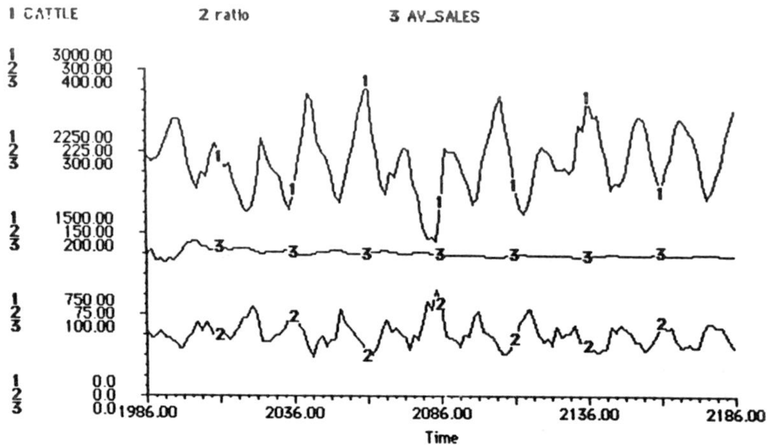

Figure 10.13 Cattle and range development 1986–2086 with average 8 per cent (+/− 2 per cent) off-take per year.

easily acceptable to all cattle farmers in Botswana. Especially those with small herds may be interested in ways to minimise the risk of losing approximately 20 per cent of their herd. In this paper the implications of two policies are presented.

Policy 1. Increased off-take rate

It has been suggested that an increase in commercial off-take rate may be an effective management action to achieve both a better range quality and more income for the farmers. The national average off-take rate has been about 8 per cent over the last few years.

An 'adaptive' off-take rate policy has been tested with the model. This policy is based on the assumption that by extra slaughter in low-rainfall years and less than average slaughter in high-rainfall years, the range is optimally exploited.

In the simulation experiments we have used the long-term national average annual rainfall (about 450 mm) as the threshold value. If rainfall is less than 450 mm then the 'high' off-take rate is applied, if rainfall is more than 450 mm, then the 'low'

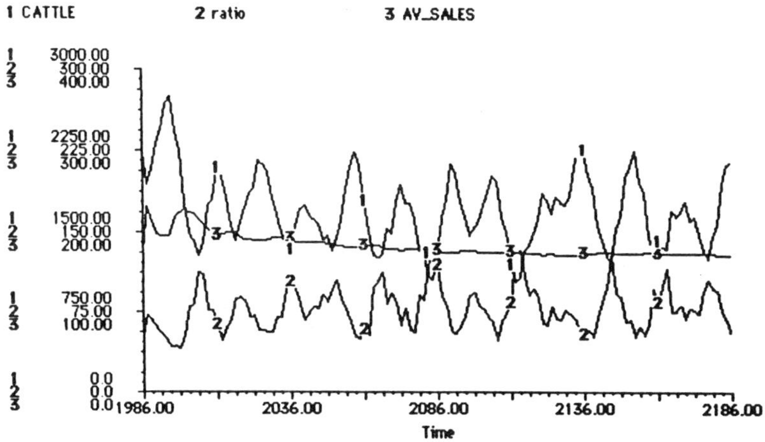

Figure 10.14 Cattle and range development 1986–2086 with average 10 per cent (+/− 2 per cent) off-take per year.

off-take rate is applied. Figures 10.13 and 10.14 show the results of simulating with an 8 per cent average and a 10 per cent average. The results of the first one are not much different from the fixed 8 per cent policy. In the adaptive 10 per cent case the herd and off-take are slightly larger and the range condition is much improved.

Policy 2. Adding grazing land by borehole development

An obvious option to decrease overall stocking rates and increase food supply per head of cattle is to enlarge the grazing area available to the cattle herd. Assuming that the best grazing land is already being utilised, additional grazing land will have a lower Potential Carrying Capacity. This implies a relatively low sustainable density of cattle on the added land.

The PCC of such additional land is not quite clear, so two alternative developments have been simulated, the first one assuming an average PCC of 12.5 ha needed per LSU (Figure 10.15), the other assuming an average PCC of 13.5 ha per LSU

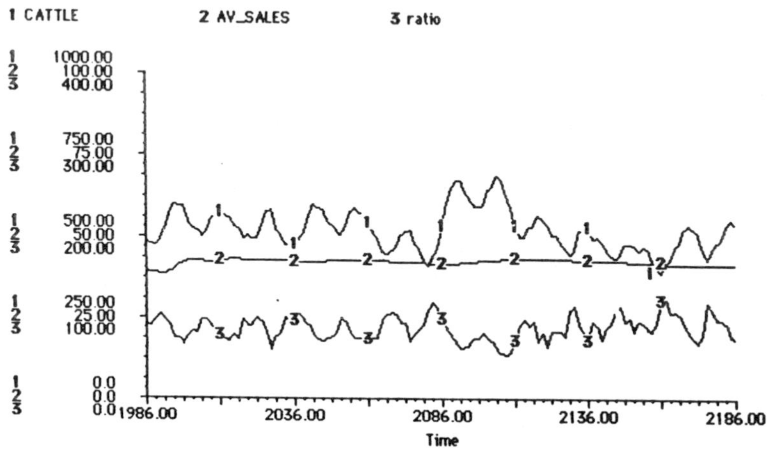

Figure 10.15 Cattle development 1986–2086 on 57,520 km² added grazing land with average potential carrying capacity of 12.5.

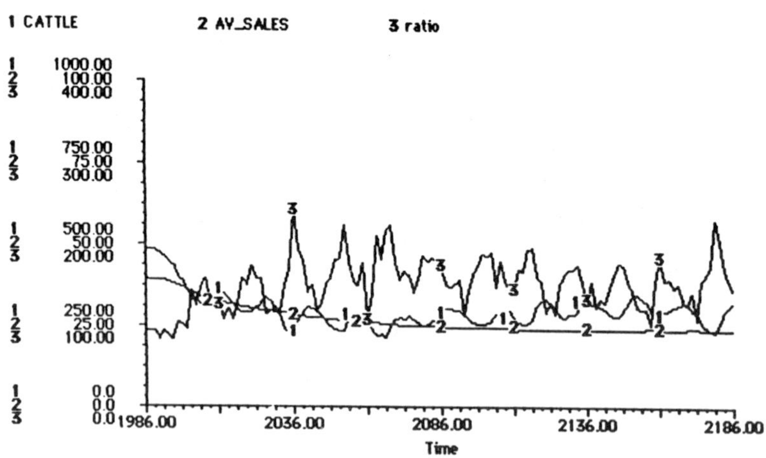

Figure 10.16 Cattle development 1986–2086 on 57,520 km² added grazing land with average potential carrying capacity of 13.5.

(Figure 10.16). The simulations indicate that a proportionally smaller cattle herd can be held on the added land.

Concluding remarks

The study provides an extended, but basically simple predator–prey type simulation model including negative feedbacks. The model does not fully represent the details of the range–cattle system. In fact, several factors which influence cattle survival such as competition, land loss by desertification and substitutes for grazing, are not included. Since only numbers of cattle are accounted for, the quality of the herd has to be interpreted from the stocking rate/grazing capacity ratio. If less than 100 per cent, the area is overstocked, implying a proportionally less well-fed herd.

The simulations indicate that

1 the regulatory feedback loops built into the model lead to a stable oscillatory behaviour, and
2 in the structure of the present model, droughts will cause serious loss of cattle but will not lead to a collapse of the national herd.

The rapid growth of the cattle herd between 1966 and 1982 will probably not be continued after the drought of the early 1980s. If present off-take rates are continued, then the herd will stabilise at about 2.3 million LSU. Maintaining such a herd, however, implies severe risks, especially for small farmers because the range is calculated to be under heavy stress (overstocked), implying poor quality (great numbers) of cattle.

Varying off-take rates (policy 1) are an improvement in terms of higher sustainable off-take and less stress on the range if they vary between 8 and 12 per cent. However, market dependency and the difficulty of profitably investing revenues from high off-take years in order to finance purchase in good rainfall years, may cause risks for those who adopt adaptive policies. Lack of good quality water and the suspected poor quality of the range in the western part of Botswana are expected to lead to less than proportional increases in herd size and off-take.

10.4. CONCLUSION

Sustainable development planning must involve the analysis of the sustainable use of renewable resources. Such analyses require the aid of mathematical ecological models. The present ecological models range from biological population models to multidisciplinary systems models. The first type of model is easy to use in management for the calculation of maximum sustainable yield. However the degree of realism is extremely low. More realistic models require more data and a finer distinction between useful and useless results. They do, however, provide some insight into the risks and long-term variations of the system to be developed as well as offering ideas for risk minimising and sustainable yield maximising management actions under changing ecological conditions.

REFERENCES

Arntzen, J. W. and E. Veenendaal. *A profile of environment and development in Botswana.* IES/NIR, Amsterdam/Gaborone, 1986.

Braat, L. C. and J. B. Opschoor (1988). 'Risks in the Botswana range-cattle system', In: J. Dixon and D. James (eds) *Economics of dryland management* (forthcoming).

DHV. *Cultivated land survey Botswana.* DHV/ Ministry of Agriculture, Gaborone, 1980.

Jorgensen, S. E. *State of the art in ecological modeling.* Pergamon Press. Oxford, 1979.

Lindeman, R. L. 'The trophic-dynamic aspect of ecology.' *Ecology* 23, 1942, pp. 399–418.

Lotka, A. *Elements of physical biology.* Williams, Baltimore, MD, 1925.

Ministry of Agriculture. *Agricultural Statistics.* Gaborone, since 1969.

Ministry of Finance and Development Planning. *National Development Plan 1985–1991.* Government Printer, Gaborone.

Odum, H. T. *Systems Ecology.* Wiley. New York, 1983.

Rinaldi, S. (ed.) *Environmental systems analysis and management.* North Holland Publ., Amsterdam, 1982.

Tyson, P. D. 'Southern African Rainfall: Past, Present and Future', In M. T. Hinchley (ed.): *Symposium on Drought in Botswana.* Botswana Society, Gaborone, 1980.

Van Steenkiste, G. C. (ed.). *Modeling, Identification and control in environmental systems.* North Holland Publ., Amsterdam, 1978.

Volterra. *Leçon sur la theorie mathématique de la lutte pour la vie.* Gauthier-Villars, Paris, 1931.

Vossen, P. Pers. Communication. Department of Meteorological Services, Gaborone, 1986.

Walters, C. J. *Adaptive management of renewable resources.* Macmillan, New York, 1985.

Watt, K. E. F. *Ecology and resource management.* McGraw Hill, New York, 1968.

11

ECONOMIC MODELLING AND SUSTAINABLE DEVELOPMENT

J. B. Opschoor

11.1. INTRODUCTION

In a phenomenological approach, economies can be regarded as spiral-like money recycling processes. This is the 'nominal' side of a coin that also has a 'real' other side: the flows of materials, labour and goods through societies. As an alternative to this phenomenological approach, economists often apply a teleological one, in which economies are viewed as processes whereby societies satisfy their needs, and try to increase their welfare by reducing scarcity. This satisfaction is seen to result from the 'consumption' of goods and services by society's members. Both approaches ultimately boil down to the recognition of a basic 'metabolism' (to use Marx's phrase) between nature and society: these goods and services ultimately originate from two sources – nature and labour, merged in the process of production. Thus, nature serves societal needs indirectly, that is, via the production process. There are also more direct ways in which nature satisfies societal needs. One can enjoy a landscape or ecosystem by viewing it, either in reality or through pictures and memories; and one can derive dissatisfaction from learning about the decrease in the number of plant species in a particular region, etc. Downstream swimmers may benefit from a river's absorptive capacity for wastes discharged into that river somewhere upstream. These are examples of drawing on nature directly for (dis)satisfaction. The majority of instances of consumption, however, relate to cases of produced goods and services, involving human labour and intelligence, but still virtually in all cases directly or indirectly requiring material inputs (energy, etc.).

This chapter presents a brief overview of the way in which economic modelling has handled this metabolism, and seeks to identify possible extensions of these models in order to enhance their appropriateness from an environmental perspective. The structure of the chapter is as follows. Section 11.2 will deal with models of natural resources (more precisely, renewable natural resources) and their 'support systems'. These support systems are typically overlooked in economic modelling of environment–economy interactions. The next section presents the neoclassical economic approach to the environment; this approach is the prevailing one in economics as it is practised today. Section 11.4 contains a critique of this neoclassical approach in terms of its relevance from a sustainability-oriented viewpoint. Section 11.5 reviews some concrete models as used in economic studies. The final section, drawing on a review study of integrated models carried out at the Institute for Environmental Studies, provides some suggestions in terms of pointers for future development of environmental economic modelling.

11.2. NATURAL RESOURCES AND RESOURCE SUPPORT SYSTEMS

From an anthropocentric, utilitarian perspective, nature can be seen as the ultimate source of all materials rotating through society, whether these materials need processing or refining before being turned into economic goods, or whether they can be consumed without such transformation. In addition, nature itself can be seen as directly or indirectly providing services, such as the enjoyment of certain scenery, species and ecosystems, the absorptive capacity of nature to deal with human wastes, etc.

These various functions performed by nature in relation to human society can be labelled 'resources'. Natural resources can be renewable or non-renewable.

Non-renewable resources will eventually be exhausted, if periodic extraction from the initial stock exceeds zero for a sufficiently long span of time. Even in cases where recycling is possible and theoretically extraction could be negative, ultimate exhaustion is the most likely end result. Whether exhaustion poses a real threat to society depends on the degree to which an exhaustible resource is essential for human production and consumption. In many cases, non-renewable stocks can be replaced by augmentable or renewable ones (e.g. fossil fuel energy by biomass) or by permanent ones (e.g. wind).

One can thus take the view that ultimately, humanity will have to learn to remain within the boundaries set by the reproductive capacities of nature in terms of its flows of renewable resources. In this paper we shall deal mainly with renewable resources.

For simplicity's sake let us assume that we can reduce the functional aspects of nature–society links to that of, say, the Dutch economy and a population of North Sea herring, the catch of which feeds that economy. That catch, then, is an economically essential resource, and the herring population is the source that the fishermen tap in order to supply the economy with that essential (renewable) resource. The North Sea is the ecosystem containing the herring population that is tapped by our economy. And as such it is not only the habitat of numerous species, some of which provide food to the herring population, but it also provides and maintains the abiotic environment of that population.

Part of that ecosystem is essential for the survival and reproduction of the herring population. It is, in fact, a reduced ecosystem: that part of it which contains the minimally necessary elements and processes to keep the herring population not only alive and kicking, but also reproducing. I call that part the resource regeneration system of the herring (Figure 11.1). It is this system that a society would wish to preserve, even if it were only interested in a sustained yield of herrings. Note that in Figure 11.1 the resource regeneration system itself is not a separable unit in the ecosystem.

The notion of resource regeneration systems has been mathematically captured in so-called regeneration functions, that relate the annual growth of the population to its initial size. They can be derived from the basic relationships of the theories of population dynamics. In the absence of environmental stress suppressing resource availability, a population P would expand exponentially with time:

$$P_{\mathrm{t}} = P_0 . \mathrm{e}^{(b - m)t} \tag{1}$$

where P = population, b = birth rate, m = death rate, t = time index.

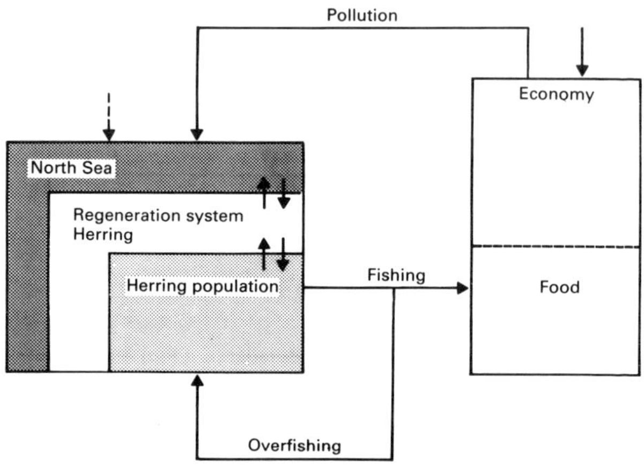

Figure 11.1 Resource regeneration system between economy and ecosystem.

However, with environmental stress E added:

$$P^*t = F(P_0, b, m, E) \qquad (2)$$

where F is some mathematical function frequently assumed to be a sigmoid curve. In that case:

$$I = dP^*/dt = b.P(C-P)-mP \qquad (3)$$

in which I is the annual increase of the population and C is the carrying capacity of that particular environment, with

$$C = f(E), \qquad dC/dE(O) \qquad (4)$$

Equation (3) is the regeneration function. If eq. (2) has the appropriate specification, eq. (3) becomes the simple quadratic function in P that resource economists like to incorporate into their models, e.g. as shown in Figure 11.2.

Our resource regeneration system is basically represented by eq. (4). In fact, (4) should be seen as a module of its own, containing an appropriately detailed specification of all relevant (i.e. from the resource's point of view) functional relationships within the ecosystem considered. Unfortunately, this entire

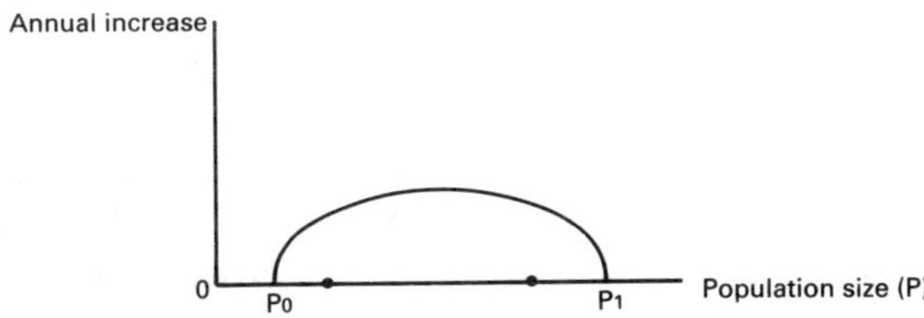

Figure 11.2 Regeneration function renewable resource.

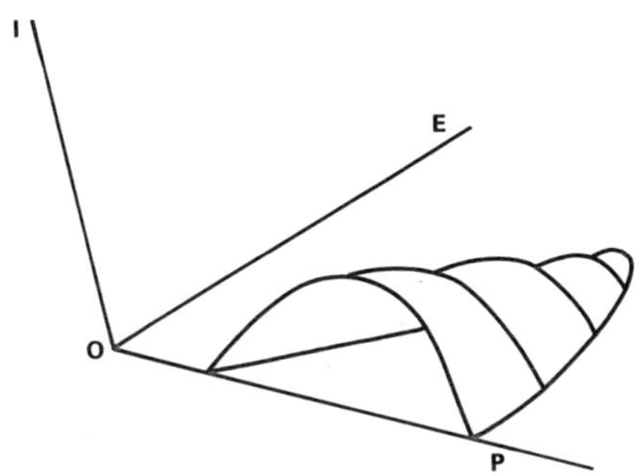

Figure 11.3 Resources utilisation space (after Siebert 1982).

module is typically represented by one constant only, in environmental economic modelling.

Eq. (3) describes *I* as depending on the environmental quality and on population size. If, through some exogenous influence, *E* would change, then *I* would change in the opposite direction (*E* is defined as environmental stress, or decreased environmental quality). In fact, then, eq. (3) develops into a family of regeneration curves demarcating ecologically feasible harvesting possibilities in the *I, P, E*–space (Siebert, 1982); I call this the 'resource utilisation space', see Figure 11.3 (Opschoor, 1987).

If one wishes to develop this model into one of resource utilisation, one may add a harvesting activity to this process. In our example, fishing would take catches (*H*) of fish out of the population, thereby reducing I to I_N (with $I_N = I - H$). A complete economy–environment model could be built by adding submodels for environmental processes relevant to the E–C relationship. This would make E an endogenous variable rather than an exogenous, invariant one, which corresponds to reality. Such additions might entail incorporating models of entire food chains, the hydrology, climate impacts, etc. Such a model can be analysed for its dynamic properties, for example, whether it yields steady state solutions in terms of environmental quality (i.e. constant levels of E and P). Also, and that is where economists tend to come in again, such models can be subjected to some ecologically constrained optimisation procedure yielding optimal and sustainable levels and time paths for H, P, E – if such levels exist. I shall come back to this latter point when discussing neoclassical environmental economics, but first I shall discuss the realism of this scientist's dream.

For a variety of reasons (of which I shall mention only three) it is very unlikely that in reality we shall ever be able to rely on this clean, mathematical approach to solving empirical environmental and resource issues.

i. The demarcation lines between the resource regeneration system and the rest of the ecosystem are very unclear, which may mean that any model ignores important relationships and processes. This point becomes progressively more important as the number of resources harvested – and hence the number of regeneration systems involved – rises. In reality one cannot reduce nature to a single resource support system, and this leads to awkwardly large and unmanageable models, even if all boundary issues can be solved.
ii. Even when relationships are known to exist, they may be surrounded by much uncertainty and risk. Technically, this could be handled by model builders, but very often either at the expense of accuracy, or to the detriment of the adequacy of the model's results in the eyes of the user. In practice many of the issues mentioned will be resolved by opting for relatively simple, aggregated models, highlighting main features – but main features only – of the systems involved. Such aggregated models, however, are often felt to be inadequately gross approximations of reality.
iii. For a variety of technical reasons (dynamic properties

and feedbacks, externalities, substitution possibilities, 'joint product' aspects associated with multifunctional use problems, etc.), the resource utilisation space will not be as well shaped as Figure 11.3 assumes. Under those conditions, various real possibilities may even be invisible to the analyst, unless he arms himself with extra information or huge simulation budgets.

One final point to be made in this section relates to the extent to which resource utilisation space can be expanded by human activities. It is clear that, in the past, humankind has been capable of overcoming the consequences of moving too far into this space or too close to its edges, in a variety of ways and means. Historically, resource scarcities have plagued societies and have led to adaptations such as

i. moving out to other areas where a new space could be occupied;
ii. trade, colonialism and similar ways of extracting resources from elsewhere;
iii. technical change allowing for a more efficient use of known resources or even the use of altogether new ones.

In this last case, the overall resource utilisation space itself has been expanded. Scientific and technological advances have very frequently pushed forward in time (to even well beyond the time horizon in many cases) the physical limits to economic growth. Optimists assume that this will also be possible in future, on an adequate scale. Pessimists deny that and often arrive at 'doomsday' conclusions. Sceptics (in which category the present author would gladly be included) would favour a critical attitude, from which future patterns of economic growth and technical development are to be challenged on their performance in terms of enhancing or diminishing the sustainability of the implied uses of natural resources, resource regeneration systems and life support processes.

11.3. NEOCLASSICAL ECONOMICS AND THE ENVIRONMENT

Following the German nineteenth century economist Eucken, neoclassical economics normally analyses the economic – that is, scarcity driven – aspect of human behaviour in a context that is static or 'given' in terms of, inter alia:

i. institutional arrangements (i.e. the economic system),
ii. preferences and wants,
iii. the state of technology, and
iv natural resource endowments.

That is, the empirical world is deep frozen as it were, in a number of its aspects, or kept ceteris paribus, as economists would say. Mainstream economics is only interested in studying behaviour within these terms of reference (or, as it is called, within Eucken's Datenkranz).

In terms of most economists' views of nature this, until recently, implied that they assumed that the supply of natural resources as they knew it, would basically continue indefinitely. This predominant view, was of course deeply shocked by reports such as that to the Club of Rome, in the early 1970s, and a new branch of neoclassical economics emerged: environmental economics. In this section, the recent mainstream additions to economics as inspired by resource scarcity, pollution and environmental degradation in general will be reviewed.

Neoclassical environmental/resource economics has occupied itself with questions such as the existence of resource-shortage determined limits to economic growth. Obviously, if there were essential, exhaustible resources for which no substitutes exist, mankind would be in trouble. However, the mainstream perceives a fairly broad survival corridor (Krelle, 1984), or survival road (Kemp and Long, 1984) in that it is normally possible to replace adequately exhaustible resources by augmentable ones, or to create these through technical progress. As long as the savings ratio and investments in environmental research are high enough, an endless future with permanently positive rates of consumption per capita is promised to us.

The next question is whether the market mechanism could be relied upon to result in an efficient use of natural resources and, if not, what types of interventions would be required (Smith and Krutilla, 1979; Kemp and Long, 1984; Dasgupta and Heal, 1979). The market does appear to be incapable of generating a permanent and prudent pattern of resource use (Smith and Krutilla, 1979; Dasgupta and Heal, 1979), although many resource economists feel that this should not be an overriding concern (Kemp and Long, 1984).

When it comes to renewable resources, regeneration functions as described above are the nucleus of economic analysis (Smith and Krutilla, 1979). To such a model of nature, one adds a model of the economy with producers and consumers, and makes an assumption on individual and societal objectives. This is typically maximisation of net present values of a stream of welfare values over time. With the aid of mathematical control theory one simulates society–resource base interactions in a number of economically relevant contexts. One then wonders whether these models have steady state solutions in terms of relevant economic and environmental variables, including the resource supply and consumption per capita, or one determines optimal exploitation paths within preset steady state conditions (Plourde, 1970; Dasgupta and Heal, 1979; Siebert, 1982). This appears to come close to the model of natural resource supply as developed above, but it fails in a number of respects, which I shall come to below. Here too, the conclusion is that absence of intervention and regulation would lead to undesirable scenarios and attempts have been made to identify types of regulation that would be required to correct the market mechanism (that is, fishing quota, charges, market entry restrictions).

In addition to resource scarcity, pollution is another example of environmental problem. Traditional environmental economics treats pollution as an example of so-called external effects. That is, effects on third parties, of decisions taken and activities carried out by some decision maker or actor. They are called external effects since they do not normally influence the decision maker, as he or she will not be confronted with the consequences. If such a confrontation were to take place, then the effect would to a smaller or larger degree actually influence the decision and hence be internalised in it. Such internalisation could be the result of:

i. social or psychological pressure;
ii. legislation forbidding certain actions or prescribing others;
iii. the legal arrangement of liability;
iv. economic incentives, such as charges, subsidies, etc.

Pigou, the famous early twentieth century welfare economist, has argued that externalities would indeed provide a case for government intervention in the market place. This position was heavily debated by Coase, writing on environmental externalities, who argued that to compensate for initial market failures, it would simply be necessary to change the law on property rights, liabilities, etc., and that thereafter, bargaining and the court would ensure optimal behaviour on the market.

In conclusion, neoclassical economics has thus looked at resource and environmental problems as though they were essentially emanations of suboptimal allocation; as though they were mainly manifestations of inefficiency. Within a set of rosy and reassuring assumptions regarding possibilities for substitution and the power of technological progress, the mainstream did in fact conclude that all was well in a basically market-driven world. To be fair, it did produce some suggestions for reforming the prevailing economic system in order to ensure the sustainability of its reproduction, but this would be a face-lift type reform rather than a fundamental one. It is this complacency that has led a more critically-inclined and scientifically-trained environmental economist to denounce neoclassical economics as 'dangerously misleading'.

In fact, there is a small but at least noise-generating group of sidestream economists who advocate a less restricted, more integrated approach (Daly, 1980; Norgaard, 1984) which would lead to a more critical view of current practice in economic choice (and the theory thereof) vis-à-vis ecological problems. They would argue in favour not only of a more integrated, but also a more concrete and historic analysis and the inclusion of ethical points of departure transcending market forces, such as the notion of society–nature coevolution, or stewardship/partnership as appropriate metaphors for sustainable economic development. It is in this sidestream that I feel that new and more appropriate ideas and tools are currently being developed.

11.4. NEOCLASSICAL ECONOMICS AND SUSTAINABILITY

11.4.1. An ecology based critique of neoclassical environmental economics

Neoclassical analysis of environmental problems starts with basic neoclassical premises such as:

1 a reductionist, analytical worldview, still containing too many remnants of Eucken's Datenkranz;
2 the notion that rational choice based on individualistic values is to underlie decision making exclusively;
3 the desirability of laissez-faire policies, etc.

When one starts with premises such as these, environmental problems can actually only be seen as unintended 'externalities', to be internalised without altering the basic features of our economic system. In my view, the relevance of neoclassical environmental economics can and must be criticised on each one of these three premises (Opschoor, 1988). Here, the focus will be on aspects relevant to modelling.

i. Circular interdependence

An ecology-based model of nature – as an interdependent combination of life support processes and ecosystems, including a number of interrelated resource support systems that society could to a certain degree exploit – is incompatible with the mechanistic and linear views implicit in neoclassical thinking.

First, almost by definition, our model sees societal activities as affecting natural resources, processes and systems, thereby making the notion of a reductionist Datenkrantz a totally unacceptable abstraction from reality. Even the inclusion of resource regeneration functions into neoclassical economic analysis is inadequate as the ecological processes and ecosystem feedbacks operating upon these functions are still not given their proper place. In other words, most neoclassical models fail as adequate descriptions of the physical realities which form the constraints within which societies, and hence economies, must remain.

Second, our ecology-based view implies a dynamic, concrete and even historic approach to society–nature interactions. It is a process-based approach rather than the abstract one of mainstream economics, and is mainly interested in patterns and distributions.

ii. Individual values versus co-evolutionary instrumental values

Applied to environmental choice situations (say, the preservation of landscapes, ecosystems, species) where society has to decide between several options, the appropriate criterion in neoclassical environmental economics would be to maximise some aggregate A of all individual (net) benefits B_i, where B_i would be the summation by individual i, of his (net) user benefits U_i and his non-user benefits N_i. Definitions vary a little from one author to the other and some of the concepts incorporated in U and N are still debated, but basically, U_{ij} is the sum of the market value M_j of the changes associated with each alternative j (versus some reference situation) and the surplus value S_{ij} of these changes (measured as the appropriate area under corrected market demand functions for the goods and services involved). And N_i is taken to be the sum of the option value O_{ij} that i places on retaining the option of having that alternative j available to him in future, his bequest value H_{ij} of having that alternative j available to future generations as well, and T_{ij} or his estimate of the 'existence value' or intrinsic value of that option, for example, the value i places on keeping a species j of animals or plants alive even if this has no use or value to him or his successors.

The neoclassical question becomes the one of maximising:

$$A_j = Z(B_{ij}) = Z(U_{ij}+N_{ij}) = Z(M_{ij}+S_{ij}+O_{ij}+H_{ij}+T_{ij}) \qquad (5)$$

where Z refers to the actual aggregation procedure, that is, some weighted or unweighted summation.

In economic choice on ecological issues concerning the preservation of landscapes, ecosystems and species, especially O, H, and T can be important, as is shown in several empirical calculations. So can, generally, S. However, normal economic decision analysis, for example, financial cost benefit analysis or cash flow analysis, is frequently restricted to the M_is and so called social cost benefit analysis adds S_is only. The H_is and T_is are thus mostly ignored. This, then, would be a critique of current decision-making practices from within the paradigm of neoclassical environmental economics, and it can be a very important one from an ecological point of view.

An additional point to be made more explicitly here because of its relevance in modelling excercises is the problem of discounting: the sensitivity of B and A to the time horizons of individuals and society. It is well known that if the Bs and As are calculated by discounting future values, substantial parts of the ecological costs and benefits and hence the costs and benefits (undiscounted) to future human societies, are ignored. Future generations are absolutely absent from these calculations, unless currently living individuals make compensations for this by altering deliberately their assessment of the arguments of *B*. This 'loss of present value' as a consequence of standard discounting procedures is important. It reflects that the time scales of market processes and ecological processes do not coincide. Consequently, either the discounting procedures have to be altered, or future events beyond the time horizon of the market have to be valued differently, or environmental restrictions in physical terms have to be decided upon a priori, in order to demarcate the boundaries within which economic calculus can be accepted as reflecting societal preferences and values. In terms of our model, specific procedures for *Z* have to be prescribed, or elements of *B* are to be replaced by their public corollaries, or the maximisation of *A* is to be subjected to explicit, additional constraints.

However, the valuation principle as outlined above, can also be criticised from non-neoclassical positions. As one such critique, I present some arguments associated with so-called evolutionary or institutional economics. Their basic approach in the face of environmental externalities would not be to express them in monetary terms and internalise them (via cost benefit analysis, or systems of charges and subsidies) within the market mechanism. Institutional economics looks for social or institutional reasons behind phenomena (such as externalities) judged to be undesirable from a social values perspective, and aims at redesigning institutions accordingly. But here, values are not the same as preferences in terms of 'willingness to pay'. Values are ultimate goals of individuals and societies. Nor can values be reduced to single common yardsticks (such as money, 'utils', energy content, etc.). Values are a hierarchically ordered system, and decision-making procedures need to follow that hierarchy. Ultimately, values such as the continuity of human life, the community, and species and ecosystems are at stake and this will imply public decision making of a non-market type, in order to identify the limits of human activities in terms of resource utilisation.

11.4.2. Towards sustainable economies

Sustainable development is a phrase that is gaining interest in a wide circle of environmentally concerned organisations and policy bodies. It is, however, a remarkably unclear concept, leading to a substantial amount of confusion. One of the basic questions (Opschoor, 1987) is whether the notion of sustainablility refers to the process of economic development, or whether it in fact relates to the impact of economic development on ecological processes. If a concern over the sustainability of societies' resource use is warranted (and I certainly belong to those who think it is), then the following questions need answering:

1 What exactly is it that we want to retain and see sustainably used?
2 Which decision mechanisms and institutions would be sufficient to ensure sustainability?

Answering the first of these two questions is basically beyond economics although that discipline may have a modest role to play in modelling linkages between sectors and regions, and in providing approaches to natural resource accounting, for example. In principle, a normative approach is required in which, at the appropriate spatial scale, norms are to be set that determine to what extent aspects of nature (in terms of ecosystems' integrity, the preservation of life support systems, etc.) be preserved, and derived from this, quality standards should be applied curtailing the amount of pollution, resource extraction and ecosystem infrastrucure modification that can be allowed. Modelling economic activities within the boundaries of the standards set a priori can yield prescriptions with respect to the sustainable levels of these activities.

Answering the second question is also beyond neoclassical environmental economics since its focus has been, and is, on other questions. Institutional economics and even political economics may provide us with more useful insights, and thus form an absolutely necessary complement to neoclassical analysis. Critical questions are involved in, for example, the possibility of alternative institutional arrangements to internalise concerns over sustainability, or to what extent adequate external manipulation (e.g. by environmental policy agencies) of economic processes and decision making on their course, is possible.

In what follows I shall limit myself to some observations on the actual role of economic and integrated modelling in attempting to approach sustainable development.

Myopia and time-scale frictions between economics and the

sustainability of humankind's use of natural processes and resources need to be overcome by a different approach, based on explicitly set, societal objectives vis-à-vis the acceptable types and extents of such utilisation. The notion of what sustainability implies has to be made operational by giving it exact content in each society, and these contents are to be consistent with what the natural environment can (re)generate. It is a problem to be resolved in a political process, fed with information from a variety of earth and life sciences. This, then, would result in some kind of space within which economic modelling could be used to identify preferred, or ideally even optimal locations. Let us see what economics has to offer in this respect.

11.5. APPROACHES TO ENVIRONMENTAL-ECONOMIC MODELLING

Looking at economics broadly defined and restricting myself to concrete, problem-oriented modelling, the following types of economic model can be discerned in addition to the dynamic stock/flow-type models that I have outlined above.

11.5.1. Materials–balance models

Here, physical properties are related to economic activity (e.g. through attaching pollution coefficients or energy use coefficients, etc., to variables representing the level of this activity). The underlying idea is to represent relatively accurately the flow of materials through the physical space occupied by a certain economy or a certain part of an economy. The crux of the logic behind these models is a physical truth, namely that matter does not get lost: every Joule of energy and each kg of substance moving through an economic system ideally can or should be accounted for. Coupled with simulation models for the development of the economy in terms of the sectors relevant to certain material flows, these materials-balance models may be used to predict future environmental burdens.

11.5.2. Spatial impact models

If a spatial grid and a dispersion/diffusion/transformation model are linked with a materials–balance model, and if economic activity is associated with certain positions or movements within the grid system, then patterns of immixtion and even accumulation may be described. Predictions and simulations can be made when economic activity is described in terms of (alternative) future developments.

11.5.3. Extended input–output models

The models described so far are hardly economic in the sense of their incorporating interactions between economic activities. Input–output analysis (IOA) is the simplest approach towards modelling such interactions; it normally works from the assumption that the input relationships in producing a certain output are fixed and given. Coefficients describing these interactions can be drawn from empirical flows of money or commodities between sectors of the economy (e.g. the value of sales from the tyre industry and the metal-plate industry to the car manufacture industry); these coefficients are taken to represent the structure of the economy. Such IO-models can be turned into environmental economic models by, as in the case of materials–balance models, associating a vector of environmental inputs and/or emissions coefficients per unit of activity, for all activities. By linking investment and consumption expenditure to the outputs, by linking incomes to employment and by making some behavioural assumptions about savings, investment, etc., the IO model is circularised and can be used for economic consistency checks, etc.; by dynamising such an IO-model, consistent scenario analysis becomes a possibility. To give one example, the debate in the Netherlands about the country's energy future has been fed with scenario results on the basis of an IO-model of the Dutch economy, disaggregating the economy to ten sectors/activities, making explicit assumptions about such exogenous phenomena as exchange rates and the oil price, by feeding the model with alternative energy and economic strategies and by running it some twenty years ahead.

11.5.4. Causal/behavioural models

Behavioural models of environment–economy interactions so far have been developed from microeconomics mainly. Within frameworks typical of neoclassical economics (welfare or profit maximisation under constraints allowing for alternative behavioural strategies and/or substitution) environmental changes are introduced, either in the sphere of the constraints (e.g. a charge imposed on discharges, or a standard limiting options), or in the objective function (e.g. environmental quality may directly influence welfare levels). The implications for behaviour of a variety of environmental changes and environmental policies are thus to be predicted, within the general frame of reference of neoclassical economics as outlined and analysed above.

11.5.5. Evaluation/decision models

Evaluation models with environmental applications range from attempts to value single environmental quality aspects (e.g. noise, visibility changes, acidification), via traditional cost benefit analysis with environmental externalities built in, to optimisation models using, for example, linear programming approaches to economy–environment models such as the input–output models. The latter approaches have been attempted by the Netherlands Council for Government Policy in exploring possibilities for economic growth under a range of constraints including environmental standards and objectives; this study used a twenty-three-sector input–output model and allowed for technological change. The former approaches have been discussed critically in some detail above.

11.6. POINTERS FOR FUTURE WORK

Even the rather brief (and hence shallow) survey given above discloses that these concrete modelling approaches are at best the beginning, but certainly not more than that, of a road towards adequate models of environment–economy systems. I suggest that these approaches are not sufficiently broad in scope; they are economists' approaches to environmental problems, using economists' toolboxes.

Multi- or interdisciplinary tools would be more appropriate. In terms of the model of renewable resource utilisation with which this paper began, it is especially the absence of appropriate modelling of ecological processes and phenomena in general that is conspicuous. Secondly, the anthropocentric bias, and even more pressing, the overemphasis on immediate and near immediate consequences of actions and decisions, over their long term repercussions (as evident from the sections on the neoclassical approach) pose a real dilemma.

Based on experience at IES with economic-ecologic modelling (Roberts et al., 1987, and Braat et al., 1987), I suggest that some guidelines for the development of more appropriate tools would be:

a. on descriptive models
  * they should be resource/impact oriented;
  * when resource based: they should include as a submodel a fair representation of the resource regeneration system;
  * they should contain causal links transcending interfaces;
  * they should be behaviorally valid.

b. on prescriptive/normative models
  * they should be 'sustainable development'-oriented; implying that these models should look at environmental quality impacts, nature conservation impacts and socio-economic development impacts simultaneously, and must be multi-dimensional;
  * they should be sensitive not only to risk but also to policy/behavioural options;
  * they should include appropriate constraints that are consistent with the notions entailed by the criterion of sustainability;
  * they should be open enough to allow for (or even induce) searches for new (unanticipated) options;
  * they should be relatively rich with relevant and feasible controls and feedbacks;
  * they should be user oriented.

The multi-dimensionality pleaded for is a reflection not only of the multi-dimensionality of values, but also of the irreducibility into one dimension (be it money, energy, or any other single denominator) of the full range of aspects of environmental quality or natural capital. This point ultimately implies the need for multi-dimensional resource accounting systems as the data base to feed such models and policy development. In terms of data requirements it also implies the need for monitoring research focusing on environmental/resource indicators, where the set of these indicators will be limited and each one a compromise between significance in a scientific sense and relevance in the eyes of policy makers.

There is another way of finding suggestions for developing (more) approprate models: looking at the currently available interdisciplinary resource models. We have done so at the EC-level as part of a FAST-project: Integrated Modelling System for Renewable Natural Resources for Europe (IRENE) (Roberts, Hafkamp et al., 1987). From a survey and analysis of existing models the following conclusions were drawn:

* models do exist for most relevant fields;
* they show great variance in spatial scale;
* they lack policy relevance;
* they are too specialistic/single-aspect oriented;
* they are too short-term oriented;
* they cannot be integrated or linked to form one comprehensive network.

If modelling is to assist society in developing sustainable roads into the future, it has to become less economic in the sense of short-term oriented and reductionist, but on the other hand it should economise in terms of comprehensiveness, so that a politically powerful, optimum level of scientific sophistication and impact on policy makers and economic decision makers is realised.

REFERENCES

Braat, L. C., F. M. Brouwer, A. J. Gilbert, E. Hulzebos, and W. A. Hafkamp. *Integrated modeling of renewable natural resources; the economic-ecologic interface*. FAST Occasional Paper No. 172, Commission of the European Community, March 1987.

Daly, H. E. *Steady State Economics*. Freeman, San Francisco, 1972.

Daly, H. E. (ed.). *Economics, Ecology, Ethics: Essays towards a Steady State Economy*. Freeman, San Francisco, 1980.

Dasgupta, S. and G. M. Heal. *Economic theory and Exhaustible Resources*. Nisbett/Cambridge Univ. Press, Welwyn/Cambridge, 1979.

DeGregory, Th. R. 'Resources are Not; They Become: an Institutional Theory', *Journ. Econ. Issues*, XXI, no. 3, 1987, pp. 1241–65.

James, D. E., H. M. A. Jansen, J. B. Opschoor. *Economic Approaches to Environmental Problems*. Amsterdam, Elsevier Scientific, 1978.

Kemp, M. C., and N. V. Long. *Essays in the Economics of Exhaustible Resources*. North Holland, Amsterdam/New York, 1984.

Krelle, W. (1984). 'Economic Growth with Exhaustible Resources and Environmental Protection', *Zeitschr. Gesamt. Staatswiss.* 140(3), 1984, pp. 399–429.

Norgaard, R. B. 'Coevolutionary Development Potential'. *Land Econs.*, 60(2), 1984, pp. 160–172.

OECD. *Environment and Economics*. OECD, Paris, 1984.

Opschoor, J. B. *Duurzaamheid en Verandering: over ecologische inpasbaarheid van economische ontwikkelingen*. Amsterdam, VU Boekhandel/Uitgeverij, 1987.

Opschoor, J. B. *Myopia versus Survival: Economic Decision making and Ecological Sustainability*. Centre for Human Ecology, University of Edinburgh, Feb. 1988.

Plourde, C. G. 'A Simple Model of Replenishable Natural Resource Exploitation', *AER*, 1970, pp. 518–22.

Roberts, P. C., W. A. Hafkamp et al. *Joint Final Report on the RES 2 and RES 3 FAST Activities: Models and Knowledge Based Expert Systems for Policy Assessment in the Field of Renewable Natural Resources Management*. EC /Fast Internal Paper 171. Brussels; DG XII/I8EC, 1987.

Siebert, H. 'Nature as a Life Support System: Renewable Resources and Environmental Disruption.' *J. Econ.* 42 (2), 1982, pp. 67–298.

Smith, V. K. and J. V. Krutilla. 'The Economics of Resource Scarity: an Interpretative Introduction', in V. K. Smith, *Scarcity and Growth Reconsidered*. Johns Hopkins Univ. Press, Baltimore/London, 1979.

12

ENERGY IN MODELS FOR SUSTAINABLE DEVELOPMENT

J. Peet

12.1. INTRODUCTION[1]

Major changes have taken place in the energy sector in New Zealand (as elsewhere) during the last fourteen years. These changes have challenged past assumptions and expectations of the energy sector. They have raised, in turn, a new set of questions about the future. What can people in the energy sector expect? What are the sort of changes with which they may have to contend? What R&D should be carried out to ensure that New Zealand has an adequate energy supply in the years to come? What is the range of energy demands with which energy managers may have to deal?

To answer these and related questions it is necessary to step out of the normal forecasting mode of energy planning and reflect, review and rethink. Above all, it is necessary to stop thinking about what is likely and explore what is possible.

Four scenarios of social, economic and technological change between 1981 and 2031 were developed in the *FOUR FUTURES* study (Boshier et al., 1986), to address these and related issues. The focus on society, the economy and technology was chosen to avoid the risk that energy futures would be developed in isolation from the factors which determine supply and consumption. The very uncertainty of the future, seen in these four scenarios, prompts questions which go one step further back, to an assessment of the importance of energy in our society. Only from this basis is it possible to develop appropriate strategies and detailed tactics to manage the change of the coming decades.

The goal of the project was to assist energy managers to

develop robust energy policies and to identify energy R&D needs. The five major objectives of the project were:

- to assess potential future patterns of energy supply and use in relation to possible economic and social change in New Zealand and overseas;
- to assess the consequences of various energy use patterns on New Zealand's energy resources, and examine the implications of uncertainty and/or resource constraints on energy and economic development;
- to establish an analytical framework that would enable a broader range of social and economic factors to be integrated in energy planning;
- to highlight issues requiring early recognition so that their resolution could be accomplished within the necessary time frame;
- to identify the key R&D programmes for both the short and long term, both to identify priorities and to help New Zealand better react to the uncertainties with which it is faced.

In meeting this brief, the research team explored a wide variety of issues, which took research beyond these objectives into a critical assessment of possible changes in the energy sector and the definition of key themes for management in the energy industries.

12.2. MODELLING

Two computer models were used in the development of scenarios. They had two prime functions – to quantify changes in the economy and the energy system, and to ensure the internal consistency of the scenarios.

The first model, a broad-brush four-sector computable general equilibrium macroeconomic model called LENZ, provided an overall view of the economy, and used relative prices to allocate demand between locally-produced and imported goods.

The second, an interactive spreadsheet model called INNOFLEX, was based on an economic input–output table and generated a physical energy balance. INNOFLEX modelled the economy in twenty-three sectors, including each of the five energy industries, and the basic agricultural, forestry, food manufacturing, wood processing, basic metals, transport and so on. Unlike the conventional approach, each energy industry 'sold' its physical energy output to one or more of five fictitious energy end-use sectors – feedstocks, motive power, high- and low-temperature heat, and miscellaneous electrical uses (lights and motors). These in turn, provided the industry sectors with energy products.

In use, scenarios were developed using assumptions about the critical social dimensions: time, world situation, social and economic change in New Zealand, and population. Using these assumptions, a narrative was prepared – a brief history as if written by someone looking back from 2031. From general information about the scenario, input values for LENZ were then prepared, and its results evaluated for consistency with the narrative, and vice versa. The final LENZ outputs then provided some of the data which were used in preparing inputs for the INNOFLEX model, in conjunction with further development of the narrative. When the INNOFLEX runs were complete, a second round of reconciliations was made. A final check of the INNNOFLEX output graphs with the narrative was carried out, and inconsistencies eliminated, before the scenario was finalised. The process is illustrated in Figure 3.1 in Boshier et al. (1986).

The models had undoubted strengths, and significant weaknesses (discussed in more detail in the *FOUR FUTURES* report and associated documents). In essence, however, the main problems were that they were very time-consuming to run, and also required a considerable degree of expertise on the part of the operators. Whilst this did not seriously limit their usefulness for the team which developed them, it meant that the expertise could not easily be transferred to others. After the team disbanded, the models, being effectively non-transportable, were no longer available for others to investigate future energy–society options.

12.3. TURBO-INNOFLEX

In order to preserve the strengths of the above scenario approach, and try to eliminate some of the more obvious weaknesses, Dr Louis Arnoux and the author (both of whom had been closely associated with the *FOUR FUTURES* research team during their work) decided to try to simplify the model structures, while keeping to – and if possible developing further

– the broad principles of the scenario approach. While the method is not completely finalised, it is built around a development of the INNOFLEX model, using the principles of input–output energy analysis as developed by Bullard and Herendeen (1975), extended by Bullard and Sebald (1975, 1977) and applied by the author to the New Zealand economy (Carter et al., 1981; Peet, 1985 and 1986).

12.3.1. Theory of input–output energy analysis

The model used is an open static Leonteif linear model, using N.Z. Department of Statistics data for 1976–77, modified for energy use (Carter et al., 1981). The input–output (I/O) model characterises the economy at a particular stage of development, in a form such that the physical processes of production, exchange and consumption of goods and services have been identified and measured. The measurement is in dollar terms, by convention and for convenience, but the reality is nevertheless physical. The data represent a snapshot of physical reality. While 1976–77 is the latest year for which detailed data were available when the work was started, the adaptation described later allows for ready adjustment of coefficients which describe the use of energy.

The general principles of input–output energy analysis may be illustrated by referring to the generalised economic sector j:

$$\Sigma \varepsilon_i X_{ij} \rightarrow \quad \dashrightarrow \quad \boxed{\text{Sector j}}$$

$$\uparrow$$

$$E_j$$

The symbols represent:

X_{ij} – transaction from sector i to sector j
X_j – total output of sector j
ε_j – embodied energy intensity per unit of X_j
E_j – energy extracted from the earth by sector j; non-zero only for primary energy sectors

(All measurements are taken over a standard time period.)

If the energy intensity of output of a sector j is ε_j MJ per dollar of output and the total output is X_j, the total energy embodied in that output is $\varepsilon_j X_j$ and is equal to the sum of all the energy inputs from the other sectors, i.e., $\varepsilon_i A_{ij} X_j$, where A_{ij} is the ratio X_{ij}/X_j, i.e.

the fraction of the total output of sector j that is derived from inputs from sector i.

To this is added the energy E_j extracted from the earth, if j is a primary energy sector, i.e.:

$$\Sigma \varepsilon_i A_{ij} X_j + E_j = \varepsilon xzj X_j$$

In matrix notation, the energy balance is $\varepsilon A + E = \varepsilon X$, where X is a matrix of sector outputs. This set of n equations can be solved for the n unknowns, ε.

For a typical product j, the production technology is represented by a vector A, where a typical element A_{ij} represents the amount of product i needed directly to produce a unit of product j. The $n \times n$ matrix A then provides a linear representation of the technology of producing all goods and services in the economy.

Solving for the energy intensities, $\varepsilon = e(I - A)^{-1}$ where e is a unit vector that defines the energy sector row of $(IA)^1$ as the energy cost of goods and services (energy intensities). I is the identity matrix.

These energy-intensity values represent the total (direct plus indirect) energy requirements of output of a unit of product from sector j for final demand consumption. They therefore provide the link between the dollar values of output of industries and the energy requirements of that output. By convention, final demand consumption includes household consumption, government consumption, exports, and gross fixed capital formation, plus stock change, which is usually very small. The sum of final demand consumptions is numerically equal to GDP.

For a multi-fuel economy, this analysis can be repeated for each type of energy (coal, oil, electricity, gas, etc.) and the total primary intensity can be calculated for each sector.

The total primary energy used by an economic system can be obtained using these results, together with the outputs to final demand, i.e. $E = \varepsilon Y$, where Y is the column vector(s) of outputs to final demand.

In practice, the total demand for output from each of the energy supply sectors is obtained by multiplying the vector(s) of energy intensities by the vector(s) of outputs to final demand, i.e.:

$$E_k = \Sigma \varepsilon_{kj} Y_j$$

where

ε_{kj} is the total energy of type k, where k is not an energy supply sector (except in the case of direct transactions to exports) required directly and indirectly to produce a unit of goods or services j; and

Y_j is the amount of output from sector j to final demand (consumers, government and investors) that makes up the economy's GDP.

E_k is thus a vector of total energy outputs from economic sectors, that may be summed to give the total primary energy demand of the economy. Data for the New Zealand economy are available for both the 1971–72 and 1976–77 I/O surveys (Carter et al., 1981; Peet, 1985 and 1986).

The value of E – the total primary energy demand of the economy – can also be determined using the values of ε, together with the population P; the per capita consumption g (in dollars and equal to per capita GDP); and a life style vector y, representing the composition of the 'basket' of goods and services purchased by each member of the population, i.e. $E = \varepsilon ygP$. The product ygP is the final demand column vector(s), as above. See another report on our work (Peet et al., 1982 and 1985) for details about the use of this methodology for establishing the direct and indirect use of energy in households.

12.3.2. Uncertainties in input–output energy analysis

The basic I/O model is constructed from a survey of the economy in a given year. It is thus a 'snapshot' of something which must inevitably change over time, although changes of a structural nature big enough to invalidate the model are known not to occur rapidly. However, there had been substantial changes in the energy supply sectors in NZ in the late 1970s, and it was seen as important to incorporate these in our analysis, to ensure that sector energy intensities were as accurate as possible. Department of Statistics surveys are carried out at approximately five-yearly intervals in New Zealand, with a similar delay before publication. The latest survey was carried out in 1976/77; the 1981/82 survey became available in 1989.

As with all I/O work, there are restrictions inherent in the technique, which can limit the validity of the conclusions (Carter et al., 1981). Three main assumptions are required in the derivation of the theory: the Homogeneity assumption, that the output of each sector is taken to be homogeneous and unsubstitutable with the output of another sector; the Proportionality assumption, that the input requirements vary linearly with the output of a sector; and the Additivity assumption, that the total effect of carrying out production in several sectors is the sum of the separate effects, i.e. external economies/diseconomies do not operate.

Whilst adequate for many purposes, the model structure described so far is clumsy to use directly for some types of investigations, especially those involving changes in the technology of energy supply and use in society, as would be expected in a scenario study. Changes in primary resource accessibility and energy utilisation efficiencies, and substitution among fuel sources and among non-energy intermediate inputs in industrial production sectors are obvious examples.

The basic input–output structure is also not suitable in situations where there are changes in the structure of production over time, which falsify the usual assumptions of linearity, i.e. of 'other things being equal'. This problem reflects the fact that material life style (the relative size of items in the 'basket' of goods and services produced and consumed by an economy) changes with time. These changes, and those due to technological factors can in practice be incorporated into input–output models, by methods that will be discussed below.

While there can be significant problems in the use of input–output data in energy analysis, the data are still much more sophisticated and useful than those from any comparable method, and they provide valuable insight into the structural relationships that exist throughout an economy. In order to increase the flexibility of the model, to take account of some of the most important limitations, a technique developed by US workers (Bullard and Sebald, 1975 and 1977) was used for development of the model that is the principal subject of this chapter.

12.3.3. Input–output energy end-use analysis

Following the example of Bullard and Sebald (1975, 1977) – at the Centre for Advanced Computation, University of Illinois – the basic input–output energy analysis model described above was modified by separating out the demand of each sector of the economy for a given fuel, into the separate demands for its end-use forms. For example, the energy output of the oil supply industry, when sold to a food manufacturing industry, may be used either as a boiler (process heating) fuel or as a motor fuel for transport vehicles. The modifications to our basic model required that fictitious, intermediate energy end-use sectors are inserted into the transactions matrix. These sectors are defined in such a way as to be physically independent of the energy supplies used to produce the end-use energy services.

Energy supply sectors are now seen to be 'selling' directly to the end-use sectors in the expanded matrix, and they in turn 'sell' their outputs to the industry sectors. By definition there are no energy inputs from energy supply sectors to industry sectors; industries are supplied with energy entirely from the end-use sectors. Direct outputs from energy supply sectors to final demand are generally limited to exports, for example of coal and international transport bunker fuel, and these are left unchanged.

12.3.4. Model development

Whereas in its basic form (Peet, 1985 and 1986) the model used in the ongoing programme of energy analysis work defines and solves the system of energy balance equations for each of 178 sectors of the economy, it was aggregated into the more convenient size of twenty-three sectors for use in this work. In the model there are five energy supply sectors and eighteen industry sectors, to which five end-use sectors are added, giving an expanded A matrix of dimension 28×28.

The main advantage of this formulation is that technological changes associated with fuel substitution and end-use efficiencies are localised in two small (5×5) submatrices; the problem of adjusting coefficients is thus much reduced, over the alternative of changing all elements in the (5×18) submatrix, where substitution and efficiency factors are combined in single coefficients.

Transactions between the energy supply sectors and the industries which consume energy services proceed via fictitious intermediate sectors in which the primary energy sectors of hydrocarbon mining, coal mining, petrochemical and fuel conversion, electricity and gas reticulation are 'converted' into energy end-use products. The five end-use products taken as being representative of NZ energy use are listed in Table 12.1.

The largest practical problem in getting the modified *A* matrix into a form suitable for this work was the disaggregation of the twenty-three-sector energy-modified input–output transactions matrix into the twenty-eight-sector modified end-use transactions matrix. This required a major effort in estimating the nature of use of energy by each of the eighteen industry sectors and five final demand sectors in the model.

Table 12.1 End-use sectors and examples

End-Use Product Sector	*Example*
Feedstocks	Coal for cement, steel
Motive power	Oil for transport,
High temperature process heat	Electricity for railways
Low temperature heat	Electricity for steel. Coal, oil, gas for process heat for home and commercial use
Miscellaneous electrical, air conditioning etc.	Electricity for light building, services, machines

In essence, the task required that the contributions of each of the five energy supply sectors to each of the eighteen industry sectors be broken down into the separate requirements for each of the five energy end-use product sectors. The method is described in some detail in a report to NZERDC (Peet et al., 1987).

The model structure is such that improved data may be easily and rapidly incorporated as they become available. At the same time as the (Energy Supply – Industry) transactions were disaggregated into the separate transactions to and from each of the end-use sectors, all transactions entered into the (End-Use – Industry) submatrix were at the same time adjusted for efficiency of conversion (measured in first law terms) into the end-use product. In other words, this submatrix contained the actual requirement for end-use energy, of the industry which received that energy product. The end result of the exercise was that the model represented the supply of a given type of end-use energy as being homogeneous, and derived from a mix of all of the energy supply sectors which contributed to that end-use energy.

12.3.5. Computation

All energy data are in enthalpy terms, with gross calorific values assigned to fuels. Matrix inversion used a modified Gaussian elimination with partial pivoting routine. Computation was carried out using a desktop personal computer (Epson QX10) in FORTRAN. Each computation took around one minute.

12.4. THE ENERGY INTENSITY OF ECONOMIC ACTIVITY IN NEW ZEALAND

Table 12.2 summarises the calculated total energy intensity values for the sectors in the model, expressed as MJ/$ of output for industrial sectors and MJ/MJ for energy supply and end-use sectors, for the base year 1976–77 and the year of the updating to be described below, 1980–81.

The data columns represent the sum of individual supply sector intensities, expressed in primary energy terms. This process (Carter et al., 1981; Peet, 1985 and 1986) eliminates the double-counting that otherwise occurs if the separate intensities are summed, for example when some electricity is produced from thermal stations fired by oil, coal or gas. In this analysis, electricity from hydro- or geothermal sources was given primary energy status, i.e. hydro- and geothermal were not given their fossil equivalents.

More detailed tables for the 1976–77 data are given in reference (Peet et al., 1987), including coefficients for the five individual energy supply sectors and a vector of total outputs of all sectors to final demand. The data confirm that expansion of a sector such as non-ferrous metals or air transport by one dollar's worth of output requires a great deal more primary energy than the same dollar's worth of expansion in a sector such as wholesale and retail trade. Thus, the effect on primary energy requirements of economic activity in any sector is obtainable as the product of the dollar output of that sector (deflated to 1976–77 or 1980–81 values) and the sector energy intensity. Similarly, an increase in the output of the electricity generation sector by 1 MJ requires a total of 1.8 MJ of primary energy.

Table 12.2 Total primary energy intensities

	1976–77	*1980–81*
Supply Sectors (MJ/MJ)		
Hydrocarbon Mining	1.04	1.04
Coal Mining	1.04	1.04
Electricity Generation	1.80	1.42
Petrochemical, Fuel Conversion	1.06	1.06
Gas Reticulation	1.24	1.13
End-Use Sectors (MJ/MJ)		
Feedstocks	1.87	1.66
Motive Power	5.27	5.25
High Temperature Process Heat	1.77	1.67
Low Temperature Heat	1.71	1.51
Miscellaneous Electrical, etc.	3.09	2.51
Industry Sectors (MJ/$)		
Agriculture	11.0	10.0
Forestry	27.0	25.0
Dairy	31.1	27.1
Meat	16.4	14.5
Other Food Manufacturing	19.5	17.2
Solid Wood Processing	16.4	14.7
Reconstituted Wood Processing	46.9	40.2
Ferrous Metals	51.1	44.3
Non-Ferrous Metals	63.5	56.0
Non-Metallic Minerals	55.0	48.5
Other Manufacturing	13.0	11.3
Construction	16.9	14.9
Road Transport	43.8	41.1
Rail, Sea Transport	19.2	17.8
Air Transport	56.6	53.2
Wholesale, Retail Trade	9.1	8.1
Communications, Government Services	10.6	9.1
Private Services	11.3	9.8

The main result of the modification of the twenty-three-sector *A* matrix into a twenty-eight-sector matrix incorporating end-use sectors is that the input–output technical coefficients most likely to change as a result of energy price changes and policies are localised in two small submatrices. These parameters, which specify fuel substitution technologies and efficiencies of use, are now isolated, respectively, in the two (5 × 5) submatrices (Energy Supply – Energy Supply) and (Energy Supply – End-use). Changes in the use of end-use energy by specific industries, as opposed to the general technology of production of end-use energy in the (Energy Supply – End-use) submatrix, are isolated in the (End-use – Industry) submatrix. Thus, changes in the technological coefficients matrix A can be quickly incorporated. The dimensionality of the problem of altering coefficients to take account of technological change is very substantially reduced, due to the fact that several factors which were previously incorporated into a single coefficient are now separated out, and can be addressed individually. Whenever the A matrix is altered, the energy intensities must, of course, be recalculated by inversion of the $(I - A)$ matrix, as already discussed.

12.5. CALCULATION OF TOTAL ENERGY DEMAND

As an example in the use of this method, the total output to final demand of the agriculture sector in the 1976–77 input–output table was $558.923 million (Peet et al., 1987). When multiplied by that sector's total coefficient (Table 12.2) of 11.0 MJ/$, the primary energy demand of that sector is:

$$558.923 \times 11.0 = 6148 \text{ TJ} = 6.148 \text{ PJ}$$

The total output of the economy to final demand in 1976–77 was $15890.095 million. By multiplying the entire vector of outputs to final demand of the economy (Peet et al., 1987) by the appropriate sector total energy coefficients, and summing, we obtain the total primary energy demand of the economy, 365 PJ.

12.5.1. Changes in an economy

As an economy expands or contracts, individual economic sectors will similarly expand or contract. Two main situations can arise under these circumstances, requiring different treatments for evaluating the total primary demand of the economy.

12.5.2. Uniformly expanding economy

Where the economy expands uniformly (i.e. all sectors grow by the same percentage) the I/O matrix remains in balance, that is, the relative values of items in the matrix remain the same. Thus, the numbers in the A matrix also remain the same, and the total coefficients matrix is unchanged. To obtain the changed total energy demand for the economy in such a case, all that is required is to multiply the energy intensities by the new final demand outputs, and sum over all sectors. Thus, if the economy expands uniformly by, say, 5 per cent, all that is needed to evaluate the new total primary energy demand is to multiply final demands by 1.05, and then sum the product of these new final demands and the energy intensities.

12.5.3. Non-uniformly expanding economy

To a first approximation, when different sectors of the economy expand at different rates, the new total demand is obtained simply by using the base coefficients with the new sectoral final demand outputs. Where one sector expands its output more than others, however, the *A* matrix becomes unbalanced. The increased demands from the expanded sector must come from its supplying sectors, but other sectors do not need any such increased supply, so the simple direct proportionality relationships (valid for uniform expansion) no longer apply. Two main options are available – rebalancing of the entire transactions matrix and updating of only the 'most important' factors.

While rebalancing of the entire matrix is in theory to be preferred (e.g. the bi-proportional RAS method), the method is not really suitable for the purposes of this work, because it depends upon the ability to balance rows and columns alternately. Since the energy-modified input–output matrix contains a mixture of money ($) and energy (MJ) units, the inputs to and outputs from a sector are not in the same units. Thus, the inputs do not sum to the same amount as the outputs. The method could be applied in practice, by returning to the basic monetary transactions matrix and subsequently incorporating revised physical transactions data into the energy sector rows, but this would be both time-consuming and prone to additional error. On balance, we decided that at the present state of development of the model, full RAS-type balancing was not of sufficient importance to be warranted.

According to Bullard and Sebald (1975 and 1977) prediction uncertainty in situations of this type can be reduced (in an example which they describe) by as much as a factor of 5, through selective updating of a small (e.g. 2 per cent) subset of the model parameters, important to particular problems. Their method involves evaluating an 'importance function', which enables an element A_{ij} to be identified as 'important', if its uncertainty causes some element of the importance function to exceed a prescribed threshold.

Bullard and Sebald suggest that the most important parameters involved in evaluating the primary energy demand of the economy, as a result of expanding specific sectors (one of the prime aims of our work) are normally those which describe the energy supply and end-use sectors (especially efficiency of transformation), and those involved in the production and use of energy-intensive materials such as metals and chemicals.

Given that most of these parameters are isolated in the two small submatrices (Supply – Supply) and (Supply – End-use), we concluded that at this stage of development of the model, detailed further work was not needed in this area. A simple method, capable of identifying and accounting for a small number of parameters of major importance was all that was required, for practical purposes, and this is described in our report (Peet et al., 1987). Inaccuracies will arise in the application of our model, to the extent that specific economic sectors (particularly those which are especially energy-intensive) expand or contract at rates markedly different from those in the rest of the economy. Since such situations are in themselves impossible to predict with any certainty, it was not seen to be an important limitation. Nevertheless, the model could be developed further, to take this problem into account, if it should be seen to be important at some later date.

12.6. TESTING OF THE TURBO INNOFLEX MODEL

It is not possible to determine the exact input–output structure of the economy in a year beyond that of the base model data, until the new survey results become available. For this reason, it will be necessary to await the publication of the 1981–82 survey, before knowing whether coefficient adjustments made in the present work (based on the 1976–77 survey) are 'correct'. Nevertheless, it is possible to illustrate the methodology involved, and compare the results with the known energy supply and demand data, in order to obtain a rough 'validation' of the model.

With this in mind, the basic (1976–77) model was approximately updated to the year 1980–81. That year was used because the *FOUR FUTURES* team had obtained detailed sector ($) output data, in a form which could be used directly in this work. For purposes of illustration, our updating process is described here, in several stages.

The first stage was to take the 1976–77 data and use the assumption of a uniformly expanding economy, with the 1976–77 coefficients unchanged. From the *FOUR FUTURES* data, total output to final demand increased (expressed in $ 1976–77) from $15,890.1 million in 1976–77 to $17,162 million in 1980–81, an increase of 8 per cent over the period. Using this simple assumption, the total primary energy requirement of 365 PJ in the base year would increase by 8 per cent, to 394 PJ in the later year. The comparable published figure for 1980–81 was in fact 369.3 PJ.

The next stage was to incorporate the actual data on changes in sectoral output to final demand, again with the 1976–77 coefficients unchanged. Using these data for individual sectors, together with the 1976–77 total energy coefficients (the left-hand data column in Table 12.2), a total primary energy demand of 404 PJ is obtained – well above the known figure of 369 PJ.

To develop further the update, it is necessary to adjust those coefficients which most strongly affect the energy requirements of industries. As discussed earlier, the first step is to adjust coefficients in the small (Energy Supply – Energy Supply) submatrix. The most important factors in this sector relate to the supply of fossil fuel for thermal electricity generation. From our own 1976–77 data, and Ministry of Energy data for 1980–81, the following fractional changes in fossil fuel supply occurred:

Coal – down from 16.511 to 5.642 PJ; change = 0.342;
Oil – down from 14.048 to 0.629 PJ; change = 0.045; and,
Gas – down from 28.946 to 19.912 PJ; change = 0.688.

With these changes (in addition to the previous ones) the total coefficients were recalculated by inverting the now modified *A* matrix, using sectoral output data. The calculated total primary energy demand was determined as 377 PJ, which is much closer to the actual value of 369 PJ.

Over the same period the supply of indigenous condensate for oil refining reduced from 25.250 to 16.451 PJ, a fractional change of 0.652. Town gas manufacture from coal incurred a factor of 0.518, and from oil 0.621. With these further corrections incorporated into the technical coefficients matrix, the total primary energy demand was again recalculated. The result was a total primary energy demand of 375 PJ.

A further stage of updating involved following up the generally-held view that oil had lost a lot of ground as a boiler fuel over the period. For the sake of illustration, it was assumed that 25 per cent of the use of oil for high-temperature and low-temperature heat was transferred, in equal parts, to the hydrocarbon mining (i.e. gas and LPG) and coal mining supply sectors. Hydrocarbon mining was used rather than gas reticulation, since it was believed that the Natural Gas Corporation had secured a number of large direct customers during this period, whereas the gas undertakings had experienced a more modest rate of growth. The results (see Table 12.3) give a total primary energy demand of 374 PJ.

The final stage of updating adopted in this illustration was to incorporate the assumption of a 5 per cent improvement in the efficiency of utilisation of energy, in the motive power, high temperature and low temperature heat end-use sectors. With this incorporated, the total primary energy demand is 364 PJ.

Table 12.3 Total energy requirements, PJ

Method used	*Hydro-carbon M^ng*	*Coal M^ng*	*Electr*	*Petro Fuel*	*Gas Retic*	*Total Primary*
1976–77 actual	70	58	75	204	15	365
Uniform 8% expansion	76	63	81	220	17	394
Sector expansion	76	65	81	229	16	404
Adjust thermal elect	63	54	81	214	16	377
Adjust oil and gas	55	52	81	213	16	375
Oil subst.	60	57	81	200	16	374
5% efficiency	58	56	80	194	16	364
1980–81 actual	59	65	82	192	15	369

Detailed total primary energy results, including individual energy supply sector data for each stage of updating described in this section, are included in Table 12.3 (rounded to the nearest PJ). The total energy intensities obtained in this exercise (for the final stage of updating) are also listed in the right-hand column of data of Table 12.3 above, expressed in MJ/$1976–77, to be directly comparable with the base year data. Some of the coefficients for 1980–81 differ significantly from those for the base year.

The discrepancy between the final adjusted and actual total primary figures is only 5 PJ (1.3 per cent), compared with a discrepancy of 35 PJ (9.5 per cent) using the best available economic sectoral growth data alone. As will be observed, the coal mining sector results are still significantly in error, indicating that further work is necessary in that sector. The point of the exercise, however, has not been to 'validate' the model, since as explained above, this will really only be possible when the new inter-industry survey results become available. The aim has been to show that by incorporating 'sensible' changes in a small number of important coefficients, realistic results are obtained, and a much closer approximation of the model's output to the known primary energy consumption achieved, quickly and easily. With more detailed information it would be possible to further improve the model.

12.7. CONCLUSIONS

We would make the caveat that, while it is relatively straightforward to identify a set of coefficient changes that will ensure that the energy requirements calculated by the model are the same as those from official data, that fact in no way confirms the validity of the changes. It is arguably possible for many different combinations of adjustments to result in the same 'correct' energy requirement of output to final demand, without in any way proving that such a combination of coefficients represents the actual structure of the economy. Since any such changes depend upon some degree of arbitrariness in the choice of adjustments, it has been left to future users to investigate.

Note that this exercise only examined a small number of changes, most of them in two small submatrices of the model, in order to reduce prediction error from 9.5 per cent to 1.3 per cent. We have not incorporated any changes in the manufacturing sectors' internal technology for production, for example. With specific data, the appropriate (industry – industry) coefficients could also be adjusted, quickly and easily.

An important point hidden by the model, at this stage of development, is that in its present structure, it does not take account of the major new gas-using projects which started after the 1976–77 survey (the ammonia-urea plant and the stand-alone methanol plant, in particular). These projects are now consuming around 23.4 PJ of gas/yr, and the synthetic gasoline project (started in 1986) averages 52.5 PJ/yr. For these to be included specifically (rather than as part of an industry such as 'other manufacturing', which we felt was inappropriate), a new industry sector will need to be created. While this could be done at the present state of the model, in the absence of good data on the likely structure of these industries we decided that it would be better left until the next I/O survey results are available.

The illustration in this section has shown that the model is rapidly and easily capable of incorporating significant changes in structure of the energy sectors, to give meaningful results.

ACKNOWLEDGEMENTS

The energy analysis data base used in this work was developed with the support of the New Zealand Energy Research and Development Committee, University of Auckland, New Zealand, under Contract 3157. Gratitude is expressed for this support, and for the assistance of the joint NZERDC/MWD/MoE Long Term Energy Futures study team.

NOTES

1 The Introduction and part of the Modelling section (which follows) adapted from the *FOUR FUTURES* report (Boshier et al., 1986).

REFERENCES

Boshier, J. F., R. R. Allan, M. Ellis, J. Gallacher, P. H. Phillips. *Four Futures: Energy Implications of Social and Economic Change*. NZERDC Report 135, September, 1986.

Bullard, C. W. and R. A. Herendeen. 'The Energy Cost of Goods and Services', *Energy Policy*, Vol. 3, No. 4, December, 1975, p. 268.

Bullard, C. W. and A. V. Sebald. 'A Model for Analysing Energy Impact of Technological Change'. *Proc. Summer Computer Simulation Conference*, San Francisco, 1975, pp. 1339–45.

Bullard, C. W. and A. V. Sebald. 'Effects of Parametric Uncertainty and Technological Change on Input–Output Models', *Review of Economics and Statistics*, Vol. 59, No. 1, 1977, pp. 75–81.

Carter, A. J., N. J. Peet and J. T. Baines. *Direct and Indirect Energy Requirements of the New Zealand Economy; An Energy Analysis of the 1971–72 Inter-Industry Study*. NZERDC Publication P55, August, 1981.

Peet, N. J. *Direct and Indirect Energy Requirements of Output of the New Zealand Economy, 1976–77: An Energy Analysis of the 1976–77 Inter-Industry Survey*. NZERDC Publication P96, October, 1985.

Peet, N. J. 'Energy Requirements of Output of the New Zealand Economy, 1976–77', *Energy*, Vol. 11, No. 7, 1986, pp. 659–70.

Peet, N. J., J. T. Baines, J. C. P. Perrott, P. N. Sinclair, B. J. Smith and H. J. H. Stewart. *An Input–Output Energy Scenario Model*. Department of Chemical and Process Engineering, University of Canterbury, Christchurch, New Zealand, June, 1987.

Peet, N. J., A. J. Carter and J. T. Baines. *Energy in the New Zealand Household; The Energy Cost of Living. 1974 to 1980*. NZERDC Publication P73, 1982.

Peet, N. J., A. J. Carter and J. T. Baines. 'Energy in the New Zealand Household, 1974–1980', *Energy*, Vol. 10, No. 11, 1985, pp. 1197–1208.

Phillips, P. H. *FOUR FUTURES: Energy Implications of Social and Economic Change*, NZERDC Report 135, September, 1986.

13

PAST AND POSSIBLE FUTURE CONTRIBUTIONS OF THE FAO AEZ METHODOLOGY TO THE DEVELOPMENT OF THE ECCO MODEL

J. Antoine

13.1. BACKGROUND TO THE DEVELOPMENT OF ECCO

The FAO, in its activities to assist member countries in developing and managing their land resources for agricultural planning, has been very active during the last decade in preparing computer-aided models for this purpose. This work has been undertaken on an inter-divisional basis in FAO and in co-operation with a number of national, international and other UN agencies.

In fact, the production and testing of the computer simulation model ECCO – Enhancement of Population Carrying Capacity Options – has been a joint Unesco/FAO venture since the beginning of the project in 1980. This co-operation was a natural one, given FAO's earlier population supporting capacity study based on its agro-ecological zone methodology; it has resulted in a series of publications on the basic ECCO model in 1984 and 1985, and a pilot study for Kenya in 1985. The choice of Kenya for the first pilot study with ECCO was based mainly on the fact that the country possessed a significant agricultural planning data base, arising from the country's agro-ecological zones study on population supporting capacities which started in 1980.

The agro-ecological zones methodology was initiated by FAO

in 1976, with the purpose of studying the potentials for various land uses by agro-ecological zones and so obtain a first approximation of the production potentials of the world's land resources. In the process a computerised world data base, based on the 1:5 million FAO/Unesco Soil Map of the World, was established as an organised source of the physical data necessary for broad-scale planning of future agricultural development. This data base was used in the subsequent UNFPA sponsored study of Potential Population Supporting Capacities of the Developing World which was conducted by FAO in collaboration with the International Institute for Applied Systems Analysis (IIASA). The project assessed the food production potential of 117 countries and determined how many people could be fed and supported by the production potential of land resources in each country under the assumptions of an objective of food self-sufficiency and various input levels. The FAO study indicated that in view of population growth, at least half of the countries in question face a critical future: they will, by the end of the century, exceed their land carrying capacity if low levels of input production systems are used. FAO's population supporting capacity approach attempts to quantify supporting capacity simply on the food producing potentials of the land and on the population that it could support in that context. The results of the study provided a major contribution to the agricultural and population components of the ECCO model.

13.2. AEZ AND ECCO ARE COMPLEMENTARY MODELS

The FAO AEZ methodology of population supporting capacity is based on optimisation as opposed to the dynamic simulation approach of ECCO. The AEZ models are intended to provide guidance to the users in deciding about specific questions of agricultural planning, such as: how best can a government use its limited inputs to increase production of specific food crops? In such a case, an objective or single criterion of success is set – increase production of rice, for instance – which one tries to attain using available resources given known constraints. One then formulates the problem as an optimisation model, essentially using linear programming techniques, to allocate the available resources to satisfy that objective.

The AEZ methodology was not designed, nor was it intended, to address the broader question of whether the inputs or capital resources necessary to attain the objectives can be supplied. The AEZ methodology is essentially an integrated resources agricultural production model and not, like ECCO, an integrated system encompassing population, resources, environment and development through the energy concept. The ECCO model is a more complex tool of analysis which deals dynamically, through a feedback system, with the structural complexity of the inter-relationships – a number of these obviously non-linear – between these various components of the integrated system.

Scenarios are quickly prepared using ECCO which can readily explore a large range of policy options, while computer runs with the AEZ population supporting capacity optimisation routines are a time-consuming exercise. This is an obvious advantage of the ECCO approach.

On the other hand it seems that the ECCO user always needs to look far ahead as the full impact of any policy change or policy option may come in evidence in the long run only. ECCO is a tool for long-term, not short-term planning. In situations where decisions are to be made in the short and medium term in a certain political or socio-cultural context to obtain specific desirable results, the approach of optimal allocation of resources would be more advantageous and practical. ECCO is a user of pre-processed data in a highly condensed and aggregated form. AEZ generates basic, semi-processed data, but also the compressed data required to feed ECCO. AEZ can also produce the reliable data which are needed to test the practicality of theoretical models such as ECCO. The systems are therefore complementary.

13.3. SUGGESTIONS FOR FUTURE FAO/UNESCO CO-OPERATION

13.3.1. Data bases

The most positive way in which FAO can continue to contribute to the development of ECCO is by helping to establish sound data bases in the important sectors of agriculture and population in the countries where the model will be used. The on-going FAO population supporting capacity assessment for Kenya has involved extensive refinements of the original methodology for its specific application at national level. The land resources appraisal and crop suitability assessment components of the FAO model are continually being refined as they are increasingly applied at national (Mozambique, Kenya, Bangladesh) and sub-national (Indonesia, Thailand, Malaysia, the Philippines) levels to create adequate computerized agricultural planning data bases, from which the relevant data can be drawn and condensed into reliable estimates of agriculture and population parameters necessary for ECCO to produce useful results.

13.3.2. AEZ and input to ECCO

As ECCO operates on the basis of physically feasible processes, it needs – in most cases – pre-investigation on the feasibility of the basic components to be incorporated into the model. The AEZ approach can provide the means to assess resource potentials and the degree and intensity of their utilisation and identify constraints at sub-national and local level. This is all the more necessary to achieve an adequate level of data quality and consistency as ECCO uses only nationally aggregated data. Some examples of such applications follow:

Assessment of biomass potential

The energy transformation system in most non-oil producing, developing countries is based to a large extent on biomass. Expansion of the biomass sector to satisfy increasing household energy demand will involve the introduction of fast growing energy crop plantations.

The AEZ criteria for site suitability to annual crops have also been applied to perennial crops, mainly those with both food and fuel wood values, such as fruit trees. Recently a forest ecologist in Bangladesh has used the AEZ criteria to classify non-agricultural sites for their suitability to various indigenous and exotic plantation tree species.

Assessment of the possibility of trade-off between land for food and land for energy crops and forest

Because land is a finite resource and because of the increasing population pressure and competition for land in developing countries, the allocation of more land resources to forest versus food and livestock production must be based on sound resource inventories and realistic assessments to enable optimal and sustainable use of these resources.

FAO's land evaluation method which takes into account the economics of the proposed enterprises, the social consequences for the people of the area and country concerned, and the consequences beneficial or adverse for the environment, in addition to purely physical factors of land suitability assessment, can provide answers to such problems.

Assessment of environmental factors and their impact

As the AEZ methodology enables the classification and grouping of sites with similar environmental conditions, it facilitates local transfer of agricultural technology and therefore can help in making local and national assessments of environmental impacts, for instance, the effects of intensification of land use through the use of more labour, machines, fertilisers and improved seeds and practices.

13.4. POPULATION SUPPORTING CAPACITY ESTIMATES

A basic question for many developing countries is the question of food autarky, the desire to provide all the food necessary for present and future populations from indigenous production. Accurate estimates of potential population supporting capacities are essential to calculate the difference between the actual or projected future population and the actual or future population that can be sustained by the indigenous agricultural systems. These are the two essential population input parameters to ECCO in quantifying the gap between the real carrying capacity at the material welfare level defined by the ECCO model for the time considered and the actual population of the country. The different input levels at which population supporting capacities are made, yield the data needed to see how good nutritional levels in terms of balanced diet for populations at a sustainable rate can be achieved.

13.5. INTEGRATION AND DISSEMINATION

As the two models are computer-based systems, AEZ being a data generator for ECCO, it would be relatively easy to link the two systems to each other or even integrate them with the help of currently available data base management techniques. In recent years the Land and Water Development Division of FAO has put a lot of effort into the conversion, the rationalisation and integration of the AEZ software products, which have been of good practical value, from mainframe into the micro-computer environment. The result is a PC-based set of agricultural planning tools called APT, a new version of which is expected to be released shortly. The APT package is characterised by:

- a data base approach in order to minimise the duplication of input data between different application systems;
- a standardised user interface to allow all systems to be accessed and operated in the same, simple way by non-computer application specialists through the use of menus.

This is achieved through the rationalisation of the data management tasks and the creation of a common data base for several applications and through the use of a shell that is a standardised user interface to the various software systems. At present, the following application systems are available in APT:

CDA A Climatic Data Analysis System which calculates sets of agro-climatic characteristics from basic climate station data.

AEZ The Agro-Ecological Zones System which compiles a computerised land resources inventory and estimates agro-climatic and land suitabilities for specific crops at specific input levels. It is most suited to analysis at scales of 1:250 000 and smaller and is therefore an aid to national and regional planning.

LECSA Land Evaluation Computer System which performs both agro-ecological and agro-economic crop suitability assessments, including soil degradation assessments and the identification of soil conservation options. This system represents an extension of the AEZ approach to scales 1:50 000–1:250 000. It is an aid to watershed or district planning and has been tested in local projects in Indonesia.

LPP2A Land Productivity Programme which draws input data from the results of the AEZ programme and converts crop yields to crop productivity assessments, taking into account such factors as cropping pattern, soil degradation, fallow period requirements, and seed and waste losses.

MCP2 The Optimum Crop Mix Programme which takes the results of the LPP2 programme and computes the population supporting capacity of land on the basis of optimisation techniques. Optimisation runs may be performed to allocate crops such that nutritional energy production is maximised, subject to a calorie/protein ratio constraint and/or a required crop mix constraint.

Other modules, such as the micro-computer version of ECCO, can be added to the package and it would be of mutual benefit, to both the AEZ and ECCO systems, to do so, and accordingly to integrate the Users and Systems Manuals of both packages to facilitate dissemination to users.

REFERENCES

FAO. 'Potential population supporting capacity assessment, Kenya'. Mission Report, 10–24 May, 1984.

FAO. *Users' guide and installation guide to the agricultural planning Toolkit,* APT version 2.0, 1987.

FAO/Unesco. *Carrying capacity assessment (Kenya): Interaction between population, food, energy and material standards. Report to Unesco and FAO.* Contract (Unesco) prepared by Strathclyde University and Resource Use Institute, Glastry for Unesco, Paris, 1984.

FAO/Unesco. *Carrying capacity assessment with a pilot study of Kenya.* Final Report, FAO, Rome, 1985.

FAO/UNFPA/IIASA. *Potential population supporting capacities of lands in the developing world.* Technical Report, Project FPA/INT/513. FAO, Rome.

Higgins, G. M., A. H. Kassam, and A. Christoforides. *Land Resources for Populations of the Future. Phase II – Detailed Country Studies, I – Kenya. Climatic data bank and carrying period analysis.* Technical Report No. 1, FAO/UNFPA: INT/75/813.

Higgins, G. M., and A. H. Kassam. 'The FAO agro-ecological zone approach to determination of land potential', Pédologie, XXXV, 2, 1981, pp. 147–68, Ghent.

Higgins, G. M., A. H. Kassam, M. F. Purnell, and H. T. Van Velthuizen. *The FAO agro-ecological zones approach to quantification of land resources and assessment of crop and population potentials.* FAO, Rome, 1986.

Shaw, R. *Carrying capacity assessment. A resource accounting approach to long-term development planning.* Unesco, Paris, 1986.

14

THE DEMOGRAPHIC APPROACH

W. Lutz

Demography is often defined as the scientific study of the composition and change of human populations. In this sense the criterion that defines the discipline is not a unique methodology but rather the object of interest: the human population. Demography distinguishes itself, however, from other disciplines that also study human populations, such as medicine, population biology, anthropology, etc., by being a social science and being heavily quantitative. Over time demography has also developed its own methodology. The models of population dynamics that originated in demography (e.g. the stable population model) are hardly used in other social sciences; but they can be found in a generalised form in biometrics. However, there the questions asked are mostly different because the components of population change are not made subject to the influence of social behaviour. People who call themselves demographers have this relatively small core field of the discipline in common and from this basis utilise the tools of other disciplines (statistics, economics, biology, etc.) to help answer population-related questions in a broader perspective. Based on this definition we may distinguish between demographic analysis in the stricter sense, which concerns the measurement of changes in population structure and its internal dynamics, and the analysis of the non-demographic determinants and consequences of population change.

The change in size of a closed population has only two components: fertility and mortality. If the population is open then net-migration (the balance of in-migration and out-migration) constitutes an additional component of population growth or decline. When not only the absolute number of

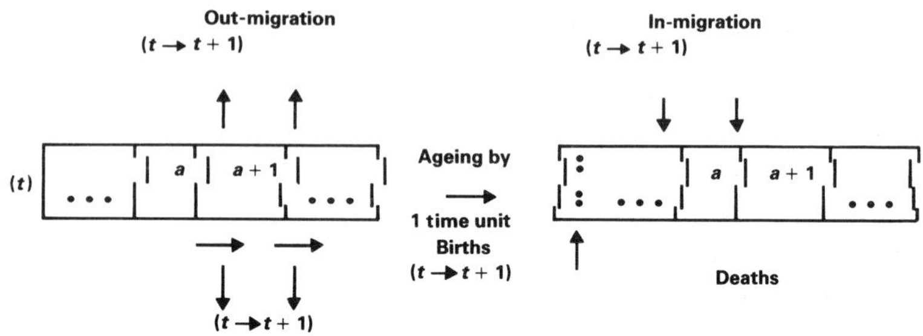

Figure 14.1 The basic model of population change over time.

persons in a population but also their age structure is of interest, then the aging of cohorts from time t to time $t+1$ is a further factor of population change. Figure 14.1 illustrates these very basic components of population change between times t and $t+1$ for the female part of the population. For the male part of the population the process would be analogous but births would come from the female population.[1]

Children can only be borne by women in the reproductive age span (usually assumed to be 15–49). Within this age span the intensity of fertility, that is, the magnitude of age-specific fertility rates, usually shows a pattern of a relatively fast increase up to the modal age of childbearing followed by a slower decrease. The sum of all age-specific fertility rates measured in a given year t is the total fertility rate, which may be interpreted as the average number of children to be born to a cohort of women that, over its whole reproductive career, had children at the age-specific rates observed in year t. Hence the area under the curve of fertility rates gives the level of fertility. The shape of the curve (especially of marital fertility) after about age 25 also indicates if the population has a 'natural' fertility regime (convex curve) or controls births as a function of the children already born to a woman (concave curve). The latter is found in all modern societies.[2]

Unlike fertility both sexes are exposed to the risk of mortality at every age of their life. The curve of age-specific death intensities (force of mortality) has also a specific shape with a high risk at very young ages (mostly under age one), low risk during youth and early adulthood, and an almost exponential increase of risk with age beyond ages forty to fifty.

The crude birth or death rates (i.e. total number of births or deaths divided by total population) gives only a very crude indication of a society's fertility or mortality level because they heavily depend on the population age structure. Two countries with the same life expectancy might show very different magnitudes of crude death rates depending on their age compositions; for young populations the crude death rates are biased downwards, for old populations upwards.

Fertility is more concentrated in a given age span and is therefore less sensitive to age structure, but it remains a major factor also for estimating future numbers of births. Especially in high fertility countries where the population is extremely young, the number of births might even further increase in a situation where fertility or the mean number of children per woman had already decreased. This is because increasingly large age groups continue to enter the reproductive age and this might easily override the effect of a reduced fertility per woman. Demographers call this phenomenon the momentum of population growth. It is crucial to consider the momentum factor in all models that include a reduction in population growth. Even in the extremely unlikely case that Kenya would reduce its fertility level from currently above eight children per woman to the replacement level of slightly over two children in the next few years, the population would continue to grow far into the 21st century.

This brings us into the methodology of population projection. The standard method is the so-called components method which essentially follows that outlined in Figure 14.1. The population is projected year by year (or in five-year steps if the age structure is given in five-year groups) where cohorts are made older and made subject to assumed fertility, mortality, and migration rates. As in any other projection the degree of uncertainty depends on the time horizon. But the inertia of population changes is much greater than that of many other phenomena especially in the field of economics. Projections of the population age structure over the next ten or fifteen years can be made with reasonable accuracy because the majority of the people living at that time is already alive today and assumptions about future fertility will only affect the youngest segments of the population. Also, as has been pointed out above for the momentum of population growth, the fertility level is only one determinant of the future number of births, the other being the size of cohorts that will be in reproductive age; the second part we know already quite well today if no major mortality crisis occurs. From this we can see that projections beyond the horizon of twenty to twenty-five years have a much higher degree of uncertainty because then the number of women in the reproductive age is also unknown. The UN assumes in its projections that ultimately all countries are heading towards fertility around the replacement level. This of course is a normative assumption.

Some European countries such as the Federal Republic of Germany show no sign of an increase in fertility towards a net reproduction rate of one, while in most parts of Africa an extremely steep fertility decline towards the replacement level seems very unrealistic. In Figure 14.2 the levelling off in

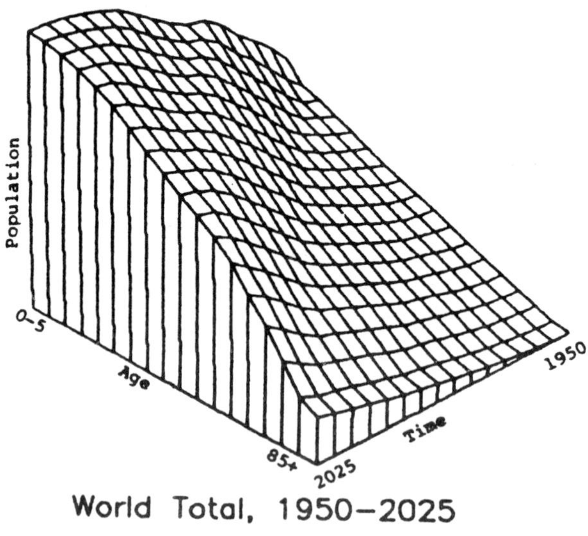

Figure 14.2 Observed and projected age structural changes of women, 1950–2025.
Source: UN Population Division.

the number of children aged nought to four after 2020 is a consequence of this assumption.

Mortality patterns have shown a relatively stable slow improvement over recent decades. Most projections assume a continuation of this trend. Large-scale mortality crises are hardly foreseeable now and therefore cannot be incorporated into projections. Past experiences, however, showed, for example, that the effects of wars and disease on population age structure tend to be less than usually expected. For the world as a whole (see Figure 14.2) the effect of World War II is hardly visible and even for Central Europe the effect is only significant in a few age groups of young men at the time of the war. The major fluctuations visible in Europe were induced by fertility changes. The notch in the world's age structure that originated around 1950 and runs diagonally along the cohort line has little to do with the War; it is the effect of the post-war acceleration of growth rates due to the steep decline of infectious diseases and some increase in fertility.

Population projections usually do not model any feedbacks of population growth on fertility or mortality. Their intention is to point out what would happen if current trends continued over a period of up to forty to fifty years. No serious projection goes beyond this horizon. The question of feedbacks, however, has a prominent place in demographic thinking. The arguments mostly go back to Malthus' basic propositions. Simplifying this argument, Malthus contended that populations grow exponentially while food supplies can grow only linearly and therefore the only possibilities are two so-called 'checks': the 'preventive check' that would affect fertility through sexual abstinence and the 'positive check' through increased mortality. Since Malthus assumed that the 'passion between the sexes' would continue, he believed that 'positive checks' through famine and war could not be avoided.

Today we know that Malthus was wrong in many ways. First, population grew to a much larger size than he had expected: the positive checks did not work. Secondly, population growth could be limited or even reversed in some countries by birth control: a 'preventive check' is possible. Both errors originate from the fact that Malthus did not account for the possibility of technological change that increased productivity and made exploitation of further resources possible. He also failed to foresee social and cultural changes that allow voluntary limitation of family size. But despite these changes Malthus had not expected his basic paradigm to remain valid in a more general sense and could be stated as follows: population cannot grow indefinitely in a finite world and the speed of growth cannot be greater than that provided by the physical possibilities of a country. We should also include in our models the possibility of technological and cultural change to avoid a repetition of Malthus' pitfall in our much more complex models.

NOTES

1 This is a statistical convenience because the reproductive age span for women is more clearly defined than for men and the father is not known for every birth. Theoretically, however, there is no objection against studying male fertility, if the necessary data can be found.

2 The paradigm of 'natural' fertility as opposed to 'controlled' fertility has been very helpful in understanding the fertility side of the demographic transition. As we can see from the above definition, this need not be identical to the level of fertility; 'natural' fertility populations show quite a large range of fertility levels, depending on the age at marriage, birth intervals, etc.

15

EVALUATIONS, CONCLUSIONS AND RECOMMENDATIONS

A. J. Gilbert

15.1. INTRODUCTION

This chapter summarises the participants' discussions and conclusions. The following section addresses the three objectives outlined in Chapter 1. Section 15.3 summarises discussion of future ECCO activities, including guidance to new projects. Section 15.4 condenses this material into a set of specific recommendations.

15.2. OBJECTIVES OF THE SEMINAR/WORKSHOP

15.2.1. Technical evaluation of ECCO

In Chapter 1, a set of criteria for a technical evaluation was identified. ECCO's scores on these criteria are presented in Table 15.1. They are based on information presented on the ECCO approach, and also on the models developed in the pilot studies.

ECCO generally satisfies these criteria for technical evaluation. Two areas of possible improvement or further work are:

1 incorporation of relevant aspects from the micro level; and
2 validation studies using a developing country with a growing population.

The latter is expected to be hampered by limited historical data.

15.2.2. Policy evaluation of ECCO

Evaluation of the policy relevance of ECCO at this stage of its development is premature. The pilot studies showed that they

Table 15.1 Technical evaluation of ECCO

CRITERION	*COMMENT*
flexibility	basic structure of the ECCO approach is flexible
adequacy (in representing the phenomena to be described)	only partly adequate as certain subnational (such as micro-economic, resource distribution) aspects are not considered
transferability	the approach is transferable, but the end-product – a national ECCO computer model – was not designed to be transferable; the approach is intended to be adapted to each country's specifications and issues
skill and quality of personnel required	needs at least a systems analyst with a strong background in economics, energy analysis and data management techniques; ideally, a team of specialists is required to build ECCO
data	amount of data needed is variable, but a model can be built with only a small amount of data (particularly if it is intended only for training purposes); use of reliable data in a final model is essential. Sufficient data were available for the pilot studies
validation	preliminary validation conducted satisfactorily for Britain

were directed more towards putting the ECCO approach into technical operation, rather than for its implementation in the policy-making process. Consequently, ECCO is not in a position to score well with regards to the three criteria identified in Chapter 1.

Transparency refers to the ease with which the essentials of a model and its mathematical formulation can be communicated. Many large models have been severely criticised on this point in the past; they have been 'black boxes', particularly to policy analysts. One approach to increasing transparency is to design models with a series of menus and accompanying information, so that a user can operate and understand the program without additional help. Micro-ECCO, demonstrated by Dr Slesser, is a simplified ECCO model for use on a micro-computer. It was developed more for training and demonstration purposes, and uses a menu approach. Consequently, it is reasonably transparent. However, the larger ECCO models demonstrated, mounted on a mainframe computer, did not use such an approach. Participants decided that effort was needed to make these larger ECCO models (and future ECCO models) more transparent.

It is not necessary for a user to understand the detail of a model, but he must have sufficient confidence in the model's results. The heart of the ECCO approach is the representation of economic activities in energy terms. Such an approach, while it may have every validity in a physical sense, provides problems for policy analysts who are more familiar with traditional economic approaches and monetary units. The use of the energy numeraire will constrain ECCO's credibility, at least initially.

Having confidence in a model's outputs is followed by the need to understand them. 'Soft' presentations are valuable in communicating results. This usually involves some pictorial or graphical presentation, usually in preference to tables, and certainly in preference to large quantities of numbers.

The results of simulations with the various ECCO models yielded numerical output which could usually be presented in graph form. However, it was sometimes difficult during the computer demonstrations to obtain a clear picture of the simulation's results and particularly trends. Consequently, it was decided that more attention was needed in this area in the future, and that more sophisticated graphics software should be considered for incorporation.

To be policy relevant, the phenomena being modelled should reflect the interests of policy makers. ECCO (as well as many approaches to population and sustainable development) suffers in that:

1 policy makers, even in developing countries, have lost momentum on population issues;
2 sustainable development is a new concept and still fraught with ambiguities and implementation problems; and
3 ECCO has a long-term perspective, whereas policy makers tend to have a short-term perspective.

While the potential for ECCO's policy relevance was not disputed, it was suggested that attempts should be made to couch ECCO in terms more familiar and of more direct interest to policy makers.

15.2.3. Conclusions from the evaluation of ECCO

The issues which ECCO attempts to represent have a good scientific basis, and the approach which it adopts it satisfactory from a technical perspective. In addition, the pilot studies have demonstrated that there are sufficient data available to construct proto-models.

There is now a need to move on from the pilot project stage, which has successfully demonstrated the technical feasibility of the ECCO approach. The next stage is to undertake case studies in which models are developed for use in policy analysis; the purpose of such case studies is to begin the evaluation of ECCO's policy relevance.

15.2.4. Other modelling approaches and ECCO

The third objective of the meeting consisted of two parts: to identify areas where ECCO was weak; and to suggest ways in which other modelling approaches could be incorporated to compensate for these weaknesses. Three main weaknesses in ECCO were identified; the first two are associated with its aggregated approach.

A number of participants argued strongly for greater sectoral detail. Sectors specifically mentioned included population, agriculture and natural resources, particularly renewables such as water, forests and pasture and arable land. While the purposes of an aggregated modelling approach were generally accepted, questions were continually raised concerning the simplifications inherent in each ECCO sector and their implications for the whole. ECCO does not preclude greater detailing of sectors. In fact, the pilot studies demonstrated quite a wide range of sectoral detail.

ECCO's national perspective also prevents incorporation of spatial elements of PRED issues, in particular those related to resource use and environmental quality; for example, inconsistencies between water availability and water supply. Such issues are more appropriately analysed at the regional level. It is not yet clear whether the proposed regional version of ECCO will address such issues adequately, and what relationship exists (or could exist) between regional and national ECCO-models.

The use of the energy numeraire provides a number of

(scientifically sound) advantages over monetary units: energy units are not subject to the vagaries of inflation; the description of a natural resource in energy units is certainly less controversial than in monetary units where the question of discount rate inevitably arises. However, the energy unit also has its limits. The most appropriate unit is not necessarily the one which has the greatest scientific basis. The needs of the ultimate user must be accommodated if any model or analytical approach is to reach the implementation stage for policy.

Consequently, the question arises: what sort(s) of units convey the most useful information? Monetary units cannot be dismissed. There is no other way of representing commodity prices which are at the centre of economic activity. Similarly, what is the value of representing a resource stock, say a forest, in energy units when the model's user is interested in the timber it can produce and in the export earnings and employment which can be derived from its exploitation. The answer to the above question may be a mixture of units, requiring regular updating and tuning for consistency.

Integration of (aspects of) other modelling approaches requires communication between modellers and between models. Linking models, or parts of models, or even using the output of one as an input for another, is often very difficult to accomplish. The models have usually been built for different purposes and incorporate very different sets of assumptions. This may lead to basic incompatibilities even before the technical specifications of each model are considered.

Participants at the seminar/workshop expressed strong doubts as to whether such formal communication was desirable, let alone feasible. It was generally agreed that more informal communication offered the greatest potential for integration. Such informal channels involve networks and personal contact between researchers with subsequent exchange of ideas.

15.3. FUTURE ECCO ACTIVITIES

ECCO efforts have concentrated on the technical feasibility of constructing models based on the ECCO approach, and on preliminary validation of the approach. These activities have been conducted in research organisations, and have been supported primarily by Unesco. They have successfully demonstrated

Table 15.2 Procedural guideline for new ECCO studies

STEP 1:
Develop a project description which is as clear as possible and which specifies:
- objectives of the project;
- conceptual framework;
- workplan and timing of the project;
- inputs, distinguishing between national and extra-national sources; and
- contributions from other organisations, networks, etc.

STEP 2:
Identify the network of contacts which will supply information, funding and skill:
- relevant organisations;
- potential users (national government departments or ministries);
- potential funding sources, which, for a case study, should include at least one potential user;
- academic representatives; and
- reliable data sources.

STEP 3:
Set up the project team to co-ordinate the projects. The team should consist of the following:
- energy analyst and system modeller, providing methodological background;
- for a case study, at least one policy analyst from a government department or ministry, preferably from an expected user of the end-product; and
- researchers for data collection and analysis.

STEP 4:
Set out a two to three (minimum) year plan, showing the basic workplan and the contributions from the team, as well as:
- hardware and software required;
- contributions from other organisations and government personnel;
- dates of meetings with (potential) clients, funding sources, and other contributors;
- dates of workshops where the project's results are to be presented for discussion and review; and
- plans and procedures for model validation and preliminary policy analysis.

the technical feasibility of constructing ECCO models and have completed a preliminary validation.

Three future ECCO activities were identified:

1 continuation of the pilot study programme, whereby training workshops and other activities encourage the construction of ECCO models in more countries;
2 validation of ECCO using historical data for a developing country, or at least a country with a growing population;
3 undertaking a case study to develop an ECCO model specifically for policy purposes.

Activities towards integration of other modelling approaches were left to individuals and the individual level.

Inevitably the above activities will be in competition for funds, despite the value which each offers. The feeling of the meeting was that ECCO's need to move into a case-study phase, to assess its policy relevance, should receive priority.

Two such case studies were suggested: one in a developing country, and another in a developed country. Thailand was suggested as the developing country, and New Zealand as the developed country. An important criterion in selecting these countries was the presence of skills with energy analysis and ECCO.

With regard to the proposed pilot studies in Rwanda, China and Zimbabwe, Dr Chirapol Sintunawa presented the following checklist for project development. The checklist, see Table 15.2, is also relevant for the case studies. In both cases, there was an emphasis on involving policy analysts at an early stage in the project's development; for the case study, it was considered important that such an analyst should be a formal member of the team. Without such close co-operation, the end-product would run a severe risk of having limited value as a planning tool.

15.4. RECOMMENDATIONS

15.4.1. To the developers of ECCO

Further validation of ECCO should be conducted, if historical data for a developing country can be obtained. The validation using BRITECCO was considered limited, since Britain had zero population growth over the time period used.

A regional version of ECCO should be developed, to demonstrate that ECCO can accommodate PRED issues on a more micro-scale. Some form of linkage between this model and a national ECCO model may be desirable.

Contacts with other organisations, especially FAO, should be developed further.

15.4.2. To the new pilot studies

Contact should be established with policy analysts and government departments at an early stage in the project's development, and they should be kept involved and informed on the project's progress. The more active their involvement, the better.

Table 15.2 proposes a procedural guide for new studies.

15.4.3. For the case studies

Two case studies are recommended: one in a developing country with population growth (e.g. Thailand), and one in a developed country (e.g. New Zealand). Both are aimed at developing an ECCO model for use as a policy and planning tool.

Some funding for the case study should come from the national government.

There should also be a commitment to the project in terms of personnel for three reasons: firstly, so that the government's perspective on PRED issues can be incorporated into the model; secondly, so that relatively realistic policy scenarios can be experimented with; and thirdly, so that the skills and knowledge gained from involvement with the model's development can be transferred to the future user.

15.4.4. For Unesco

Unesco was congratulated on its support for ECCO activities, including not only the development of the ECCO approach, but also the pilot studies and the programme of training workshops.

However, Unesco should redirect some of its efforts into setting up the case studies. It should provide some initial financial support for these studies, but also provide what assistance it can to finding other sources – other international and development organisations as well as national government sources.

ANNEX

List of participants at the seminar/ workshop on Modelling for Population and Sustainable Development

Mr Jacques Antoine,
AGLS,
FAO,
Via delle Terme di Caracalla,
00100 Rome,
ITALY.

Dr Jaap Arntzen,
Institute for Environmental Studies,
Free University,
Amsterdam,
THE NETHERLANDS.

Mr J. Baguant,
School of Industrial Technology,
University of Mauritius,
Reduit,
MAURITIUS.

Mr J. Bartlema,
International Programme of Training in Population,
Institute of Social Studies,
PO Box 90733,
2509 LS The Hague,
THE NETHERLANDS.

Mr H. Becker,
GEFA,
Avenue Lemaitre 13,
1348-Louvain-La-Neuve,
BELGIUM.

Dr L. C. Braat,
Institute for Environmental Studies,
Free University,
Amsterdam,
THE NETHERLANDS.

Dr D. Faber,
SOW,
PO Box 14,
6700 AA Wageningen,
THE NETHERLANDS.

Ms A. J. Gilbert
Institute for Environmental Studies,
Free University,
Amsterdam,
THE NETHERLANDS.

Dr J. Glasgow,
International Programme of Training in Population,
Institute of Social Studies,
PO Box 90733,
2509 LS The Hague,
THE NETHERLANDS.

Dr M. Griffiths,
Ministry of Housing and Land,
Bridgetown,
BARBADOS.

Ms Pertida Huston,
Coordinator,
Population and Sustainable Development,
IUCN,
Avenue du Mont-Blanc,
CH-1196 Gland,
SWITZERLAND.

Dr N. O. Kabwasa,
Population and Human Settlements Division,
UNESCO,
BP 3.07 Paris,
FRANCE.

Mr Katusisako, di Malenga,
Chef de Cellule d'Etudes et Coordination des Activités en Matière de Population,
Department du Plan,
B.P. 9378,
Kinshasa 1,
ZAIRE.

Dr J. King,
Centre for Human Ecology,
University of Edinburgh,
Buccleuch Place,
Edinburgh,
UNITED KINGDOM.

Prof. V. E. Leoning,
Centre for Human Ecology,
University of Edinburgh,
Buccleuch Place,
Edinburgh,
UNITED KINGDOM.

Dr Wolfgang Lutz,
Population Program,
IIASA,
Laxenburg,
AUSTRIA.

Prof. Ngo Manh-Lan,
Research Professor,
ISMEA,
11/13 Rue Pierre et Marie Curie,
75005 Paris,
FRANCE.

Mr B. K. Njoka,
Department of Agricultural Engineering,
University of Nairobi,
KENYA.

Prof. J. B. Opschoor,
Institute for Environmental Studies,
Free University,
PO Box 7161,
1007 MC Amsterdam,
THE NETHERLANDS.

Mr Joseph Owino,
Centre for Human Ecology,
University of Edinburgh,
15 Buccleuch Place,
Edinburgh EH8 9LN,
UNITED KINGDOM.

Dr E. Peelink,
DGIS,
Ministry of Foreign Affairs,
PO Box 20061,
2500 ED The Hague,
THE NETHERLANDS.

Dr John Peet,
Principal Investigator,
Centre for Resource Management,
PO Box 56,
Lincoln College,
Canterbury,
NEW ZEALAND.

Dr F. J. C. M. Rath,
Population and Human Settlements,
UNESCO,
BP 3.07 Paris,
FRANCE.

Dr A. M. Ruboko,
Director,
Zimbabwe Institute of Development Studies,
PO Box 1880,
Harare,
ZIMBABWE.

Dr Chirapol Sintunawa,
Faculty of Environmental and Resource Studies,
Mahidol University,
THAILAND.

Dr M. Slesser,
Centre for Human Ecology,
University of Edinburgh,
Buccleuch Place,
Edinburgh,
UNITED KINGDOM.

Prof. P. Twagiramutara,
Département de l'Aménagement du Territoire,
Faculté d'Agronomie,
Université Nationale du Rwanda,
Butare,
RWANDA.

Dr Li Wenhua,
Executive Deputy Director,
Commission for Integrated Survey of Natural Resources,
The Chinese Academy of Science,
PO Box 767,
100011 Beijing,
THE PEOPLE'S REPUBLIC OF CHINA.

Mr Rene Wery,
Coordinator – Population Activities,
Employment Planning and Population Branch,
Employment and Development Department,
ILO,
4 Route des Morillons,
CH-1211 Geneva 22,
SWITZERLAND.

Mr M. Wuyts,
International Programme of Training in Population,
Institute of Social Studies,
PO Box 90733,
2509 LS The Hague,
THE NETHERLANDS.

INDEX

Note: Page references in italics indicate tables and figures. *Abbreviations*: ECCO = Enhancement of Population Carrying Capacity Options; FAO = United Nations Food and Agriculture Organisation